# IMPROMPTU
# MAN

# More Praise for *Impromptu Man*

"Jonathan D. Moreno has written an informative book about an amazing man who, over one hundred years ago, saw improv theater as a way to change the world. Today his ideas are more relevant than ever." —JONATHAN FOX, founder of Playback Theatre and editor of *The Essential Moreno*

"A splendid account of one the most creative social scientists of the twentieth century. *Impromptu Man* is filled with fascinating anecdotes, many of them about famous and infamous people, and brilliant insights as to how Moreno's work transformed vast segments of society and eventually eluded his control. This book is frank, funny, fascinating, and long overdue." —STANLEY KRIPPNER, PhD, Professor of Psychology, Saybrook University

"J.L. Moreno, who fathered psychodrama, set a new world in motion. I doubt he ever dreamed his life's work would change the lives of trial lawyers and the people they represent, providing us with a new way to communicate and give justice a chance. This book restores him to his rightful place in history." —GERRY SPENCE, author of *How to Argue and Win Every Time* and founder of Trial Lawyers College

"J.L. Moreno was a pioneer of twentieth-century theater and psychotherapy. A remarkable work, *Impromptu Man* should be required reading for therapists and dramatists alike." —JEFFREY K. ZEIG, PhD, founder and director of The Milton H. Erickson Foundation

## Praise for *The Body Politic: The Battle Over Science in America*

"An impassioned defense of scientific study . . . an essential dose of logic." —*Salon*

"Articulate, timely and impassioned . . . [an] important book."
—*Times Higher Education*

"An excellent guide. . . . In his highly readable and provocative book, Moreno makes clear that progress, including biotechnological progress, is still America's most important product." —*Reason* magazine

"A timely take on the debate raging over biotechnology breakthroughs." —*Nature*

"This groundbreaking must-read book situates the biological revolution in its historical, philosophical, and cultural context and, with almost breathtaking elegance, shows how society may come to define itself by the body politic."
—NITA A. FARAHANY, Professor of Law & Philosophy, Duke University; Member, Presidential Commission for the Study of Bioethical Issues

"A clear-eyed map of the emerging biopolitics—greens, transhumanists, bioconservatives, technoprogressives—and a thoughtful defense of inquiry, innovation, and the liberating power of science." —WILLIAM SALETAN, author of *Bearing Right: How Conservatives Won the Abortion War* and *Slate* National Correspondent

## Also by Jonathan D. Moreno

*Mind Wars: Brain Science and the Military in the 21ˢᵗ Century*

*The Body Politic: The Battle Over Science in America*

*Is There an Ethicist in the House: On the Cutting Edge of Bioethics*

*Undue Risk: Secret State Experiments on Humans*

*Deciding Together: Bioethics and Moral Consensus*

### Coauthored Books

*Ethics in Clinical Practice*

*Discourse in the Social Sciences:
Strategies for Translating Models of Mental Illness*

### Edited Works

*Progress in Bioethics: Science, Policy, and Politics*

*Science Next: Innovation for the Next Generation*

*Ethical Guidelines for Innovative Surgery*

*In the Wake of Terror: Medicine and Morality in a Time of Crisis*

*Ethical and Regulatory Aspects of Clinical Research:
Readings and Commentary*

*Arguing Euthanasia: The Controversy over Mercy Killing,
Assisted Suicide, and the "Right to Die"*

*Paying the Doctor: Health Policy and Physician Reimbursement*

*The Qualitative-Quantitative Distinction in the Social Sciences*

# IMPROMPTU
# MAN

*J.L. Moreno and the Origins of Psychodrama,*
*Encounter Culture, and the Social Network*

————⬤⬤⬤————

JONATHAN D. MORENO

BELLEVUE LITERARY PRESS
NEW YORK

First published in the United States in 2014
by Bellevue Literary Press, New York

For information, contact:
Bellevue Literary Press
90 Broad Street
Suite 2100
New York, NY 10004
www.blpress.org

Library of Congress Cataloging-in-Publication Data
Moreno, Jonathan D.
Impromptu man : J.L. Moreno and the origins of psychodrama, encounter culture,
and the social network / Jonathan D. Moreno. – 1st ed.
p. cm.
Originally published: New York : Bellevue Literary Press, 2014.
Includes bibliographical references and index.
ISBN 978-1-93413-784-0 (pbk.) | ISBN 978-1-93413-785-7 (e-book)
1. Moreno, J. L. (Jacob Levy), 1889-1974. 2. Psychiatrists—United States—Biography.
3. Social scientists—United States—Biography. 4. Social reformers—United States—
Biography. 5. Drama—Therapeutic use. 6. Humanistic psychology.
RC438.6.M67 M67 2014
616.89/14092 B                    2014025363

Bellevue Literary Press would like to thank all its generous
donors—individuals and foundations—for their support.

Book design and composition by Mulberry Tree Press, Inc.

Bellevue Literary Press is committed to ecological stewardship in our book production
practices, working to reduce our impact on the natural environment.

∞ This book is printed on acid-free paper.

Manufactured in the United States of America.
First Edition
3   5   7   9   8   6   4

paperback ISBN: 978-1-934137-84-0

ebook ISBN: 978-1-934137-85-7

# Contents

*To spontaneous and creative
men and women everywhere.*

# Invitation to an Encounter

A meeting of two: eye to eye, face to face.
And when you are near,
I will tear your eyes out
and place them instead of mine,
and you will tear my eyes out
and will place them instead of yours,
then I will look at you with your eyes
and you will look at me with mine

J.L. Moreno, 1914

# THE EMPTY CHAIR

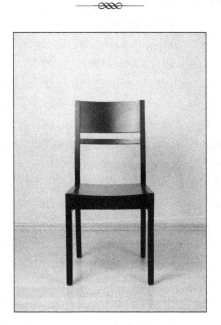

*God is spontaneity. Hence, the commandment is: "Be spontaneous!"*

J.L. Moreno, 1919

I T WAS A SPONTANEOUS, last minute thought that only occurred to the famous eighty-two-year-old actor–director as he waited to ascend the stage at the Republican National Convention in Charlotte, North Carolina. Here was the surprise speaker they had just learned about, an American icon. After an endless and arduous primary campaign, this was the night that Mitt Romney would officially become the Republican candidate for President of the United States. The theme song from *The Good, the Bad and the Ugly* played in the background and a huge image of the young Clint Eastwood as the outlaw Josey Wales filled the video screen behind the platform. More than thirty million Americans watched on television.

"There was a stool there, and some fella kept asking me if I wanted to sit down," Eastwood said later. "When I saw the stool sitting there, it gave me the idea. I'll just put the stool out there and I'll talk to Mr. Obama and ask him why he didn't keep all of the promises he made to everybody. The guy said, 'You mean you want it at the podium?' and I said, 'No, just put it right there next to it.'"

The extemporaneous talk that followed was quite different from the banal speeches of modern major-party conventions. Rather than more or less public exercises of political horse-trading in action, they had become long, windy, and free political commercials for the major TV networks. Ever since the convention that nominated Richard Nixon in 1968, they were also tightly scripted for the cameras. But as is typical of truly improvisational theater, Eastwood's speech stumbled, it rambled, it was garbled, it defied the esthetic conventions of the prefabricated performance. Yet the occasionally bawdy challenge to the "sitting" but absent president could not have been clearer: For all your promises, you let us down. What do you have to say for yourself?

The crowd loved it. Their spirited applause and laughter forcing the five-minute scheduled appearance into ten. Eastwood then retired to the green room to congratulations all around, settling in to hear the introduction by rising star Senator Marco Rubio and the acceptance speech of the nominee, Governor Mitt Romney. But beyond the inner sanctum there were discordant notes. Theater professionals know that when technologically transformed into an on-screen image, a performance that succeeds in real space and time with a warmed-up audience can fail to engage those who are mainly curious. By his own account, Eastwood didn't hear the full range of reactions until the next morning. Apart from a few bloggers and spinners, what seemed a triumph to the live gathering of party activists who were hearing an iconic American artist and celebrity express their views in a creative way was immediately received with at least puzzlement and at worst derision by major media commentators. Party stalwarts buckled. Even Mrs. Romney could only offer that the effort was "original." Perhaps more damaging, the incident cast doubt on one of Governor Romney's purported strengths as a manager: If his campaign had been so careless as to permit Eastwood's unorthodox performance, how well organized could it be? Worse still, his spot pushed out of prime time a very well-produced film about Mitt Romney's story, one that was intended to "reintroduce" the candidate to the American people. The internal campaign recriminations piled on.

## IMPROV

Asked about the empty chair routine a couple of weeks later, Eastwood said he got the idea came from watching his old friends among the great standup comics. "[I]t reminds me of the days of Shelley Berman . . . Bob Newhart, all those guys who used to do those phone conversations, all that sort of stuff." Sure enough, comedians across the political spectrum appreciated the effort. "As a performer," the liberal satirist Bill Maher said, "as a stand-up comedian for 30 years who knows how hard it is to get laughs . . . he went up there . . . without a net, on a tightrope. There was no teleprompter. He did a bit with just an empty chair and killed." The political commentators who were most positive about the speech wove it into the context of performance. A *Breitbart.com* editor called it "funnier, fresher, edgier, and braver than anything those comedy cowards Chris Rock, Jon Stewart, or Stephen Colbert have done in 15 years." But when one top Romney aide referred to it as "theater of the absurd," it was not a compliment.

Eastwood confirmed an explanation I offered in a *New York Times* Op Ed two days after his convention appearance, that the empty chair is rooted in improvisational theater. The technique would have been familiar to the comics with whom Eastwood was acquainted, especially someone like Shelley Berman, who was one of the early cast members of the Second City troupe in Chicago. But they also used carefully scripted routines rather than full-on improv. True improvisational theater usually has a different flow from scripted theater. It generally lacks the conventional dramatic arc with which audiences are familiar. The essential unpredictability of improv often makes viewers uncomfortable. Indeed, that is part of the point: to challenge the audience and subvert theater conventions, often making the audience part of the performance.

In the Op Ed I noted that my father, the psychiatrist J.L. Moreno (whom I will call J.L. in this book), had first used the empty chair in his improvisational theater in Vienna a century before. The empty chair is only one of many techniques he formulated in his investigation of what he called "role-playing." Using the many possibilities inherent in role-playing, he also developed a form of psychotherapy he called "psychodrama." He agreed with Shakespeare that "all the world's a stage," and with Aristotle that the play can be therapeutic for the audience. Combining these insights, J.L. thought that the stage could be turned explicitly into a therapeutic platform to help people overcome their troubles and to learn and grow.

By the time I was twelve I had participated in dozens of psychodramas, and had been credited as the coauthor of a child-rearing monograph, *The First Psychodramatic Family*. As I grew older I participated in and led many psychodramas and trained people in the method. So when I saw Eastwood talking to the empty chair, what puzzled so many was quite recognizable to me. I had the same feeling in the early 1960s, when I was old enough to become aware that magazines and newspapers were writing stories about new experiments using group therapy to expand human potential and that experimental theater was flourishing in response to social and political upheaval. I wondered what all the shouting was about; it all seemed very familiar to me. After all, that had been my life.

Useful though it is for the training and preparation of actors, the empty chair is only one of many influential therapeutic theater techniques J.L. developed. One of those techniques is called *role reversal*, in which a person sits in the chair and takes the other's point of view. Because Eastwood did not role reverse with the president, and because being in the room is so different from seeing the act on screen (a problem that also bedeviled my father who wanted to create a broadcast therapy for the masses), the episode appeared on television as angry and mocking rather than as light-hearted and ironic. Eastwood's apparent goal was to enact an encounter between himself and the president, but because the president was absent and because he did not engage in a role reversal with his antagonist, the encounter was stillborn. Admittedly, if Eastwood had really tried to role reverse with the president the act could have lost its political edge.

Eastwood's performance alone cannot be blamed for Governor Romney's defeat, but it didn't help. A more effective presentation would have launched the candidate to a more robust popular reception and perhaps put the Democrats off their game. No one can know what the ultimate outcome would have been. The most one can say is that this was yet another in a legion of odd incidents that, if not for them, history might have changed. And surely, never before has a technique borrowed from improvisational theater and psychotherapy been the centerpiece of a potentially momentous occasion in partisan politics. Had J.L. been alive to see it (he died in 1974 at age eighty-four), he would have been delighted that the kind of attention he sought for his ideas had so permeated the culture that they had—at least momentarily—become the focal point of water-cooler conversations and perhaps changed the course of a presidential campaign. Undoubtedly, he would have published a press release the day after the convention inviting both candidates to engage in a psychodrama and reverse roles—with himself as the director of the drama, of course.

## THE SON ALSO RISES

"I grew up in a mental hospital," I sometimes tell groups of students or colleagues when I'm giving a talk. Then I notice amused smiles and nods in the room. I can tell they're thinking, "Oh yeah, my family was crazy, too."

"No," I add, "I *really* grew up in a mental hospital."

Then, reaching for a formula one-liner I say, "It's true. I grew up surrounded by drug addicts, psychotics, and psychopaths—and those were the doctors!"

Ba-da-bump.

What was it like to grow up in a mental hospital as the son of a famous, eccentric, and controversial man? It's hard to summarize, but I can say that it was far more exotic than the lives of my friends. The hospital itself was small, just thirty or so beds, in an idyllic, pastoral setting. There were other buildings, a modest frame house that was our home and an imposing mansion called the Gillette House (named for the famous family that once owned that portion of the grounds), where there were offices and guest accommodations. The twenty-acre grounds were beautiful, nestled in hills sixty miles north of New York City with the Hudson River visible when the trees were denuded in the fall and winter. Whenever a kid came to my house to play for the first time I had to explain that the otherworldly howling in the background was Joe, a longtime patient with schizophrenia who occupied a "quiet room" in the main hospital building less than a hundred yards from our house. Joe was a gentle soul who was a threat to no one but himself. His father was a successful businessman in New Jersey. When Joe arrived at J.L.'s hospital in 1948, he improved under my father's care, even donning a suit and joining him on trips to Manhattan where he attended the public psychodrama sessions in J.L.'s midtown office. Then on a pass from the hospital a foolish uncle took him to a prostitute. Joe could not perform. When he returned he had thoroughly withdrawn into his own world, never to return. As I write this sentence I can still hear his wails, responding to the tormenting voices no one else could hear. After one or two visits to my house my friends would ignore the cries. That was just Joe.

J.L. never forgave himself for the catastrophe with Joe. For the next twenty years he never let him leave the grounds unsupervised, and certainly not in the hands of a stupid relative. These were the days before there was much medication for mental illness, and before the movement to empty large asylums of patients who were residents for months or years. Families could be a problem or they could be instrumental in a patient's improvement through J.L.'s group therapy methods. On a bright spring day when I was driven home from school, I waved to a recently admitted male patient at the top of one of the hills. It took me a second to realize that the young man was not only hirsute, but quite naked. It turned out he had a Jesus fixation, and his Jesus must be naked to be pure. He insisted that those around him in his therapy must also be nude. My father assigned the roles of Joseph and Mary, Mary Magdalene, and the disciples in psychodrama sessions in which scenes from Jesus's life could be enacted. The idea was that delusional patients have an "act hunger" that can be sated in dramatic action. His girlfriend, parents, and a therapist were willing to go along with the nudity, but not J.L., a nineteenth-century man who was certainly not going to get naked in public no matter how devoted he was to his patients.

J.L.'s colleagues often referred their toughest cases to him. People with delusions about being Jesus, or Hitler, or being persecuted by mysterious forces were among J.L.'s favorites. To him these cases were examples of natural spontaneity and creativity run amok. Considering his own history of messianic preoccupation and manic creativity, he identified with them. One obese young man was convinced he was the last descendent of the czar and that the CIA was cooperating with the KGB in keeping him from his inheritance. I remember well his distraught parents when they came to visit. The look in his father's eyes was among the saddest I have ever seen. Besides the most challenging psychiatric patients, J.L. attracted offbeat students to his group therapy institute as well. Some were psychologists, psychiatrists, and social workers who rejected the standard psychoanalytic or behavioral approaches of the day. Some were actors who wanted to combine their theatre work with training as a therapist. Some were graduate students, journalists, educators, members of the clergy, or just seekers of new "personal growth" experiences, especially in the late 1960s. Often it was hard to tell the students from the patients; in truth, to J.L. the roles were interchangeable, especially in psychodrama sessions where patients who were well enough might be asked to assume important roles in, say, a psychiatrist's psychodrama. Putting the patient in the therapist role was itself considered to be therapeutic in J.L.'s theory. One of the advantages of the group is that a person can choose from among various people to be his or her therapist.

Although they tried somewhat halfheartedly, it was hard for my parents to segregate me from the "main building" and the patients. I pretty much had my run of the place. Often I'd stroll down the dirt road to visit with the nurses and hang out with the students and patients. When I was around eleven years old I became close to a brilliant and handsome young African American man who was a drug addict. Bored, he asked me to buy him a yo-yo at the local W.T. Grant's department store. When I saw him next he said, rather sadly I thought, "you didn't forget old Sam now did you?" Indeed I had not. I pulled the yo-yo out of a bag and he happily showed me some tricks like the throw down and the sleeper. I got to be pretty proficient myself. A few weeks later his tall, beautiful white girlfriend came to visit. In the mid-1960s interracial relationships were unheard of outside of the most bohemian circles. One of my friends shocked me with a racist remark when he saw them, reminding me of the distance between the world of J.L.'s sanitarium and the surrounding town.

Beyond the confines of my father's hospital and psychodrama institute, my life in a small somewhat depressed rural working-class community was like an alternate universe. I was in essence self-schooled and homeschooled, fortunate to be surrounded by my father's wide-ranging library that included philosophy, psychology, sociology, and history. I must have been eleven or twelve when I read A.S. Neill's classic *Summerhill* on his radical education theory (I especially liked the idea of a female roommate), and not much older when I paged through nuclear war theorist Herman Kahn's tome, *On Thermonuclear War*, where he dispassionately discussed atomic bomb "throw-weights" and "mutually assured destruction." Every other summer was spent traveling for my father's lecture tours in Europe, including forays behind the "Iron Curtain." J.L.'s idea of a vacation was schlepping from one mental hospital to another where he could meet with colleagues, conduct a psychodrama demonstration, and promote his ideas. There were sojourns in places like Frankfurt, Vienna, London, Paris, Milan, Budapest, Warsaw, Leipzig, Prague, and in small towns like the Czech resort Jesenik. I have vivid memories of Moscow in 1959 when I saw both Lenin and Stalin lying in state in their Red Square mausoleum, before the latter was unceremoniously moved to a modest grave next to the Kremlin wall, which I also saw in 1966.

Because of my father's odd form of celebrity, there were also awkward moments, especially in my later teenage years. There was no reason for strangers to assume that I was the son of the old eccentric. At an international psychodrama conference in Amsterdam in 1971, a young man to whom I had not been introduced launched into an anti-J.L. tirade while we were sitting with a half-dozen Dutch students I had gotten to know. It was a difficult moment as he gradually realized there was something unsaid in the group. The others looked at me, their eyes wide with alarm. Yet I sympathized with his skepticism as J.L.'s later years coincided with an era in search of gurus. On other occasions that were just as disconcerting, I was treated with adoration just because of whom my father happened to be. Then there was his theatrical appearance. All young people are at some point embarrassed by their parents, but in my case the conditions were extreme, as I found myself gallivanting around Europe with this heavy-set elderly man invariably dressed in a dark suit, suspenders, white shirt, and bow tie. Yet his teasing manner and love of a joke (he said nothing in life could be so terrible if you can make a joke about it) often made for delightful moments. Always resembling the gregarious impresario, at seventy-five he was approached on a London street by a gaggle of young women who were nearly falling over themselves with excitement. "We loved you in your last movie," one of them said breathlessly.

"Oh yes," J.L. replied with a deadpan expression. "I was good wasn't I?"

## THE SOCIAL NETWORK

The seemingly unlikely confluence of theater, therapy, and the third dimension of the Eastwood event put me in mind of J.L.'s other major contribution to our culture: the social network. For J.L., human experience is not just individual but "interpersonal," so he created the science of sociometry, the measurement of small group relations. He was the first to draw maps of the relationships in groups, maps he called "sociograms." Because of that work, he is also recognized as a forerunner of modern social network analysis. Powered by the World Wide Web, social networks have been supercharged by social media like Twitter and Facebook. The Internet has enlarged our understanding of social networks and how new ones can be created for specific purposes, from meeting potential partners to selling products and services to organizing revolutions. Clint Eastwood's speech was one of those modern, mass cultural events that the Internet leverages into something still more intense and personal. Even before the speech had ended the social media firestorm was ignited. According to *knowyourmeme.com*,

> As the speech aired on television, Twitter and Google+ users reacted by posting jokes about Eastwood's mock interview, many of whom used the hashtag #invisibleobama. From 12 pm (ET) on August 30th to 12 pm (ET) on August 31st, approximately 93,204 tweets were posted about Clint Eastwood, with 78,272 of them occurring during the hour of [12 pm] on August 30th. The speech also made it to Iran the following day, where people were even more baffled. The speech has become a notable American topic among Iranians on Facebook and other sites.

Through the Internet the expansive English language added a new term (or in current parlance, meme), with "dozens of updates every few seconds of people posting their 'Eastwooding' pictures. In some cases, an empty chair is shown with folks pointing at them. In others, users are sharing pictures of politicians, like President Obama, sitting next to empty chairs." Seeing an opening, Mitt Romney's opponent got into the act as President Obama's Twitter feed, @BarackObama responded with the post: "This seat's taken" along with a photo of the Commander-in-Chief in a chair with the plaque "The President." Within twenty-four hours the photo had been retweeted more than forty thousand times and liked four hundred thousand times on Facebook.

J.L.'s idea, also dating back to the 1910s, was that there are invisible constellations of human relationships based on mutual choice rather than contingency or arbitrary assignment. We do not choose our parents, our work partners, or sometimes even our living companions. But we do make interpersonal choices all the time, and we communicate through these informal networks, and they often work despite the "official" relationships to which we are assigned by institutional authorities or fate. Using social networks as their platform, modern social media create new communities (in this case, the network of those who followed President Obama's tweets), and the data about these networks can be used to study the way people interact in networks.

The power of social networks is immense. They can create a groundswell for relatively trivial matters like a witty neologism ("Eastwooding"), built by thousands of contributors or a nearly instant gathering of protestors in the city square (as in Tunisia's Jasmine Revolution, also in 2012). J.L. believed that if we understood the structure of a particular social network we could apply that knowledge to release the creativity that emerges from the participation of many who are focused on a single task. The solution to a problem can be built exponentially, akin to the way that information systems can grow. Understanding the social network of an organization can assist in team building. Understanding the social network of a therapy group can help the group members help each other. Combine those ideas with the concept of improvisation and the idea of spontaneity and you have a comprehensive approach to theater, therapy, and the social network.

## THE EPIC

Over a seventy-year career J.L.'s innovative genius and relentless promotion of his ideas touched an astonishing array of human activities and helped shape the way we think of ourselves, of our relationships, and of our society. As the decades rolled on, J.L. also influenced virtually all the important thinkers whose work contributed to humanistic psychology and the human potential movement that bubbled up in the 1960s. Among these famous philosophers and psychologists were Viktor Frankl, Kurt Lewin, Abraham Maslow, Carl Rogers, Rollo May, and Fritz Perls. Encounter groups involving other pop therapies using J.L.'s ideas were and remain common at growth centers like California's Esalen Institute. The founder of the next major step in this cultural trend was est, whose founder, Werner Erhard, I interviewed for this book. By the 1950s, companies commonly included sensitivity training in their employee training programs. Feminists and experts on race relations used role-playing and conducted encounter groups. In the 1960s, the engineers who developed personal computing devices ran their own psychodramas. The word became enmeshed in popular culture. I screamed when my favorite TV show, *The Many Loves of Dobie Gillis*, demonstrated a psychodrama with the iconic beatnik, Maynard G. Krebs, and again when the rock group The Association referred to "the psychodramas and the traumas" in their hit, *Along Comes Mary*. The folk rock group The Byrds recorded *Psychodrama City* in 1966, though David Crosby's lyrics were not among his best efforts. Today, corporations, the military, and academia require diversity training, and role-playing is commonly used in orientation for all sorts of occupations, including medicine and the law. Role-playing is also used to describe online gaming and sadomasochistic bondage. Counter-terrorist operatives are trained using psychodrama. A score of television shows are built around group therapy. We long for authenticity and meaning in human relationships as never before, and for spontaneity and creativity (J.L.'s core principles) in ourselves.

Just as J.L. anticipated, the boundaries between public spaces and personal growth have been blurred. Lifestyles that involve spirituality, meditation, and alternative diets are no longer considered odd or nonconformist. Today, we understand ourselves as playing roles, whether at home or at work. Role-playing and psychodrama techniques like the empty chair are part of couples and family therapy. Management and organization development courses include social network theory and diversity training. We might be socialized into a new company by participating in trust exercises. After dinner with our partner, we might sit down to watch a TV comedy about group therapy, or attend an improvisational theater performance (though few are truly improvised). While children are enjoying fantasy role-playing games on the web, both they and their parents are immersed in social media networks like Twitter, Facebook, and LinkedIn.

But can someone write a credible assessment of his father's influence on all these cultural realities, even someone who teaches and writes about history and philosophy for a living? The question is a fair one. Any history can go too far in attempting to connect distant dots. Of course I think that my father's role in the social movements that led up to our time has been underappreciated, but I intend to let the facts speak for themselves, including others' testimony. The story of the ways that J.L.'s ideas have been transmitted is a complicated one that I am both personally and professionally uniquely qualified to tell. But as I have a professional reputation to protect, I need to be especially scrupulous about overreaching. While I was writing this book, several psychotherapists told me they hoped that I would "set the record straight" about J.L.'s influence on many modern psychotherapies, but unless J.L.'s influence has been explicitly acknowledged by modern leaders in the fields he touched, I have avoided such claims.

My task is also made more difficult by the fact that J.L. had a paradoxical attitude about his creations. On one hand he believed that creativity is an infinite resource that belonged to no one; on the other hand he resented being overlooked for his creations, a source of frustration that sometimes caused him to lash out and hardened the resistance of his critics. But while J.L's intellectual priority was deeply important to him, in the final analysis his place in history only matters if it helps illuminate the ideas that are so important to us. For me, there is also a risk that runs in the other direction. Rather than exaggerating his influence, some might suspect that the son of such an imposing man has an unconscious urge to "kill the father." If so, I hope very much that I have failed.

The fact that J.L. was sixty-three when I was born is both a disadvantage and an advantage. That I didn't witness his most vigorous period allows me to be somewhat detached in identifying his triumphs and his failures. There is no question that J.L.'s ideas about theater, therapy, and the social network have helped to define the last hundred years. My goal in this book is to apply my unique insight into his experience as a guide to these motifs and their place in events that took place over a century and on several continents.

## ENCOUNTER CULTURE

As I read widely for this book, I discovered a remarkable passage in a 1982 history of improvisational theater by the distinguished University of California theater historian Robert Karoly Sarlos. In one dense paragraph the Hungarian-born Sarlos dispatched a series of observations that sketch a good part of the argument of this book, mentioning theater, therapy, and the group dynamics ideas that form the basis of the social network:

Connections between the early, pre-1920 tremblors [of the study of human relations] and the recent tidal wave of collectivity and spontaneity are indirect, but traceable. Moreno revived his *Stegreiftheater* as Impromptu Theatre with a probable impact on founders of the Group Theatre whose theatre he shared. From the playground creative theories of Neva Boyd, Viola Spolin developed a game-centered actor training technique for the Federal Theatre (1935–1939) and beyond. Paul Sills, who employed his mother's system at the Compass (1956) and at the Second City (1959), is largely responsible for an upsurge in improvisatory theatre that took advantage of, and helped spread, certain techniques of sensitivity training. Although Buber's *I and Thou* was first published in English in 1937, it had little effect until its second American edition, twenty years later. Nor did existentialism become a household word until Sartre's name made it so in the fifties. Research in group dynamics and group therapy, pioneered by Moreno and others in the thirties, intensified with the establishment in 1947 of the National Training Laboratory for Group Development. The explosion into mass movement occurred when Michael Murphy, primed for mysticism by a visit to an Indian ashram, founded the Esalen Center [sic]—a Western bridgehead for the human potential movement—in 1962. About the same time, the Living Theatre's communal approach to mythmaking attracted world-wide attention when, because of harassment by the Internal Revenue Service, it went on a tour of Europe—and the revolution of encounterculture was joined.

In a footnote, Sarlos (who died in 2009), writes that "these connections can be indicated here sketchily; they would provide sufficient material for a book dealing with the history of ideas."

Professor Sarlos, wherever you are, here it is.

## CHAPTER ONE

# WHAT THE WORLD NEEDS NOW

Empty chairs on the psychodrama stage.

*In the beginning was existence. In the beginning was the act.*

J.L Moreno, 1964

THE HANDSOME YOUNG COUPLE—he about forty, she about ten years younger—is in animated conversation as their expensive sports car rounds the bends of the coastal California canyons, the strains of Handel's *Hallelujah Chorus* in the background. As they arrive at their destination, beautiful bare-breasted young women sunbathe, men and women of various ages soak in coed nude hot tubs, a couple explores each other's faces with their fingertips, one man leads another in a primal scream, and an older Asian man conducts a t'ai chi class.

These were the opening minutes of Paul Mazursky's 1969 hit, *Bob & Carol & Ted & Alice*. For millions of Americans this was their first glimpse of a personal growth center, called "the institute" in the film, inspired by the famous Esalen Institute in Bug Sur, California. Esalen was the epicenter of the encounter group movement, along with a number of other kinds of experience aimed at expanding "human potential." Though hardly any Americans had ever been to such a place, much less participated in their signature activity—called variously encounter, sensitivity, or T-groups—the scene was nonetheless recognizable to sophisticated moviegoers of that era, for the encounter movement was a hot topic. Encounter groups were a kind of loosely structured group therapy that sought to enhance emotional sensitivity and expressiveness. Enthusiasts saw them as therapy for normal people and an opportunity to become a better, more complete person; critics saw them as a self-indulgent escape from reality or even a Communist plot to brainwash unsuspecting Americans.

## Touchy–Feely

During a decade of headlines proclaiming shocking violence, human rights movements, a "generation gap," and a youth rebellion, the human potential movement got a lot of ink. Encounter groups became their most visible activity. They were a curious and titillating respite from all the bad news, the very origin of the expression "touchy–feely." Reflecting the longing for authenticity after the "phoniness" of the 1950s canonically expressed by J.D. Salinger in *Catcher in the Rye*, many establishment institutions took encounter seriously as a novel and possibly permanent part of American life. The prestigious Russell Sage Foundation sponsored a scholarly analysis of the encounter group movement. Magazines like *Time, Newsweek, Life, Look,* and *The Saturday Evening Post* periodically chronicled the new philosophy of "inter-personal relations" and the organizations and leaders behind it. Mazursky got the idea for his movie from a *Time* magazine article. *Look* magazine senior editor George Leonard coined the term *human potential* movement in 1962, encompassing encounter groups, Eastern religions, bodywork, massage therapies, psychedelics, and all the new ways that people were in search of personal growth. In 1970 a *Life* magazine editor wrote about his and his wife's visit to Esalen: "I felt then, and I feel now, that we had been exposed to an almost-revolutionary format for educational and institutional change."

The *Life* editor was right, though not in the way he imagined. The popularity of encounter groups quickly waned, but the social forces they represented have left an indelible mark on our society. Encounter was part of a broader though ill-defined quest to expand human potential. Perhaps because it seemed to be (and often was) elite, narcissistic, and superficial, the pervasive traces of the human potential movement are easily ignored, even beyond the obvious continuing interest in New Age lifestyles and products, from Eastern-influenced spirituality to macrobiotic diets to organic bath soaps. It is also easy to overlook the depth and variety of the movement's origins. The roots and branches of the human potential movement included existential philosophy and psychology, innovative studies of group dynamics, experimental theater, humanistic psychology, management training, organizational development, training and screening of soldiers and spies, Eastern spiritual traditions, consciousness-expanding drugs, and experiments in sexual liberation. Though the leaders largely abjured leftist political activism, they sprang from the same dynamics as the rest of the counterculture. The human potential movement was "the continuation of expressive politics by other means," in the words of Sixties historian Todd Gitlin.

A core practice of the human potential movement, encounter groups appeared in a period characterized by exploding affluence and embodied by a glamorous young American president calling forth a "new frontier," by an incipient civil rights movement that demanded a more humane and respectful society, and by the birth control pill. As the initially hopeful decade of the 1960s became mired in divisions over war and race and scarred by assassinations, the desire to be authentic, not "playing games" but being "real" and living fully in the "here and now" became still more urgent. Authenticity meant being honest and open about one's desire for love and acceptance in an increasingly alienating, corporatized, technological, violent, and materialistic world. And it meant being willing and able to give love in return. Encounter groups involved touching others, both literally and metaphorically, in order to be in touch with oneself. Encounter also provoked a cultural backlash that has had important consequences for American politics: In the decades since its peak, the movement has been a favorite target of cultural conservatives like Christopher Lasch who view it as partly responsible for a "culture of narcissism."

Ironically, those who most desired these intense group experiences and wanted to escape their sense of anomie were often among the most affluent and educated members of society, those who should feel the least alienated.

They were also among those who were most likely to have access to the growth centers and other settings where they could experience encounters, especially through modalities like role-playing, which was often integrated with various forms of massage, meditation, and sometimes hallucinogens. *Bob & Carol & Ted & Alice* was a largely affectionate parody, but many leaders of the human potential movement saw it as a setback; nonetheless, the film is a window into the sensibility of the era. As the film critic Roger Ebert slyly observed in his review of the film, "[f]or some curious reason, we suddenly seem compelled to tell the truth in our personal relationships."

## THE MARATHON

Following the opening flourishes, Bob and Carol are participants in a twenty-four-hour marathon encounter group. Bob was played by Robert Culp, a charming if undistinguished actor closely identified with his role in the television program *I Spy*, in which he played a globetrotting secret agent in the guise of a tennis bum. As perhaps America's favorite child star and ingénue since Elizabeth Taylor, Natalie Wood was well cast in the role of the somewhat naïve but earnest and endearing Carol. Wood seemed no less wide-eyed as a grown woman than she did as the little girl who desperately wanted to believe in Santa Claus in *Miracle on 34th Street*, and later the virginal, love-struck Maria in *West Side Story*. As she strove for moments of insight into her relationship with her husband and the new sexual morality that was invading even the sacred precincts of marriage, Wood as Carol achieved a level of comic sincerity that lightened her evident struggle to become a new sort of woman and wife.

The possibility that they could achieve an enhanced level of meaning and openness in their relationship seems not to have occurred to filmmaker Bob or his wife Carol prior to their encounter-group experience. They were ostensibly there to plan his new documentary, a suitable premise considering the ongoing love affair between the human potential movement and the media. As the encounter group scene began, an open-faced young man introduced himself somewhat ambiguously as a leader or perhaps more as a guide—the movement never settled on a single term—and then suggested that the participants could learn something about themselves and one another as they related to each other with little sleep, with minimal bathroom breaks, and with no rules except nonviolence.

The group got started with a basic "warm-up" encounter exercise in which each member is encouraged to walk up to someone and "see, really see" them, breaking through the quotidian and comfortable barriers of embarrassment and stereotyping. In this way, they would also face themselves more honestly, dropping the usual defenses and impression management. The members took turns encountering one another through their gaze alone, trying to show the other person who they really are. Honest and earnest attempts to "be real" with other people in a group could in themselves evoke powerful feelings of relief and release, especially when combined with simple and nonthreatening physical contact. They might result in "peak experiences," perhaps equipping participants with permanent enhancements in their sense of responsibility for and sensitivity to the feelings of others.

Now that they had warmed up and dropped their initial defenses, the next scene in the movie showed the participants seated languidly around the room. The leader asked the group members to introduce themselves and explain why they were there. "I'm 64 years old and I still want to grow," said one man in a black business suit and tie. "I can't say no to a man," said a heavily made-up young woman. Each in their own way began to share their loneliness and longing, their fears and hopes. Emotions gradually deepened. Tears began to flow. To Bob, Carol sobbed, "I'm afraid of you." As the day wore on, inhibitions diminished. Each sleep-deprived participant found that deep, vulnerable place that was both unique to them, but somehow also shared by all who are thrown out on the human journey. The group finally coalesced into a huddling, weeping, throbbing mass. Hours before they had entered as strangers, even those who told themselves they knew one another; now they were united in a wordless bond of intimacy, comfort, and humanity. They had learned how to be more aware of their feelings, more willing to express them, and more sensitive to the feelings of others. At least for the moment.

## PSYCHODRAMA

Surely most moviegoers were amused and a bit surprised by the encounter-group scene in *Bob & Carol & Ted & Alice*. That was not necessarily the movie they were expecting. The film had been promoted through the then-popular lens of male-centered "wife swapping," as though husbands weren't also being "swapped." Movie posters showed Bob and Carol lined up in bed with their friends Ted and Alice. "Consider the Possibilities," the posters urged suggestively. Yet, as Ebert observed in his perceptive review, the film "isn't really about wife swapping at all, but about the epidemic of moral earnestness that's sweeping our society right now." That moral earnestness was supposed to be enhanced and explored in encounter groups. Like Clint Eastwood's empty chair, the film's encounter group scene was familiar to me, even though I was only seventeen when I first saw it. In one encounter group, I found myself in a sweaty clutch with two other young men as we sat cross-legged on the floor, all of us experiencing a sense of emotional release. Finally, as we rocked back and forth in unison, one of them said quietly, "Boy, you guys are so sensitive."

My group hug with the two other young men was part of a psychodrama session at the American Psychological Association 1970 convention in Miami. At what is normally a dry scientific meeting you could barely walk through the lobby or down the halls without tripping over a spontaneous encounter group. Violence still raged in Southeast Asia, the Age of Aquarius was still expected, and sensitivity training through group experiences was a way to bridge the gap between war and peace. The next year, three psychotherapists wrote that "the distinctions between sensitivity training, group encounter, and group psychotherapy are blurred. . . ." It wasn't possible to write about one without the others. Calling sensitivity training "a current phenomenon," they said that its historical roots date back to J.L.'s work in 1914. "Moreno, as the creator of psychodrama, can be considered the forerunner of the Group Encounter movement."

Then and now most people would have a hard time defining the word *psychodrama*. Nonetheless, it has become part of our cultural vocabulary, commonly used to describe the externalization of internal conflict, like anxiety about a problem with a boss or ambivalence in a marriage or any event that makes psychological forces visible. The words *psycho* and *drama* are loaded with implications of their own, but combined they pack a considerable punch. Journalists and bloggers are not above leaning on the word as an attention-grabber, even though the word drama alone often works just as well. At least several alternative rock bands call themselves Psychodrama or use it as the name of an album, and sex workers adopt the thin disguise of a psychodrama in their advertising. Role-playing has come to denote fictional games and sexual practices. Psychodrama is a favorite of sex manuals. *Joy of Sex* expert Alex Comfort advised, "[d]on't be scared of psychodrama—it works better in bed than in an encounter group—be the sultan and his favorite concubine, the burglar and his maiden, even the dog and a currant bun, anything you fancy for the hell of it."

The trivialization of psychodrama is amusing, and Comfort's pointer about psychodrama in the sack is doubtless on target, but the popular fascination with the word doesn't give much of a clue about the method of systematic role-playing. As a form of psychotherapy, a classical psychodrama is a well-defined process. It normally begins with a warming-up exercise in which, for example, an empty chair might be placed in the center of the group and each participant asked by the therapist, called a *director*, to sit in the chair and imaginatively become whomever he or she imagine sitting in that chair. The protagonist for that session might emerge from that warm-up, so that the action portion is an enacted exploration of the relationship with the person superimposed on the chair. The final part of a psychodrama is called *sharing*, in which the group members discuss the ways they identified with the drama, either in terms of their personal experience or as a participant in the drama itself. Analyzing and intellectualizing are taboos in sharing; rather the emphasis is on feelings.

Unlike psychodrama, the goal of encounter groups was personal growth and the "turn on" of an intense new experience rather than the more inclusive objectives of psychotherapy. With innovations like twenty-four-hour marathons, experiments in nudity and psychedelics, encounter groups and the human potential movement of which they were a part exploded on the public scene. Many professionals harbored reservations, pleased to see a rebellion against psychoanalytic orthodoxy and sympathetic to the goal of greater interpersonal sensitivity, but uncertain about the long-term implications. As encounter groups flourished they were described by several therapists as using "near-psychodramatic techniques. . . . All too often, however, these techniques are used piecemeal by leaders untrained in the [psychodramatic] method or its theory, frequently producing negative results." Those negative results included fears about careless and incompetent self-appointed gurus who longed for power and recognition, posing risks for those in search of solace at a vulnerable time in their lives.

## The Radical

J.L. regarded himself as the founder of encounter but not of 1960s-era encounter groups, which he saw as a spinoff of psychodrama. Like many of the group experiences that emerged after World War II, from his point of view these newcomers cannibalized his ideas. Notoriously stubborn, proud, and independent, he avoided being identified with any movement or organization he did not both found and control. He published his own books and academic journals and established his own psychiatric hospital, training institute, and professional organizations, even a movie company called Therapeutic Motion Pictures, all for the promulgation of his ideas. It was a pattern he established early in life. As a medical student in Vienna in the 1910s, he had his own impromptu theater, a journal of existential philosophy, a shelter for wartime refugees, and even his own religion in which he was not merely the medium to God but the voice of God Himself. J.L.'s flamboyant style and overt spiritualism were part of his creative genius, but they were also a professional handicap. Psychologist Karl Scheibe writes that J.L. "worked and wrote in an era when orthodoxies were most powerful, forcing his brilliant and innovative work on psychodrama to the margins of eccentricity and exclusion." He was a self-described megalomaniac, a highly controversial figure whose dramatic style alienated him from the staid academic world of mid-century America. In a moment of characteristic exaggeration, he said he narrowly escaped becoming a mental patient, allowing him to identify closely with those who were most deluded. He said he heard voices, not like someone with schizophrenia but like a biblical prophet. J.L. learned how to manage his creative impulses by pouring his considerable energy into his creations, his love of the spontaneous theater, and his lifelong desire to provide a universal stage upon which all human beings could remake their lives together.

In both his personal style and philosophy, J.L. was quite different from his sometime medical school lecturer, Sigmund Freud, who focused on analyzing the individual neurotic in the artificial setting of the consulting room. J.L. derived his inspiration more from theater than from medicine or psychology. He took his psychotherapy into the streets, homes, workplaces, and cafés. His psychodrama could recreate all of the actual, possible, and even impossible settings of human life in what he called "surplus reality," often to satisfy an "act hunger," an unresolved need to get into action. Rather than a single analyst, there was an entire group prepared to play roles that the subject of the psychodrama, called the *protagonist*, needed to fill to play out his or her emotional needs in action. The empty chair has long been a favorite warm-up. The symbolism of the empty chair taps into deep and cross-cultural feelings about absence and regret. Anyone can be projected into an empty chair, living or dead, or even a fantasy personage. To describe his techniques J.L. invented a new vocabulary. "Auxiliary egos" can take the role of one's parents, children, spouses, lovers, friends, coworkers, or anyone at all, including those who were dead or who never lived. One could "reverse roles" with those with whom one was in conflict, or "double" for someone who was unable to articulate how they truly felt, or "mirror" the behavior of another.

J.L.'s idea of surplus reality, his theatrical style, and his affection for the headline-grabbing anecdote, are illustrated by his most famous clinical case, the psychodrama of Adolf Hitler. During World War II he was presented with a Manhattan butcher who believed he was the Fuhrer and that the fellow in Berlin was an imposter who resembled him and had taken his place. When they met at J.L.'s Hudson Valley sanitarium he immediately took "Hitler" into the psychodrama theater, where he casually introduced him to several of the members of the group who were waiting for a session. Among them were "Goebbels," "Goering," "Eva," and other members of the Nazi inner circle. As reported in the *Los Angeles Times* during J.L.'s West Coast visit in 1945, the various racial theories and political intrigues of the war were replicated on the psychodrama stage. Eventually the man's act hunger was satisfied in the surplus reality of the psychodrama, and he was "back selling meat again on Third Avenue." J.L.'s confidence in his method was such that he believed even the ruthless, hateful dictator himself could be treated. "If such a treatment had been used on another superego—the real Hitler—he could have expended his megalomania on the stage and retired to some quiet activity like that of an artist," he told the newspaper.

The goal of many psychodramas is personal growth and learning, often by means of a catharsis, the term used by Aristotle to describe the emotions of pity and fear aroused by the drama, and also by trying out new roles, new ways of being in the world. His "Hitler" patient experienced such a catharsis, though it was not obviously emotional but more nearly cognitive in nature. J.L. deeply believed in human goodness and the capacity for growth. He told me that his disagreements with Freud included the psychoanalytic notion that birth is the first traumatic experience. Rather, J.L. saw the birth event as the first accomplishment, a triumph of spontaneity and creativity. He did not believe that sex or libido was the ultimate basis of human relations, but that Platonic love and altruism are possible and in fact common. J.L. intended the title of his masterwork *Who Shall Survive?* as an homage to Darwin, who understood that survival requires cooperation and mutual choice as well as competition.

As he anticipated the end of his life, J.L. was at different times philosophical and frustrated about his unrecognized priority. Writing in 2000, psychologist Karl Scheibe observed that "Moreno's name is simply not to be found in contemporary psychology texts. . . . Yet Moreno not only had powerful insights about the theatrical character of human life but developed from his ideas a set of revolutionary therapeutic practices." The same traits that enabled J.L. to battle the forces of orthodoxy—his insistence on independence, his resistance to association with institutions he could not control—also worked against him. And he knew it. "There is no controversy about my ideas," he once wrote. "They are universally accepted. *I am the controversy*" [emphasis in original]. But who can say that they would have chosen differently, or mobilized the energy to promote radical ideas over most of a tumultuous century? At least as important, by the time he was in his seventh decade the culture was changing. J.L. had been ahead of the curve all his life, but by the mid-1960s all kinds of group experiences were being touted in all sorts of organizations, as often as not using concepts and modalities that he had pioneered. Once a social science celebrity, J.L. began to fade from the public mind, even as his ideas were finally being accepted. Psychologist George Gazda has written that J.L. was "very likely the most colorful, controversial and influential person in the field of group psychotherapy. . . ." As Scheibe points out, ". . . it seems an ironic twist that while his influence has been mighty, his name has receded into the shadows."

Worse still, in the latter 1960s J.L. was caught on the horns of a dilemma, eager for recognition as he entered his last years but hesitant about identification with some of the manifestations of the movement he had helped to sow for half a century. In a 1970 interview, he sounded an uncharacteristically sour note about what was happening to his ideas and the limitations being placed on their universal application: "The giants are dead and 200 million midgets are in charge. We have to wait for the Psychonauts to take over from the Astronauts before we get to what we need: a psychiatry and sociatry for all mankind."

## ESALEN RISING

One institution in particular captured a part of the public imagination that J.L.'s innovations had once occupied with little competition. Esalen, the inspiration for Mazursky's film, was born in 1962 when two Stanford University alumni decided to create a new kind of institution on a stunning Pacific Ocean property that included a hot springs and had long been a bohemian retreat. At Stanford in the early 1950s, Michael Murphy heard a life-changing lecture on the Vedic hymns by the scholar of Eastern religions Frederic Spiegelberg. After a stint in the Army during the Korean War, Murphy began the Stanford doctoral program in philosophy, only to resign when he realized that postwar, Anglo-American philosophy was uninterested in mysticism. Murphy went to India and enrolled in an ashram. Returning to Palo Alto, he played golf, meditated, and got a job as a hotel porter. In San Francisco he met Richard Price and the two discovered that they had been at Stanford at the same time and that they were both psychology majors. Since then, they had followed similar paths. Price served in the Air Force, and like Murphy he had had an unsatisfactory graduate experience, his in the Harvard Department of Social Relations. That department housed some of the most important thinkers in social science, including several who were close to J.L., but Price found that academic psychology was unfulfilling.

The hot springs at Big Sur already had a reputation for nonconformity owing to their most famous resident, Henry Miller, whose erotic novels *Tropic of Cancer* and *Tropic of Capricorn* had been banned and burned. A group gathered around Miller to form an artist's colony, made famous in a 1947 *Harper's* article entitled "The New Cult of Sex and Anarchy," though Miller denied it was a cult. As a child, Murphy had vacationed on the property with his parents, and discovering that the place had fallen into disrepair, offered the owner his and Price's management services. Just before their first formal set of programs, the vision for what became Esalen was suitably initiated by the Eastern-oriented philosopher and mystic Alan Watts in January 1962. The British-born Watts became a guru for the California artists broadly included in the Beat movement.

The first formal Esalen program was a "leaderless group," an unstructured format that resembled group dynamics experiments inspired by J.L. and others who developed personality assessments for the armed forces during World War II. Then there was a seminar on psychic phenomena. Eastern religions, encounter groups, and parapsychological explorations were all to become important themes in Esalen programs, along with various forms of bodywork and Gestalt therapy. The diversity of experiences demanded some unifying principle. In the thought of the eminent British intellectual and author of *Brave New World*, Aldous Huxley, they found an overarching concept: human potentialities. Its 1960s mission statement was "ESALEN INSTITUTE [sic] is a center to explore those trends in the behavioral sciences, religion and philosophy which emphasize the potentialities and values of human existence."

Considering its embrace of Eastern wisdom, mystical experience, and the paranormal, historian Jeffrey J. Kripal has aptly called Esalen the focal point of a "religion of no religion," a quintessentially American phenomenon with precursors in Walt Whitman and William James, including a pluralistic sensibility in its fascination with Buddhism, Chinese Taoism and Indian Tantra, Carl Jung's archetypes and collective unconscious, Aldous Huxley's psychedelic spirituality, and Abraham Maslow's self-actualized man. In 1972, Duke University sociologist Kurt Back saw the visitors to growth centers like Esalen in the tradition of Geoffrey Chaucer's pilgrims in the *Canterbury Tales*, in need of "the singular experience a pilgrimage can give," especially these "strong group experiences" that flourished in post-World War II America. Kripal recalls the periodic spiritual revivals called American Great Awakenings, the first in the 1730s and 1740s, coming to full fruition with Jonathan Edwards's sensational and psychologically sophisticated sermons that evoked divine wrath in fire and brimstone. Various revival movements appeared in the decades before and after the turn of the nineteenth century, then again in the mid-1800s, producing finally the early twentieth-century "social gospel" of community activism in the quest for social justice. Were the social forces of early 1960s America that led to Esalen and dozens of other spiritual retreats a fourth American Great Awakening? The point is debated among historians, but the argument is a potent one. In the American-Protestant denominational tradition there is always room for another church.

The mysticism and group orientation for which J.L. was well known anticipated the spirituality of Esalen and the human potential movement. A budding social scientist named Walter Truett Anderson described his own journey from psychodrama to encounter groups in the later 1960s in his book *The Upstart Spring*. Anderson described his first experience with J.L. and psychodrama, "the grandfather of the group psychotherapies," which he credits with helping him and his wife get to the altar, and his later immersion in the culture of Esalen, where Michael Murphy chose him to become a leader of encounter groups. At the time, the roots of the human potential movement were thoroughly identified with Esalen and the 1960s, but Anderson noted, "all of the methods that became popular at Esalen were anchored firmly in Europe in the early decades of the twentieth century." Anderson singled out Martin Buber's diagnosis of social malaise in *I and Thou*, first published in 1923. Where were modern men and women to find the new forms of social life that could give meaning to an industrialized and urbanized civilization that seemed so intent on alienation and perhaps even self-destruction? "One person who had ideas about this—lots of them—was an excitable young Austrian psychiatrist named Jacob Levy Moreno."

> Moreno believed that alienation, the separation that prevented people from interacting deeply with one another, was not only a social problem but a spiritual crisis. As early as 1908, when he was scarcely out of his adolescence, he tried to start a "religion of the encounter." Later, as a practicing psychiatrist, he experimented with therapy done in groups instead of on a one-on-one basis between patient and therapist. Moreno also edited a literary magazine called *Daimon* (whose most famous contributor was Martin Buber) and for some years was involved with an avant-garde drama group called the Stegreiftheatre (Spontaneity theater). Moreno believed that all written plays were rigid artifacts of past culture that inhibited genuine self-expression and were therefore on the side of the forces of alienation. Spontaneity was what the world needed.

Anderson adds that J.L. "also developed a research method, called sociometry, for measuring the hidden substructures of interpersonal relationships." But for all his energy and ingenuity, many people who were interested in his ideas were not charmed by his megalomania. "Sociometry [now known as social network analysis] slipped away from his control and was absorbed into the growing academic discipline of social psychology; psychodrama found its way into new experimental methods, such as sensitivity training." As the final assessment of the tale Anderson's summary is accurate, but it was not always so. How J.L. developed and promoted these transformative ideas, how he lost control of them, and how his insights have been vindicated, is the core story of this book.

## THE GROWTH INDUSTRY

The human potential movement took root in a society that was primed for self-examination. After World War II a combination of popular appetite for personal growth, the closing of traditional asylums, and public spending to train a legion of new psychologists resulted in a subtle shift from an emphasis on treating mental illness to promoting mental health. The American Psychological Association began requiring clinical training for psychologists in 1949, though it wasn't clear what that would involve. "The mental health program is going forward," said the director of the National Institute of Mental Health at the time, "and neither you nor I nor all of us can stop it now because the public is aware of the potentialities." In 1940, virtually all psychiatrists were working in mental hospitals, but by 1957 nearly 80 percent were in private practice. The Veterans Administration trained university mental health counselors and the National Defense Education Act created sixty thousand jobs for school guidance counselors. In 1969, a University of California at Berkeley psychologist drily observed that psychotherapy was being "sought by people who do not think of themselves as ill but who wish to avail themselves of something they believe to be good for them, and it is offered by people who consider not that they are treating disease but that they are aiding in the realization of certain ethical values."

As the mass market for psychotherapy crystallized in the 1950s and 1960s dozens of psychological innovators sought to provide an alternative to Freudian psychoanalysis and Watsonian behaviorism, neither of which satisfied the longing for spiritual growth. Spawned by Ivan Pavlov's dog that salivated at the sound of a bell it came to associate with food, and carried forward by John Watson's contention that all behavior is shaped by pleasurable reinforcements, behaviorism seemed an even more desolate account of the person than did psychoanalysis. At least Freud believed that human beings need to be understood in terms of their mental lives, however grim his ultimate assessment of their drives. During the 1960s the bête noire of the human potential movement was the greatest and most radical behaviorist of his time, B.F. Skinner, who flatly denied that there is a mental life behind human actions. Skinner's 1971 book *Beyond Freedom and Dignity* popularized precisely that which was abhorrent to the gurus of encounter: that the solution to humanity's self-imposed ills lies in a technology of human behavior based on conditioning. Nonetheless, reflecting Mike Murphy's liberal philosophy that Esalen should be a sanctuary for visionary dialogue and sharing, in 1967 both Skinner and J.L. were invited speakers at Big Sur.

Skinner's book appeared along with a wave of popular accounts of the encounter movement. In 1967, a well-liked young leader of the movement, Esalen practitioner Will Schutz, published *Joy: Expanding Human Awareness*. Two years later, the same year as Bob and Carol's filmic adventure at the institute, *Joy* appeared as a highly successful mass-market paperback. Its cover boasted, not without reason, that it was "the book that made encounter groups famous." By 1969 the educated public was as familiar with encounter as it was with the other movements that signified a decade of social upheaval. Schutz explained the encounter movement's philosophy: "A man must be willing to let himself be known to himself and to others." (For all its vaunted sensitivity the movement was still terminologically and in other ways a reflection of a sexist society.) Schutz continued, "[h]e must express and explore his feelings and open up areas long dormant and possibly painful, with the faith that in the long run the pain will give way to a release of vast potential for creativity and joy. This is an exhilarating and frightening prospect, one which is often accompanied by agony, but which usually leads to ecstasy."

Wow.

Not everyone put so much emphasis on the elevated outcomes of these group experiences. "Encounter groups, particularly of the Schutz variety, were often wild events," Tom Wolfe wrote in 1976. "Such aggression! Such sobs! Moans, hysteria, vile recriminations, shocking revelations, such explosions of hostility between husbands and wives, such mudballs of profanity from previously mousy mommies and workadaddies, such red-meat attacks. Only physical assault was prohibited."

*Joy* was a success with a wide audience not only because of its timing, clarity, and positive, life-affirming message, but also because Schutz's approach combined elements of just about every modality that was making the rounds of encounter: J.L.'s psychodrama, Fritz Perls' Gestalt therapy, the bioenergetics of Alexander Lowen, Moshe Feldenkrais's movement therapy, Ida Rolf's muscle manipulation or "Rolfing," and Abraham Maslow's theory of self-actualization, among others. In *Joy* Schutz also provided something of a cookbook of techniques, when they are recommended and when they are too risky, so it was useful for general readers, group participants, and specialists alike. One technique Schutz described is the "wordless meeting," depicted at the beginning of the encounter session in *Bob & Carol & Ted & Alice.*

An article of faith in the encounter movement was that words often get in the way of openness and honesty, that either deliberately or unconsciously we use spoken language to protect ourselves and close ourselves off from others. In one group, Schutz wrote, "[i]t seemed a much clearer picture emerged of each of the group members after the wordless first meeting than ordinarily exists after a more traditional first meeting. Perhaps this underscores the use people make of words to prevent others from knowing them." An advantage of nonverbal meetings is that feelings can be turned into actions, Schutz said. "The group's desire to 'include' a member of the group was expressed when several members literally picked him up with his chair and carried him into the group circle."

As suggested by Schutz's anecdote, another premise of encounter was that if at all possible no one should be excluded. That was true about the world in general and in the encounter group in particular. Members who were somehow left out needed to be integrated, so group leaders were supposed to have an intuitive "feel" for the structure of the group. Sometimes inclusion happened spontaneously, as it did in the incident Schutz described, but at other times certain techniques were used to facilitate inclusion, like creating two-person dyadic meetings: "The charge to each member of the dyad is to try to understand the other, learn how to give to and take from the partner, and how to produce creatively with him." That way old patterns of isolation and withdrawal can be overcome and the lessons taken into experiences with other groups.

## HERE AND NOW

One of the ideas that J.L. insisted upon enacting at every opportunity, including in his presentations at scientific gatherings, was an emphasis on the "here and now." A focus on what is going on in the present moment became a key premise of the encounter movement. Instead of reflexively examining one's past and especially early childhood, as in psychoanalysis, encounter groups focused first on what's happening in the moment, between you and me and within the group. The option of rediscovering past hurts was always there, and was commonly pursued by encounter groups, but it was not the starting point in practice or in theory. Of course, the idea of "seizing the moment" is nothing new or unique to encounter. The feeling that time is passing us by is a familiar part of the human condition. When integrated into the encounter philosophy it could also rationalize a good time. In *Bob & Carol & Ted & Alice*, after learning of Bob's infidelity, Ted confesses that he nearly had an affair with a young coworker. "Go for it, we're only here for a second," says Bob. At the next possible opportunity Ted takes Bob's advice.

The characters of Ted and Alice were played by two newcomers, Elliot Gould and Dyan Cannon. Gould's Ted was a sweet, somewhat goofy and sexually frustrated young lawyer. The everyman quality he brought to the role and his puzzlement at his best friends' sudden discovery of emotional honesty and their aggressive and loudly public assertions of their love for him and his wife, helped audiences recognize their own bemused uncertainty about the promise of encounter and their resistance to such openness. A breakout role for Cannon, who brought a sultry comic intensity to the part, Alice's parochial attitude toward her friends' changed outlook, especially their sharing of information about their extramarital affairs, embodied viewers' waning resistance to the new sexual mores that accompanied "the Pill." As though to emphasize this point, in a hilarious bedroom scene between Ted and Alice that is the lynchpin of the film, the decisive climax of Ted's failed longing for sex is Alice's discovery that she has run out of pills. The energy and freshness that Cannon and Gould brought to their roles earned them both Academy Award nominations.

Director Mazursky squeezed a remarkable range of social commentary into his very accessible movie, even comparing group encounter sessions to more traditional individual psychotherapy. A stereotypically "uptight" but affluent young woman of the late 1960s, Alice is in individual therapy. Her session with a detached, puffy-faced, rigid psychotherapist presents a vivid contrast to the encounter group at the institute. Here the "here and now" between Alice and her therapist seems almost systematically ignored. After Alice recounts her recent denial of sex to Ted, her therapist points out that she said she "liked" her husband but "loved" her friends. Alice seems on the verge of a stunning insight into her ambivalence about Ted—at which point the analyst officiously points out that the hour is over and that they would continue the topic on Thursday. This on-screen satire of the established therapeutic model took place several years before Woody Allen mined the same territory in many of his films, and it too demonstrates that pop psychology was well known to film audiences of the era.

Working through its affectionate parody of encounter, *Bob & Carol & Ted & Alice* exploits universal themes. What are most dated about the movie are the clothing and language (as in Bob's casual remarks about "balling" and "chicks"), not the confused attitude toward love and sex that has hardly changed since the 1960s. The moments of highest comedy come when Bob and Carol achieve the "insight" that sex is only physical and has nothing to do with commitment. In the movie's penultimate scene Alice decides she really does want an orgy, putting aside her "uptight," middle-class attitudes. Although wanton sexuality certainly had its place in some encounter groups or at least in the practices of some leaders and group members, libertinism was not a core idea of encounter. In this instance, the movement was both influenced by the wider societal interest in sexual liberation and influenced it in return.

## Please, Less Touching

Just as *Bob & Carol & Ted & Alice* hit the screens a real-life self-confessed uptight journalist named Jane Howard was putting the finishing touches on her popular 1970 book, *Please Touch: A Guided Tour of the Human Potential Movement*. Because it not only permitted but encouraged touching, encounter was a distinct, even shocking departure from convention. In these days of full-body hugs by candidates for high political office, it is hard to recapture the physical reserve that was typical of pre-1960s behavior. Howard brought a homey, WASP American attitude toward her project, one she used as a point of pride that provided leverage for her story: A "straight" reader could feel comfortable in her hands. Howard's expressed view of the prominent people and places in the human potential movement was at once one of deep skepticism and horrified fascination, broken by scattered moments of sympathy and even what might be called joy. Why would a nice middle-class girl be attracted to studying the human potential movement? "[B]ecause," she wrote, "the movement is a curiosity, and if there is one thing I am it is temperamentally, professionally and all but pathologically curious. . . . The scope of its ambitions impressed me, and so did the idealism of its people. Naïve and silly and even dangerous though some of them might be, I sensed a gallantry in their efforts to change the world."

Howard's first reported on encounter groups in a 1968 *Life* magazine piece called "Inhibitions Thrown to the Gentle Winds," in which she mentioned that in some groups people do without clothing, an offense for which some readers called her a "slut." The slur was misplaced; among the unconventional behaviors Howard described and often adopted in her tour of the encounter movement, casual sex was not a concession to her reporting that this midwestern girl would allow, and her one foray into a nudist group was accompanied by agonized anticipation, and in the event, a marked lack of enthusiasm. The leader of her first Esalen workshop was none other than Will Schutz, whose *Joy* had just been published and who was struggling with the disease of fame or what he called "celebritytis" (though perhaps he protested too much). Howard's ambivalence about the sheer physicality of her first group experience was palpable. "I was disturbed, first of all, that people sat around at and between the meetings draped all over one another, leaning against one another with their arms around one another, giving backrubs to people they didn't even know. But as the days went on I changed. Regretting my own chronic undemonstrativeness, I did some draping and became a drapee myself."

"'It's all right to touch,' an elderly man kept assuring me."

Public tears and hugs came hard for Howard, but she persevered. The story was good, the characters colorful. J.L. was one of them. I remember Howard interviewing him in our home. She gave the appearance of a rather prim blonde wearing dark-framed eyeglasses; in *Please Touch* Howard recalls that her penchant for heavy eyewear was an object of criticism in one confrontational group. As he did with most women, when they first met J.L. kissed her hand and held it for a while as they chatted, a gesture to his Habsburg Viennese origins. But Howard was a challenge to J.L.'s somewhat antiquated Old World charms. Though she quoted him liberally and favorably, she also described him as resembling "a giant blue frog, younger than his eighty years, and who founded that much-used technique of psychodrama" (which, she said, "can go on for hours, very affectingly"). Howard called my mother "a one-armed lady who often conducts group psychodrama sessions," apparently unaware or unconcerned that she had survived cancer at the price of her right arm and shoulder and that she was J.L.'s powerful and indispensable partner.

Understandably, my mother was offended by their treatment at Howard's hands, but J.L. decided to handle the incident by congratulating Howard on the book's publication and expressing the hope that she continue to write. But he laid it on rather too thick, much like the whipped cream in a Viennese coffee house, hoping to bring her into the fold as had done with so many writers of the previous generation. "I am reading your most delightful book *Please Touch*. There is nothing like it in the literature of encounter. People will read it and quote it. It reads like a fantastic novel, backward from 2000." Although J.L. was abrupt with his philosophical enemies, he saw the press as indispensable for communicating his ideas and was only too happy to bend over backwards to avoid alienating an influential writer. Though his self-confidence and optimism about his ultimate place in history never flagged, as he aged his expectations became less realistic. After Howard published an article on an innovative, encounter-group style theater troupe in 1971, he sent Howard copies of a couple of his books, one of them his 1927 book, *The Theatre of Spontaneity*, noting that "*LIFE* has never done a proper review" of the work. Howard responded stiffly a few weeks later. "Thank you for sending me the two books. I'm sure they trace without question your role in [the] origin of new theatre developments, but I'm afraid I can't undertake the sort of article you suggest," and offered to return the books. Not to be discouraged in the promotion of his ideas, J.L.'s correspondence with Howard continued until just two years before his death.

As J.L. predicted, looking "backward from 2000," for all its snarkiness *Please Touch* is an accessible, entertaining, insightful account of the human potential movement at its peak. Despite her protests and reservations, it seems that Howard was deeply affected by her years of experience with encounter. Her next book, *A Different Woman*, makes implicit connections to encounter through her coverage of "rap sessions" and women's consciousness-raising groups, both exercises in self-discovery and social solidarity. Howard describes getting a massage at Esalen with her boyfriend, and visiting *One Flew Over the Cuckoo's Nest* author and psychedelic activist Ken Kesey. Her 1984 biography of Margaret Mead, a friend and supporter of J.L.'s (and with whom I drew animals on a napkin when I was about ten years old), is considered by many to be the best source on the great anthropologist. Howard's death at age sixty-one cut short the career of a talented journalist who had her finger on the pulse of the era.

## THE CLIMAX

The last scene of *Bob & Carol & Ted & Alice*, in which the four back off from a climactic act of group sex, has puzzled and frustrated viewers ever since the film appeared. Among the important exceptions was Pauline Kael, the powerful film critic of *The New Yorker*, who theorized that "[m]aybe, like Dyan Cannon in the movie, the press and the audience want an orgy, and think it's a cop-out when they don't get one." Similarly, the *Chicago Sun-Times* reviewer Roger Ebert wrote that Mazursky's ending was "consistent with the situation and the development of the characters, and an orgy at the end would have buried the movie's small, but poignant, message."

The finale can only be fully understood against the backdrop of the encounter movement that inspired it. The two couples go to Las Vegas for a weekend of play *sans* their kids, when Alice challenges the others to slip the last bonds of sexual conformity. They are in bed engaging in the preliminaries of group sex when, at a critical juncture, they stop. What was a fluid process of arousal has suddenly become self-conscious and detached. The moment has passed. Gradually they arise, dress, and walk into the corridor. As Bob pushes the elevator button the first strains of

*What the World Needs Now Is Love* creep into the soundtrack. The Hal David–Burt Bacharach hit was soulfully performed by Jackie DeShannon. In the elevator the two couples join a waiter carrying a room-service tray. Gradually they grin a little, half to themselves, sneaking glances at each other. The joke is not only the shared secret that moments before they were all in bed together, but that the mundane parts of life—retrieving empty dishes from a hotel room—have a way of going on even as we pursue and struggle with our deepest longings. They wander past the lobby shops, then walk more purposefully through the dark, tawdry, and pathetic casino where hopes and addictions flourish and are sure to be unfulfilled. Jackie is now in full voice as they exit the hotel under its exaggerated, sweeping canopy: "Lord we don't need another mountain. There are mountains and hillsides enough to climb."

The movie began in the bright sunlight of the Big Sur canyons, in nature's gorgeous warm embrace, but now it is late at night in the desert, in Las Vegas, the very quintessence of artifice and vice. In the journey from love to sex and back to love, we have lived a day with the two couples, but now the love is of a higher form. As they emerge from the hotel they are not alone. Behind them is a column of dozens of couples of various ages, dress, ethnicity, and lifestyle: a priest in a collar, an Indian chief, even some who might qualify as gay or lesbian—an astonishing suggestion in 1969. We are seeing a Noah's Ark of humanity in all its diversity, two-by-two. All were once in search of love. Having found it, they are shoulder-to-shoulder, arm-in arm, hand-in-hand. The column circles around, swirling and integrating into an enormous group. Then a giant wordless meeting exercise emerges, both recalling the encounter session at the institute and anticipating large group-awareness-training programs like est and the Forum only a few years later. Here, in this whirl of humanity of all shapes and sizes, is the original social network, not prearranged or virtual, but spontaneous and embodied.

A round, sweet-faced man with a heavy beard confronts the audience. For a moment we are face to face with him. He smiles at us warmly, reassuringly, as though to say that he accepts us for who we are. Then he turns to face Alice, then Alice encounters Ted, then Bob encounters Carol, all with delighted expressions of joy in the discovery that they really do love each other. The sex was not the point at all of course, but as is so often true for human beings, a distraction from what the world really needs, and what they have finally realized they have.

It was an eminently simple thing that they were looking for, at once the simplest but most elusive thing in the world. In the end, the crucial clue was to be found in a little verse J.L wrote in 1914, in a poem called "Invitation to an Encounter," a few modest lines that started it all:

> *A meeting of two*
> *Eye to eye*
> *Face to face*

CHAPTER TWO

# THE GODPLAYER

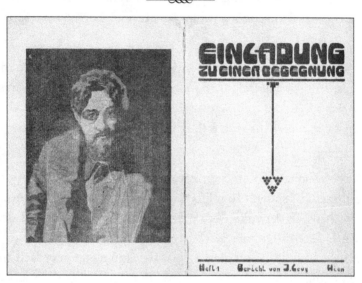

J.L.'s "Invitation to an Encounter," 1914.

*It was in the early part of our century that a young man tried to become*
*God. The place was Vienna; the period of his appearance was between 1908*
*and 1914. He made a deep impression upon his contemporaries. He had his*
*apostles, his gospel, his apocrypha. The religious books in which his doctrine*
*was expressed had profound reverberations throughout the intellectual*
*world. The cruel wars and revolutions through which mankind has passed*
*since have destroyed or dispersed most of the original witnesses, but some of*
*them are still living, and I am one of them.*

J.L. Moreno, 1972

WHEN J.L. IS IDENTIFIED AS A VIENNESE PSYCHIATRIST of a certain
era, many assume he must have been a Freudian. Although Sigmund Freud was one of his medical school lecturers, J.L. spent all of his
professional life casting his psychodrama as the logical next step beyond

49

psychoanalysis. He conceived of psychodrama as an opportunity to get into action instead of just talking, to take the role of the important people in our lives to understand them better, to confront them imaginatively in the safety of the therapeutic theater, and most of all to become more creative and spontaneous human beings. After one of Freud's lectures on a dream analysis, the medical students filed out of the room. Freud chanced to ask J.L. what he was doing. This was the way J.L. remembered his response:

> Well, Dr. Freud, I start where you leave off. You meet people in the artificial setting of your office. I meet them on the streets and in their homes, in their natural surroundings. You analyze their dreams. I give them the courage to dream again. You analyze them and tear them apart. I let them act out their conflicting roles and help them to put the parts together again.

It was an audacious and even impertinent reply from a twenty-three-year-old medical student to a fifty-six-year-old professor. However, it is unlikely that J.L.'s remarks were precisely as he reported them decades later. His ideas about role-playing were only beginning to take shape at that time. But it is clear that he was developing an approach that he believed could be superior to psychoanalysis, and that the roots of his thinking were quite different from those of Freud. The British group psychoanalyst Malcolm Pines draws a vivid contrast between the two in their cultural context:

> Freud is the son of the enlightenment, and inheritor of the intellectual and religious emancipation of the French Revolution. He is an Ashkenazi Jew and relatively distant from Jewish mysticism and spiritualism.
>
> Moreno is Sephardi, ascetic, a wild extravagant spirit who proclaims his godliness and who, beneath his role play, remains deeply spiritual. He uses science to practice medicine but not to research into the basic sciences. He uses science for his sociometric tables but his heart is in his therapy where his genius shows, especially with psychotics, for whom he evidently feels empathy. . . .

Freud and J.L. were German-speaking intellectuals in a period under the sway of Nietzsche's opposition of the forces he called the Apollonian and the Dionysian: the mind's struggle to liberate itself from instincts versus the celebration of wild nature. "Freud," Pines writes, "explored myth and drama through the Greek tragedies and through his self-analysis. Moreno took another path, away from self-analysis and towards the celebration of the self, of its creativity and spirituality." Of the two, Pines concludes, J.L. is the more modern man. His world is that of "the encounter, the absurd, of fragmentation." His is "a psychology of possibility, of openness to the future, of indeterminacy."

## MODERNISM

J.L. was a product of the nineteenth-century Ottoman Sephardic community that had over the previous several hundred years been rocked by a series of false messiahs, perhaps the most shocking and celebrated of whom was Sabbatai Zevi, who proclaimed himself the redeemer in 1648. Over the next two decades Sabbatai's fame, wealth, and influence spread. The Sultan finally took notice of the disorder Sabbatai was causing. In a dramatic scene in the Sultan's court, Sabbatai placed a turban on his head and announced his conversion to Islam. In his wake, he left chaos on all sides.

One response of the Jewish world to Sabbatai and other false messiahs was a greater emphasis on the charismatic authority of rabbis than on preoccupation with He who would finally bring redemption. Nonetheless, messianism had left its mark on the community and it clearly fired J.L.'s imagination, keenly aware of the Christian savior's Jewish origins. Thus although little Jacob was educated by a distinguished rabbi and was deeply impressed by the first words of Genesis, he was more interested in Jesus than the Torah. Yet messianism was only one ingredient of the spiritual stew in which J.L. first came to awareness. Like many Jewish girls at that time, his mother had attended a convent school. She read tarot cards, believed in fortune telling, and tried to interpret dreams. These were common preoccupations of Jewish folk life in the region; Freud, too, had his earliest acquaintance with dream interpretation through Jewish mystical traditions. Steps from the site of J.L.'s family home in Bucharest there was, and remains, a Greek Orthodox basilica. The long processions of richly decorated holy men impressed him deeply. Then there were earthier but no less revelatory experiences with his fifteen-year-old Hungarian nanny Piroshka (herself only a couple of years younger than J.L.'s mother, Pauline), whom J.L. recalled as responsible for his toilet training and also for initiating him sexually when he was four or five years old, a common practice among Middle-European peasants. To J.L., Piroshka came to represent a mystic animism, the idea that spiritual life permeates everything both animate and inanimate.

In 1894, when J.L. was four years old, he first tried his hand at Godplaying. In the large basement of the Bucharest house, there was an oak table. Bored one Sunday afternoon while his parents were out, he instructed a group of children from the neighborhood that their game that day would be God and his angels. But who would play God? Little Jacques, of course. Anticipating his later immersion in theatrical stage design, he directed them to collect chairs from all over the house so they could build a tower on the table. He would ascend to the top and they would fly around him. The structure was accomplished and two of the bigger children held up the tower as the others encircled it. The game was going well until one of the "angels" suggested that God spread his wings and fly. As he stretched his arms to take wing the angels holding up the chairs released them, and within a split second he was on the floor with a broken right arm.

## FALLEN GODS

Freud would have interpreted J.L.'s Godplaying as an expression of J.L.'s narcissism and megalomania. This it surely was; but reflecting on the experiment years later, J.L. saw it as having greater meaning. The natural self-centeredness of all small children prepares them especially well to imagine themselves in the God role, the *fons et origo* of all creation. We are all fallen gods, he often said, as we come to learn that we are not the center of the universe. Even for children Godplaying is challenging. "My warming up to the difficult 'role' of God may have anticipated the warming-up process of spontaneous role acting on the psychodrama stage," J.L. wrote in his memoirs. "That I fell when the children stopped holding up the chairs may have taught me the lesson that even the highest being is dependent upon others. . . ." These insights about the conjunction of spontaneous dramatic play upon a stage along with a network of other beings, the primordial union of the individual and the group, formed the basis of much of his later thought. Their shared modernist environment helps to account for Freud's observations in *Civilization and Its*

*Discontents* (1929) about the individual in relation to the group; but while Freud sees the group as a source of repression, J.L. sees in it the possibility of salvation.

J.L. loved, admired, and identified with his father, whom he remembered as a man with a deep appreciation of human nature in all its diversity. An only moderately successful tradesman, Nissim Moreno Levy moved the family to Vienna in search of better circumstances when J.L. was five. J.L. was the eldest of three boys and three girls. Unlike the rest of the family, Nissim never fully adjusted to the Germanic language or culture, preferring life in the Ottoman east. At some point he began long periods of absence. J.L. speculated to me that his father might well have had a second family somewhere; it is certain that he was a philanderer. In 1900 when J.L. was eleven his father took him to meet his cousins in Constantinople, now Istanbul. J.L. recalled that his great uncle was a convert to Islam, perhaps a banker. As a wealthy Muslim, he was expected to shelter unmarried women, lest they become prostitutes. This is how a pubescent J.L. came to spend time in a harem. "The girls were primarily concerned with preserving their youth and beauty, and they seemed to spend a great part of their time tending their bodies and faces, oiling and perfuming themselves, massaging, bathing," he recalled. "Women aged fast in Turkey, and by the time a woman was thirty, she had to be extremely careful to preserve her looks." Few received much attention from their patron, so they frequently coupled with the eunuchs, who posed no threat of pregnancy. Perhaps he associated Sabbatai the false messiah with his great uncle the businessman, both converts to Islam. What is certain is that growing up in an atmosphere in which he was exposed to all three Abrahamic religions, J.L. came to see God in universal terms.

Reinforcing his self-described megalomania, J.L. was both a brilliant student and the de facto head of the household when his father finally abandoned the family in 1906. As the oldest son J.L. was provided the funds that were needed to pursue academic opportunities, so much of the burden of providing for the family fell on his younger brother, William. For the rest of their lives Willie was the businessman who quietly supported his brother's work, asking no credit for himself. J.L. earned money as a tutor, but in some instances he gave his services free of charge, as in the case of little Lisette Bergner whose family had limited means. Lisette was such a difficult child that her parents worried that she would be thrown out of school. Elizabeth Bergner would later become one of the great actresses of the German stage. After leaving Germany to escape Nazism, she starred in such British films as *Escape Me Never*. In her 1978 memoir, Bergner remembered J.L.'s "Christbeard," "grippingly beautiful blue eyes," and his smile that was at once "loving and amused." She became a close friend of Freud and was analyzed by Alfred Adler, but she credited J.L. for saving her academically and opening her creative side.

## VIENNA

The first twenty years of J.L.'s life corresponded almost precisely with the period historians call Viennese Modernism, an unsettled time before World War I in which a longing for peace coexisted with an urge to destroy, a wholesale rebellion against the doldrums of contemporary Mitteleuropa. As Carl E. Schorske, the historian of *fin de siècle* Vienna has written, "[t]he moral and scientific culture of Vienna's haute bourgeoisie can scarcely be distinguished from garden variety Victorianism elsewhere in Europe. Morally it was secure, righteous, and repressive. . . ." The pompous social style of Habsburg Vienna was notorious for its ritualized flattery. Even shopkeepers would come around from behind their counters to greet female clients in an elaborate hand-kissing ritual. J.L.'s personal style reflected the exaggerated operatic qualities of the Vienna of his youth; but somewhat paradoxically, so did many modernist themes—especially the flouting of conventional morality, the desire for a more emotionally honest society including a focus on the "here and now," and the fascination with the theater as the most comprehensive and universal of the creative arts.

Modernism was simultaneously progressive and reactionary. Rebellion took countless forms. Freud's *Interpretation of Dreams* (1900) proposed that his patient's dreams were a form of wish fulfillment that was consciously unacceptable, such as bisexual fantasies. The painter Gustav Klimt's favorite subjects were women who were portrayed as either aloof or erotic. There was the pessimistic philosophy of Ludwig Wittgenstein (born in 1889, the same year as J.L.), and the absurdism of Franz Kafka, whose close friend and literary executor Max Brod was one of J.L.'s collaborators. Somewhat older was the playwright and physician Arthur Schnitzler. His plays focused on love and death and challenged the mores of a culture in decline. Schnitzler's *Rieigen* created a scandal by portraying five couples from various social classes who were about to or had just had sex.

Schnitzler's plays were expressions of another movement related to modernism, the Young Vienna (*Jung Wien*) writers who rebelled against moralistic attitudes toward love and sex and advocated more openness in society, earning a reputation for decadence. A popular leader of Young Vienna was Peter Altenberg, who wrote mainly sensitive little stories and essays and was known for his worship of boyish young girls but not, it seems, in a sexual sense. Among Altenberg's other quirks was a deathly fear of poverty. He lived simply, borrowed endlessly from friends, but died with a considerable estate. Though forty years older than J.L. they became close friends, wandering through Vienna at all hours. "P.A." was the paradigm of the Bohemian character so prevalent in the twentieth century. Fitted out with sandals and walking stick, his proto-hippie personal style influenced J.L.'s own as a young man. On an all-night walk through Vienna he told J.L. that he preferred his ideas to Freud's because "if I have to die, I would rather die of diarrhea than constipation." Near the end of his life Altenberg was the senior contributor to J.L.'s literary journal, *Der Daimon*, which undoubtedly lent great prestige to that venture.

The Viennese modernists made their influence felt in all creative fields. There were architects like Otto Wagner who combined new materials with sculpture and functionality, and Adolf Loos who focused on elegance in design. The philosopher Wittgenstein helped design a house for his sister, an experience that influenced his later thinking about problems of transmitting information. The witty Karl Kraus fiercely satirized German culture in print and gave one-man performances of others' writings accompanying himself in song and on the piano. In their classic *Wittgenstein's Vienna*, Allan Janik and Stephen Toulmin write that "[i]n Kraus's hands polemic and satire became weapons with which to direct men away from everything superficial, corrupt and dehumanizing in human thought and action, back to the 'origin' of all values, and so, in effect, to accomplish a regeneration of culture as a whole." Kraus admired Peter Altenberg as one whose life was fully integrated with his work.

Arnold Schoenberg wrote highly influential chamber music; his student Alban Berg put to music some compositions that Peter Altenberg had written on the back of postcards. Composer Gustav Mahler saw opera as the synthesis of all the creative arts, a view that J.L. apparently adopted from him, though J.L. rarely attended the opera or any theater that was not his own. J.L. later knew Mahler's widow, Alma, a Catholic feminist who was then married to the anarchist Franz Werfel, another of J.L.'s literary collaborators. Werfel wrote a powerful novel exposing the Armenian genocide, but his most famous work was *The Song of Bernadette* about the saint who had visions of the Virgin Mary at Lourdes. He and J.L. had a reunion when Werfel came to Hollywood in 1942 for the movie adaptation of his novel.

## CHAIM KELLMER

In his later teens, J.L. succumbed to a period of dissatisfaction and depression, a kind of wandering in the desert. He blamed his father's departure on his mother, resented his uncles' intrusions into the family's precarious financial position, and sank into the familiar adolescent rejection of the educational system. He read many religious texts, struggled to find the right relationship with God, and came to admire the eighteenth-century Swedish mystic Emanuel Swedenborg, whose ideas had attracted attention on both sides of the Atlantic. Swedenborg claimed to have experienced "encounters" with beings from other planets. Perhaps, as J.L.'s biographer suggests, he found in Swedenborg a role model, someone who was both a scientist and a theologian. Constructing the role of a prophet, he took to wearing a long green cloak, grew a long untrimmed beard, and violated the convention that men should wear a hat. His behavior shocked and embarrassed his mother, who worried about his sanity and the impression he was making around town. Thanks to his unconventional appearance and behavior, J.L. was already a known figure when he entered the University of Vienna in 1909. Fortunately for him, there he experienced a relationship that moored him back to the world and gave shape to his ill-defined religious ambitions. It was the most important encounter of his young life.

"I was stopped by a stranger one cold winter morning" while crossing the street to the university. The stranger told J.L. that he had seen and heard him many times, and wanted to speak to him. Chaim Kellmer was about to receive his doctorate in philosophy at the university. That cold morning Kellmer was supposed to attend a seminar, but instead he decided to introduce himself. Tall and broad-shouldered, Kellmer was considerably older, but also riven with puzzles about the moral demands of the universe. He was torn between the life of an intellectual and working with his hands, or perhaps settling in one of the Jewish colonies in Palestine. In a deep and melodious voice he addressed J.L.: "Tell me how to live and what to do."

The nineteen-year-old J.L. felt overwhelmed that this imposing, brilliant, and passionate man was putting his life in J.L.'s hands. They walked in silence for a long time. Perhaps, for all of his previous fitful Godplaying, this was the moment at which J.L. gained a crucial insight into the messianic role: that it is not a role that one can choose simply for oneself, that one must be chosen by another as the path to salvation. He came to see the role of God and His followers as an exemplar for all interpersonal choice, a moment of mutual recognition and acceptance. This insight came to be crucial in his later appreciation of the healing power of the group as well as its inherent internal structure of networks of choice and rejection, with the encounter as its bedrock.

Around the time of his first encounter with Kellmer in 1909, J.L. began a career as a storyteller for children in the Augarten, a public park famous for its baroque gardens. "[M]y favorite pastime was to sit at the foot of a large tree in the gardens of Vienna and let the children come and listen to fairy tales. . . . It was not so much what I told them, the tale itself, it was the act, the atmosphere of mystery, the paradox of the unreal becoming real." Predictably, J.L. was at the center and the tree became a kind of stage with multiple levels, as he would sometimes move up higher and sit on a branch, another heavenly ascent. From the excited imagination of the children, he came to appreciate how in a dramatic setting the unreal could become real. Their spontaneity and creativity far surpassed that of adults.

J.L. began to think that many human problems result from a deficit of spontaneity and creativity, an unfortunate and nearly universal consequence of growing up. These were pieces of the puzzle that became his inspiration for what he later called "psychodrama," an action setting in which the twin qualities of spontaneity and creativity could be revived and relearned. Besides helping him develop his philosophy, the children's theater games in the park gave J.L. his first taste of celebrity. They also resulted in one chilling encounter with an impoverished and disheveled postcard painter named Adolf Hitler. After one of the storytelling sessions, Hitler approached J.L. and shook his hand. "We introduced ourselves, and he told me he had enjoyed the session. He had no particular distinction but had an enthusiastic spirit." J.L. saw him again in 1921 in a Munich beer hall, "on the platform exhorting his listeners to their future glory. As far as I could see, Hitler was just another nationalist with a following among the factory workers. He was the same enthusiast I had met in the park, but still not particularly distinctive."

J.L. did have an opportunity to put his budding theories about groups into practice with the founding of a wartime refugee shelter called the House of Encounter, where displaced persons were helped to file for work papers and other necessary documents as well as to obtain jobs. Written on a wall of the house was its motto: "Come to us from all nations. We will give you shelter." He and Kellmer were joined in this project by three other advanced university students, one of whom, Andreas Peto, returned to his native Budapest in 1938 and founded a famous institute for children with movement disorders like epilepsy. Group meetings held in the House of Encounter to resolve disputes among the residents were a source of inspiration for J.L.'s ideas about group therapy. The project was idealism in action and it also added fuel to J.L.'s persistent messianic side. Accepting J.L.'s model, the other young men in his circle also grew prophets' beards, for a time living a monastic life under the spell of religious enthusiasm. "We were all committed to the sharing of anonymity, of loving and giving, living a direct and concrete life in the community with all we met. We left our homes and families and took to the streets. We were nameless but were easily recognized by our beards and our warm, human, and gay approach to all comers." They received many donations for the House of Encounter, including a contribution from a Catholic relief organization.

J.L. had an intuition about what today would be known as the drama of everyday life. That drama is played out not only in a vast array of types of encounters between people, but also in the interpersonal choices they make. The attractions and repulsions between human beings have consequences for them and others that it seemed to J.L. had never been properly identified. Preoccupied with this notion, one day he took the families of the House of the Encounter for a picnic in the park. At some point in the festivities, he asked the parents to line up on one side and the children to line up on the other. Then he asked the children to walk over to those whom they would like to be their parents, not necessarily their actual parents. The result was predictable, but startling when so obviously realized. Some parents were surrounded by happy children, whereas other couples stood alone. Here was concrete albeit painful truth about interpersonal choice and the internal structure of this group of parents and children. But the point was not simply to embarrass or cause trouble, but in a nearly surgical fashion, to lay bare a truth that could then be ameliorated. At the moment J.L. did not have the healing tools he needed. Later he believed the psychodrama provided them.

## CLOSE ENCOUNTERS

Though Godplaying and social activism were the most important expressions of J.L.'s personality in his university days, there were still classes, examinations and clinical assignments on the way to fulfilling his professional goal: to become a family doctor. J.L. had left secondary school before obtaining his diploma, so to qualify for the medical faculty he needed to take some other courses and to pass written and oral exams. In 1909 and 1910, he enrolled in both philosophy and premedical courses, then he was permitted to transfer to medicine where he was introduced to some of the most famous professors in anatomy, biology, surgery, and gynecology. Surprising for a Godplayer, J.L. disliked delivering babies and when he became a young doctor always managed to transfer that responsibility to colleagues.

J.L. took advantage of the intellectual hothouse that was Vienna in the 1910s. He attended lectures by Albert Einstein in 1911 when Einstein was working as a professor at the German university in Prague; there was a great deal of traffic between the two cities in those days. Einstein was beginning to be recognized for his 1905 papers, especially the one on relativity. The fact that Einstein left room in his theorizing for a mystical attitude toward the cosmos impressed J.L. and helped validate his own sensibilities.

As a medical student, J.L. was assigned to work as a research assistant to anatomy professor Julius Tandler, the architect of the Austrian welfare and public health system. Tandler was a devotee of the popular notion that the loss of so many healthy young men in the World War would undermine public health unless provisions were made to improve the general condition or "race hygiene" of the social body. The idea of race hygiene became a key concept of Hitler's National Socialists and was used as a rationale for ethnic cleansing, and ultimately the Holocaust. Although posterity has linked such eugenic notions to Nazism, in fact they were dominant in the medical science establishment before the 1930s. Tandler himself was both a social democrat and one of the few Jews on the University of Vienna medical faculty before World War I.

J.L.'s favorite professor was the young Otto Pötzl, who was to become a distinguished expert on diseases of the brain. Pötzl was his first important direct link to the psychiatric profession. He was warm and humorous, full of Jewish jokes though he was not Jewish. J.L. confided his ideas about God to Pötzl, a very unusual intimacy between a student and a professor in those days. Pötzl published a paper about dreams in which he listed J.L. as a coauthor, his first publication. Among his other research assistants was the psychoanalyst Helene Deutsch, who trained the humanistic psychologist Abraham Maslow.

Pötzl was a man of courage and integrity. Twenty years later, as chairman of the department of psychiatry at the University, Pötzl tried to protect his Jewish colleagues and their patients from the Nazi race laws. According to a history of the medical school after the annexation of Austria to Germany:

> Psychiatrists much more than any other professional group were involved in Nazi genocide, as scientific and ideological forerunners, as political advisors, consultants, institutional directors, responsible health-policy makers and health officials, or as exclusive operators of the gas valves in the euthanasia institutions. Nevertheless, the Viennese Chair of Psychiatry Dr. Otto Pötzl, did not play a leading role in Nazi racial hygiene. As Viktor Frankl, who was director of the Neurological Department of the Jewish hospital in Vienna from 1938 until 1942, told me in an interview, Pötzl behaved very decently towards Frankl and Jewish patients. He did not transfer Jews to the Steinhof sanatorium, where they

might have become victims of "euthanasia" activity, but sent them to Frankl to [sic] the Jewish hospital.

Frankl survived the war in a concentration camp, though his family did not. He returned to Vienna to create his own form of psychotherapy he called "logotherapy." Frankl and J.L. became friends in the 1950s, both beneficiaries of Pötzl's decency.

Pötzl was himself an assistant to Julius Wagner von Jauregg a formidable scientist, Nobel Laureate, and notorious anti-Semite who had divorced his Jewish wife. J.L. described him as "an aristocrat whose aloof, superior manner placed him in a realm far removed from anyone who worked with him. Moreover, he was a boring lecturer who put his students to sleep." A bear of a man and a champion wrestler, he was feared by both patients and colleagues. Pötzl told J.L. a remarkable story about von Jauregg: "Once, wearing a mask, he went to a bout where the current Russian wrestling champion was fighting and challenged him to a match. Von Jauregg won the bout, chose to remain anonymous, and had Viennese wrestling fans mystified for years."

Von Jauregg won his Nobel Prize in 1927 for experiments that began in 1917. In those pre-antibiotic days, there were no effective treatments for the psychiatric symptoms of advanced syphilis. Von Jauregg had the idea that by giving his patients malaria the high fever would impede the bacterium and halt the progression of the psychosis associated with syphilis. Indeed, many patients did have a remission from their symptoms because of his "malaria therapy." These were the days when the head of a psychiatric hospital could do whatever he thought was indicated or just scientifically interesting. J.L. counted himself fortunate that he escaped from assignment to von Jauregg's clinic before he would have been expected to participate in unethical experiments with helpless mental patients.

Besides witnessing the unethical experiments, J.L. was also exposed to the practice in the von Jauregg clinic, during the war as an anesthesiologist J.L. assisted the practice of a brain surgeon in another refugee camp in Hungary, a Dr. Wragasy. The experience led him to a lifelong mistrust of surgeons and hospitals.

Dr. Wragasy's designation of a brain surgeon was self-styled and emerged because he had developed a standard treatment for many different ailments that consisted of trepanning the skull and tossing iodine on the exposed brain tissue. Dr. Wragasy really believed that this treatment was indicated. . . . But of course the consequences of opening up the skull were to cause brain sepsis in many, if not most cases. Thus, many men died in agony because of Dr. Wragasy.

## SOCIAL REFORM

As exemplified in his performance in the encounter with Freud, theatricality was central to J.L.'s personality from an early age. He found drama not only in the children's role-playing games, in his Godplaying and in the formal theater, but also de facto in the institutions of civil life. While a medical student he sometimes observed trials in Vienna's law courts. Then with his family or friends he reenacted the performances of the lawyers, witness, judges, and members of the jury, and on the basis of their relative success in playing their roles and interacting with one another he was able to predict the outcomes of the trial. In 1913, his enthusiasm for unorthodox social reform took another turn, perhaps influenced by Karl Kraus's attacks on hypocritical Viennese attitudes toward prostitution, a trade that was in effect encouraged by late marriages that were often business arrangements. "One afternoon I walked through the Praterstrasse when I encountered a pretty girl, smiling at me. She wore a striking red skirt and white blouse with red ribbons to match it." As he was striking up a conversation with the girl a policeman appeared and took her away. J.L. followed them to the police station where she was booked as a prostitute. Sex workers were generally tolerated, but were not allowed to wear such bright colors during daylight hours. Offended by the women's lack of rights (while asserting that he was too much of a snob to utilize their services), J.L. recruited a gynecologist and a newspaper publisher to help him organize the women of Vienna's red-light district into a labor union. Meeting in small groups, J.L. and the gynecologist gained the women's trust, even persuading them to pool a small amount of their earnings into a fund for medical emergencies and pensions. A lawyer was retained to represent them in court. The climax of the experience was a meeting of the women in a large hall, with J.L. and the gynecologist the only men on the dais. As their first act, the women threw J.L. and the physician out of the room, an expression of defiance to the male power structure.

This exercise in mutual aid was one of several incidents, including the House of Encounter and the children's theater games that planted the twin ideas of group therapy and social networks in J.L.'s mind. Another was his experience in 1915 and 1916 as a medic for the Austro-Hungarian Army in a refugee camp in Mitterndorf, a spa town midway between Graz and Salzburg. The camp had been established for displaced Italians from the Tyrol. Thousands were thrown together in barracks; intractable conflicts resulted that were exacerbated by the primitive living conditions. J.L. drafted a letter to the Ministry of the Interior suggesting that it would be wise to take into account the "national and political" affinities of the refugees when assigning them to houses or to work in the camp factories. "A new order, by means of sociometric methods is herewith recommended." It was a characteristically audacious proposal by a very young man to revise the very structure of the camp. There is no evidence that the Ministry replied, nor even that the draft letter was sent. But it was J.L.'s first known proposal to design a community deliberately along the lines of interpersonal choice, an idea he would have the opportunity to apply in America nearly two decades later.

## Encounter

Although he was a prolific author J.L. was more attracted to action than to writing. This attitude was not simply a matter of temperament, but followed from his criticism of "cultural conserves," that the products of creativity are less important than the creative act itself. Once cultural productions appear in the world, he argued, they are all but dead and can too easily block future creativity. But even before his twentieth birthday he began several essays that were published as booklets between 1908 and 1911, just around the time he was entering the university and met Chaim Kellmer. At the time, they were published anonymously, and then reprinted a few years later under the title, *Invitation to an Encounter*. Among the verses is this pronouncement:

*More important than procreation is the child.*
*More important than the evolution of creation is the*
   *evolution of the creator.*

*In the place of the imperative steps the imperator.*
*In the place of the imperative steps the creator.*

The verse continues with his famous "Invitation" (*A meeting of two: eye to eye, face to face. . . .*), the basis of his claim to have been the first to formulate the concept of the encounter. It is somewhat paradoxical that his proclamation of the superiority of the creator over that which is created (apparently with the significant exception of the soul-bearing child) should be followed by the lines that he so jealously protected as evidence of his priority as a creator. J.L.'s youthful philosophical commitment to anonymity was premised on the notion that ideas should belong to the world rather than to any individual. It was an ideal that other literary figures entertained in Vienna in those days, but it caused him much grief later, when he wanted to stake his claim as the originator of encounter and his other inventions. This dilemma beset him for the rest of his life.

Another source of confusion in securing his reputation was his name. Even when he did sign his publications he was sometimes Jacob Levy, sometimes Jacob Moreno Levy, sometimes Jacob Levy Moreno and finally J.L. Moreno. (Even in his birth certificate, as later, "Levy" is at one point spelled with a *y* and at another with an *i*.) It is common for writers and revolutionaries to adopt new names as symbols of new identities, but for J.L. there were multiple motives. He wanted a more universal identity than that of a Jew in early twentieth-century middle Europe. For him the shift from "Levy" as a family name was not so much a question of avoiding anti-Semitism—though there certainly was that problem—as it was that of being stereotyped. He wanted his writings to be taken on their own merits and as emanating from an original voice. "Moreno" was a cosmopolitan name that was hard to pin down: Was it Spanish, Italian, Turkish, or something else? By a happy coincidence "Moreno" is also a homonym with "our teacher" in Hebrew. And he nursed identification with his father, Nissim Moreno Levy. Then, too, the name had been in the family for generations. "Moreno" tied him to his Sephardic origins in which he took pride. Though he had not been an active Jew since early childhood, in at least one occasion in his later years he expressed satisfaction that he, a Godplayer from a young age, was a product of a people said to be superior and the source of the Christian messiah.

For all the advantages and emotional satisfaction of his name changes, especially while he was in his formative years in Vienna, they have obscured his early contributions to philosophy, theology, theater and psychology. There was more bad luck about his name: A Viennese theologian has found that the university archives had for eighty years misfiled some of his self-published anonymous pamphlets under "Gevy," a result of a librarian's poor handwriting. This error was discovered during the preparation of a 2006 University of Vienna doctoral dissertation on J.L.'s relationship with the existentialist Martin Buber, who was deeply influenced by Hasidic Jewish philosophy, especially as expressed in its marvelous folk tales. Buber is best known as the author of *I and Thou* (1925), considered to be perhaps the greatest statement of the idea that we find meaning in relationships with other persons, the I–thou rather than the I–it relationship. Buber was eleven years older than J.L., was an assistant editor of his journal *Der Neue Daimon*, and published a piece on Hasidism in the journal in 1919. Buber claimed they never met, but J.L. said that they met at least once in one of the cafés.

For decades, some have speculated that Buber's "philosophy of dialogue" was inspired by J.L.'s previous writings on the encounter. J.L. himself claimed as much, noting that *I and Thou* was published nine years later, but "pushed *Invitation to an Encounter* out of the limelight." Historian Robert Karoly Sarlos said that J.L. "was working with the 'I–Thou' concept before Martin Buber formulated it, and began applying it to psychotherapy." In his autobiography J.L. emphasized that he and Buber had no conflicts, adding that he was "a great gentleman with a very warm and cordial manner." It was one of the few occasions on which J.L. was not spoiling for a fight over his priority, perhaps an artifact of some residual discomfort with his relationship to his own Jewish identity, in contrast to Buber who had embraced his. Or he simply might have been so involved in his multiple activities that he decided not to pursue the matter. And in fact the precise lines of influence have been difficult to sort out. Based on the evidence available in the 1980s, J.L.'s biographer concluded that "there seems to be no historical basis for putting too much emphasis on direct influence."

That judgment turns out to have been premature. Upon discovering the misfiling of J.L.'s formerly anonymous booklets in the University of Vienna archives, in 2006 the Austrian theologian Robert Waldl undertook a meticulous examination of the evolution of the two men's ideas, including side-by-side comparisons of their texts, and concluded that all of Buber's essential ideas about the "I and Thou," and even some of his linguistic formulations, were developed after those of J.L., in some cases as much as nine years later. "Buber found in Moreno's 'direct encounter' the central theme for his own 'I and Thou,'" Waldl concludes. "He took over this formula from Moreno's early writings. . . . It is particularly ironic that, with these words which he found originally in Moreno's texts, he would become the most quoted philosopher of humanistic psychology."

## THE DEMON

Longstanding confusions about J.L.'s originality must be attributed not only to his shifting personal identity as reflected in the names he used (or did not use) in his writings, but also to his public roles. At one time or another between 1918 and 1925 he was a philosopher, editor, dramaturge, stage designer and practicing physician. Vienna's was a vigorous café culture in which creativity was fueled by great quantities of caffeine *mit Schlag*. Already in the early eighteenth century a visitor observed that "[t]he city of Vienna is filled with coffee houses where the novelists or those who busy themselves with newspapers delight to meet." Café Herrenhoff was a favorite of J.L. and his circle, whereas the Freudians and members of the Young Vienna group frequented Café Central, as did Leon Trotsky and Adolf Hitler. "In Vienna," write Janik and Toulmin, "artistic life centered in the coffeehouses, where its exponents met and talked and then went home; all except Altenberg, for he *lived* in the Café Central." The café life performed a practical function, as Vienna then and for many years since was notorious for a housing shortage. Apartments with indoor plumbing were a minority and private houses were rarer still.

According to an account of contemporary Viennese café culture, "[a]mong the regulars who ensconced themselves at the Herrenhoff were such stellar members of the Vienna psychoanalytical establishment as Alfred Adler, Siegfried Bernfeld, Otto Gross, Jakob Levy Moreno, and Adolf Josef Storfer." (J.L. would not have been at all pleased to be grouped with the psychoanalysts, and Adler was seen even by Freud as a colleague rather than as his student.) J.L.'s literary friends Robert Musil, Franz Werfel, and Max Brod were also there, as was Buber, and sometimes Franz Kafka when visiting from Prague. So was Billy Wilder before his move to America and his wildly successful career directing movies like *The Seven*

*Year Itch* and *Some Like it Hot*. Territoriality was an important part of the networking in the cafes, so much time was spent there. The actor Peter Lorre and Wilder, the two youngest of the group, were consigned to the "kitten table for the children." Freud's preferred café was the Landtmann, but he sometimes made an appearance at the Herrenhoff, at which times Adler preferred a table separate from Freud's.

Out of the goings-on at the cafés, during and after the Great War, emerged a decision among half a dozen or so of the young men to create a new literary journal, *Der Daimon*, an allusion to Socrates' demon who spoke to him in something like the way moderns think of a conscience. The *daimon* so conceived is a spirit guide that assists in personal creativity and in bringing about a new world. Among this loosely knit group were the writer Franz Werfel, Kafka's close friend Max Brod, Alfred Adler who was then an active socialist, and Arthur Schnitzler intimate Max Reinhardt. Though over the several years of its irregular publication beginning in 1918 others drifted in and out, and despite name changes *Der Neue Daimon* in 1919 and *Die Gefaerhtan* ("The Associates") in 1920, J.L. was always the editor-in-chief. The collaborators did not constitute a distinct circle, but each of them was connected to various groups in Vienna, Prague, and Budapest—poets, dramatists, essayists, scientists, and political activists. Besides Altenberg, Buber, and Werfel, among the more famous contributors were the Marxist philosopher Ernst Bloch; Heinrich Mann, novelist and older brother of Thomas Mann; and critic and novelist Jakob Wasserman. Philosophically they were in greater or lesser degrees expressionists, existentialists, and mystics. As J.L.'s biographer describes the *Daimon* associates, "[i]t was a network of almost all the intellectuals of Austria at that time."

Today only a few copies of *Daimon* remain, but they were in wide circulation in German-speaking Europe for some time. In 1974, while I was a graduate student at Washington University in Saint Louis, the great authority on Jewish mysticism Gershom Sholem, visiting the local Jewish community from Israel, asked to see me between his lectures. I had written to him after his biography of Sabbatai Zevi was published. In the corner of a hotel ballroom just after his luncheon speech Sholem took me aside. I showed him several copies of *Daimon*. He nodded in recognition. "I saw some of these in bookstores in Berlin in the early 1930s." He looked up at me, a small man with an immense head, a clear olive complexion, enormous ears, and a penetrating gaze.

"Did your father die a Jew?" Sholem asked. I was taken aback; it was never a question that occurred to me.

"Yes," I answered truthfully, "he never renounced his Judaism." Handing the magazines back to me he said, "You are a very lucky young man."

In subsequent decades I came to appreciate that what Sholem was asking me was whether a rabbi had said the Kaddish, the Jewish prayer for the dead, over him. He had not, and as J.L. was cremated no rabbi would have officiated. But my naïve answer preserved a warm encounter with the great scholar.

## THE WORDS OF THE FATHER

It is difficult to overstate the influence of Jewish cultural traditions on the Viennese modernists and the movements associated with them. Like Chaim Kellmer, who had studied Hasidic texts before beginning university studies, Jews—or those from families that had largely departed from Judaism—were vastly over-represented among the Viennese thinkers and writers who played such an important role in shaping the new century, including many of those mentioned in this chapter. Yet beyond a general orientation to scholarship and philosophy and their rebellious attitudes toward the "establishment" it is hard to assess the specifics of this influence, so varied were the styles and attitudes of the modernists. What is clear is that there was at this time a great deal of confusion within the Jewish community about its future. Some believed that the modernity was about to accomplish what centuries of exclusion could not: the disintegration of Judaism as a living faith. There were of course the Zionists, whose conflicts with anti-Semites resulted at least once in the closing of the university during J.L.'s student career. But their solution to Jewish persecution, a Jewish state in Palestine, was hardly the universal or even majority response. Many Jews chose assimilation, some conversion, and some, like J.L. and Chaim, sought a new approach to faith, though essentially within the framework of Abrahamic traditions and models of the Christian saints.

Along with his theatrical personal style, his oracular writings and his unconventional scientific orientation, J.L.'s approach to the God question undermined his long-term reputation in the scientific establishment. His underlying argument was a simple one: to be truly moral, one had to take responsibility for the whole of creation. Any drawing of lines was necessarily arbitrary. Unlike Nietzsche, whose Overman would transcend morality, J.L. felt compelled to a full embrace of the Divine. Still more radically, he felt that compulsion in the first person: not the distant "He" God of the Hebrews or the "you" God of the Christians, but an "I" God who took personal, absolute responsibility for everyone and everything. J.L. traced this idea to an epiphany he experienced when he was fourteen years old, standing in front of a small statue of Jesus in the German provincial town of Chemnitz. He found himself transfixed by the statue, framed in the moonlight, attempting to will Jesus to come alive and speak to him. At that moment he conceived a question the answer to which he believed would determine the course of his life.

> The question was, how would I choose: was my identity the universe, or was it with the particular family or clan from which I had sprung? I decided for the universe, not because my family was inferior to any other family, but because I wanted to live on behalf of the larger setting to which every member of my family belonged and to which I wanted them to return.

As a young man, the seriousness with which J.L. took his position that the only truly moral approach to life was to aspire to become God had long been a favorite joke among his acquaintances in Vienna. One story had him over supper with friends in a crowded café when above the din someone could be heard exclaiming "Oh God!" at which point J.L. rose in his seat and shouted in utter conviction, "Somebody call me?" Over the next fifty years, at professional meetings, long after he was an established figure, he was sometimes asked if he truly believed he was God, and he always answered that he did. Amid waves of shock and consternation he would add, "And so should you. Why would you settle for anything less?"

The peak of J.L.'s Godplaying occurred in connection with an incident that might be interpreted as a clinical episode. In 1919 he took a position as health officer and company doctor for the textile factory in Bad Voslau, a spa town about 40 kilometers from Vienna. His life was full. He was well paid, had a successful medical practice, traveled back and forth to Vienna regularly for his Theater of Spontaneity and to visit the cafés, and abandoned a vow of celibacy upon meeting a beautiful local Catholic girl named Marianne, who became his muse. Bad Voslau occupies a lush valley, an expanse of soft, green rolling hills visible from the comfortable house J.L. rented from the city council. The house sits over a complex of wine cellars, the site of the first sparkling white produced in Austria, called Schlumberger. Altogether, the physical and emotional setting stimulated J.L.'s messianic tendencies to new heights. Recalling his epiphany in Chemnitz, he and Marianne began to hear a "Voice." Night after night they waited for it. At first it was subdued. Finally, it came more clearly than ever and seemed to transport J.L. to a new level of consciousness.

I walked down the hill, up the hill, stimulated by the scent of flowers and the silent air wanderings of the nightbirds. I was marching through space and space was marching through me, on and on and on, no stop. Millions of other people were marching through space at the same time, on and on and on, no stop. It was as if the universe was in movement in an unlimited number of dimensions. Wherever I turned a new dimension would open up. I saw sky, stars, planets, oceans, forests, mountains, cities, animals, fishes, birds, flies, protozoa, stones, and hundreds of other things. Then I saw each opening its mouth, each man, each tree, each stone, each particle of the universe shouting in unison:

*I am God,*
*The Father,*
*The creator of the universe*

*These are my words,*
*The words of the Father.*

So began the long poem that J.L. published anonymously in 1920, *The Words of the Father ("Das Testament das Vaters")*. Finally his Godplaying had reached its apex, the conclusion of a thirty-year journey. He had directed himself in the ultimate psychodrama. He had reversed roles with God. *"The only way to get rid of the God syndrome,"* he wrote emphatically nearly fifty years later, *"is to act it out."*

## Chapter Three

# SPONTANEITY

J.L.'s "Theater Without an Audience," 1923

*The natural theme was to search for a new order of things,*
*the testing of anyone in the audience who aspired to leadership,*
*and, perhaps, to find a savior.*

J.L. Moreno, 1972

ONE OF THE VIENNESE CAFÉ REGULARS was an odd little fellow named Laszlo Lowenstein. Just eighteen and impoverished, Lazlo was destined for fame as the actor Peter Lorre, the star of Fritz Lang's classic *M* and of Hollywood films like *Casablanca* and *The Maltese Falcon*. He claimed he was cast out of his home for impregnating the family maid, but in fact Laszlo's father reluctantly approved of his attempt to break into the world of theater. He was begging for spare change in the cafés when he met J.L.'s younger brother, William, who thought him adorable. "He was cross-eyed and had a dimple in his cheek," J.L. remembered. "There was something very appealing about him. . . ." After testing him

71

for his ability to respond to an impromptu scenario, J.L. recruited Laszlo/
Peter as an actor in his new *Stegreiftheater*, the Theater of Spontaneity, a
theater of free will unrestrained by a script other than the one written by
the players themselves. The Theater of Spontaneity was a response to the
traditional theater that J.L. believed had grown old and tired, a "cultural
conserve." In some respects the theater functioned as a stand-in for his
generation's contempt for what had become of their society. Young Laszlo's later mentor, Bertolt Brecht, agreed. But J.L.'s response to the problem
was more radical than Brecht's: a total rejection of scripted drama.

## REVOLUTIONARY THEATER

Unlike many other times and places for which theater is ornamental or
merely one means of cultural expression among many, for the Viennese
the nature and destiny of the theater were not peripheral but rather central
questions. As Stefan Zweig explained it:

> It was not the military, nor the political, nor the commercial that was
> predominant in the life of the individual and of the masses. The first
> glance of the average Viennese into his morning paper was not at the
> events in parliament, or world affairs, but at the repertoire of the the-
> atre, which assumed so important a role in public life as hardly was
> possible in any other city. . . . [I]t was the microcosm that mirrored
> the macrocosm, the brightly colored reflection in which the city saw
> itself. . . . The stage, instead of being merely a place of entertainment,
> was a spoken and plastic guide of good behavior and correct pronun-
> ciation, and a nimbus of respect encircled like a halo everything that
> had even the faintest connection with the Imperial Theatre.

In that culture, anyone who would insert himself into the question of
the future of the theater was engaged in a serious business, no less those
who sought its radical reform. Of the those in J.L.'s circle who joined him
in wishing to subvert the traditional theater, one of the more influential
was the playwright, actor, and theater director Max Reinhardt, a Café
Herrenhoff regular during his visits from Berlin, where he directed the
Volksbühne Theater among many others in Germany and Austria, including the Salzburg theater festival, before being forced to flee to England and
then America. He was one of the few theater directors who made a highly

successful transition to film. Like so many in his generation, Reinhardt rebelled against theater conventions in favor of fantasy and the psychological development of the characters. He introduced various art forms like dance, acrobatics, and innovative lighting techniques into his direction, often with mystical undertones. Reinhardt also brought productions into public spaces like city squares. Like J.L., he wanted to bring the drama into the places where people actually lived and worked.

At times it seemed there was nearly a competition for doing the most to overturn the conventional theater, which had in any case come up on hard times. From the perspective of J.L. and others in his circle the peak of the formal Viennese theater might have been 1888, when the historic Imperial Theater to which Zweig referred, also known as the Burgtheater, was moved to the new Ringstrasse, a circular road that replaced the old city walls. Over the ensuing two decades the road seemed to run all downhill. During the 1910s an influx of working class immigrants and economic woes in the World War I era tended to favor more popular theater productions that would assure success at the box office, including seedy, often sexually oriented shows. The decline of Viennese theater signified the decline of Habsburg civic and political life and of the fortunes of the imperial capital.

Among the protagonists in the vigorous contemporary discourse about the future of the theater was another contemporary of J.L.'s, Karl Kraus, editor of the satirical magazine *Die Fackel*. Kraus issued a broadside against Max Reinhardt in which he harshly criticized Reinhardt's introduction of spectacular effects like dramatic lighting, music, and a huge revolving stage. As summarized by the historians Alan Janik and Stephen Toulmin, "Kraus considered Reinhardt's theatrical techniques a kind of glorified sleight of hand, an extravaganza intended to divert the audience from the quality of the drama. . .Kraus desired to replace [Reinhardt's 'theater of spectacle'] with a 'theater of poetry,'" with "nothing but the text and its interpreter." J.L. was surely aware of Kraus's extreme position, but again he went further: He wanted to eliminate the playwright altogether.

J.L. began to formulate his radical ideas about the theater in one of the anonymous essays he self-published between 1908 and 1911. In *The Godhead as Comedian or Actor*, he challenged the very concept of playing a role other than one's own. J.L. claimed that he and a friend went so far as to mount the stage during the performance of a play called *Thus Spake*

*Zarathustra*, based on Nietzsche's book of the same name. According to J.L., they berated the actor for taking the role of Zarathustra, a role only Zarathustra could play, rather than playing himself. The director of the play and the author defended the actor amid J.L.'s declaration that the traditional theater was ending. Finally, the police were called and J.L. was obliged to promise a judge that he would never interrupt someone else's play again.

## The House of Comedies

The theater incident might have been the product of J.L.'s fertile imagination, or as he might have called it, his surplus reality. Whether the story is literally true or not, it signified the impact that Friedrich Nietzsche had made on this generation of German-speaking intellectuals. Famous for his contentious declaration that "God is dead," Nietzsche was a powerful thinker who came to grips with the previous several hundred years' worth of developments in Western science and philosophy. Classical Greek assurances that we live in an orderly universe, a cosmos, had seemingly been swept aside by scientific discoveries, especially the definitive refutation of the idea that the Earth is the center of the universe, and philosophical insights like those of David Hume, the Scot who argued that even the notion that events are caused can't be empirically proven. Facing what he considered to be the brute facts, Nietzsche argued that a new being is required who can constitute his or her own values, an Overman, someone who can transcend the merely human. J.L. took Nietzsche's argument as a challenge. He believed he could show that human beings do have the potential to be loving and creative. In a way, the later "human potential movement" that flowered in the 1950s and 1960s was a response to Nietzsche's skepticism about human capacities.

In 1923, a few years after Kraus's critique of Reinhardt, J.L. published his book, *The Theater of Spontaneity*. Just as Nietzsche declared that God is dead, J.L. declared the death of the playwright in a dramatic, oracular, and somewhat mordant fashion reminiscent of Nietszche's prose style.

The inner structure of the theatre is easily recognizable if one considers the nascence of any specific dramatic production. In the rigid, "dogmatic" theatre, the creative product is given: it appears in its final, irrevocable form. The dramatist is no longer present, for his work is entirely divorced from him. His work, the creation of which was the very essence of certain moments bygone, returns only to deprive the present moment of any living creativity of its own. In consequence, the actors have had to give up their initiative and their spontaneity. They are merely the receptacles of a creation now past its moment of true creativity. Dramatist, actor, director and audience conspire in an interpretation of the moment which is mechanical. They have surrendered themselves to the enjoyment of an extra-temporal, moment-less performance. The value which appears supreme is like nothing but the spiritual bequest of someone who is dead.

The story about J.L.'s unwanted intervention in the play also signified his determination to put his radical ideas about the theater into practice. He did so at least once in an event that is on the historical record, a dry run for his own experimental theater. On April Fool's Day in 1921 J.L. rented a stage in the House of Comedies (*Komoedienhaus*) and cast himself as the lead character, standing alone on the stage before an expectant audience of a thousand. The stage was bare except for a throne and a gilded crown on the seat. It was an auspicious and unsettled moment in postwar Vienna, a former imperial capital in political and financial turmoil, anxious to find a new basis for society, and perhaps a new beginning for its treasured art form, this time in the guise of a spontaneous production. As J.L. recalled the evening in the epigraph of this chapter, he had stepped into a social vacuum. "There was no stable government, no emperor, no king, no leader. The last Habsburg monarch had fled to Italy. And, like other nations of the earth, Austria was restless, in search of a new soul." The various elements of Viennese society in attendance were engaged in a collective struggle, one that he aimed to portray on stage as a sociodrama, a role-play aiming to resolve a problematic, shared social situation. Who could come forward to lead Austria into a new order of things? J.L. cast the audience as the jury. Candidates came forward, but in the end, no one passed the test.

The next day's newspaper review, "Dadaism in the House of Comedies," was less than a ringing endorsement of the experiment. "They had rented the auditorium to a physician who lives in a famous spa-resort on the south railroad line [the town where J.L. was the municipal doctor], where he might also practice, but who primarily sees himself as a poet-philosopher and who chose specifically the first of April to bombard a lenient and easy-going audience with his rather obscure way of thinking. ... At first, the presentation was received with quiet delight, later there were strong gestures of displeasure. This was followed by ironic applause which kept the speaker from finishing his speech. But there were also friends, who were supposedly followers of Werfel and defended the poet." The reviewer concluded that many in the audience left the theater angry at the "wasted evening," having expected that the poet's speech would be followed by a dance performance, "and only the fall of the iron curtain made the audience aware that they were fools, just as much as they looked at the speaker as a fool." It was far from the last time J.L. would be dismissed as a fool or a charlatan.

As it happened, fools were prominent among the typical characters in the one form of improvisational theater that J.L. cited as "the nearest approach to [psychodrama] in the history of the theater," but even the Italian commedia dell'arte failed to live up to his rigorous standards of spontaneity. In its early period this sixteenth-century form gave the actors, who played standardized roles like lovers, masters, and servants, considerable room for improvisation as they were moved to do so in reaction to other actors on stage or in response to the audience. One of the great actors and directors of the commedia was Luigi Riccoboni. In 1728 he argued that "]t]he player who acts all'improvviso performs in a more vivacious and natural way than the player who has learned a part." Goethe wrote that his visit to the commedia was "a great joy. I saw an extemporaneous piece with masks performed with much temperament, energy and brilliance. ..."

J.L. saw the commedia dell'arte as a middle ground between the fully scripted traditional theater and his spontaneity theater. But it is almost a law of nature that at some point whatever degree of scripting there is weighs on improvisation and undermines spontaneity. "The lines themselves were unwritten and it is in this feature that the improvisatory character of the form came to expression, but because the same situations and plots, and the same types of roles were repeated again and again, the improvisatory character of the dialogue which prevailed when a case was new disappeared little by little, the more often they repeated a given plot." Paradoxical as it may seem, sustaining spontaneity is hard work, especially for grownups. We succumb to the cultural conserve, the scripted way of doing things, at the first opportunity. Although little children come by spontaneity naturally, by the time they reach adulthood cultural expectations and social conventions impair it.

In this respect J.L.'s thinking was in the same Enlightenment tradition as Freudian psychology. Both viewed childhood as a period in which basic drives are thwarted by society, though J.L. and Freud differed in the nature and consequences of this process. Freud believed that societal constraints on the energies of childhood were tragic, necessary, and unavoidable; J.L. thought they were unnecessary, socially and psychologically costly, and amenable to correction. He thought theater was the best possible corrective, though the conventional theater rarely is. Rather, memorization and the natural repetition of situations reinforce clichés, unless a deliberate effort is made to prevent the return to the cultural conserve. The history of the theater recapitulates human social history in which spontaneity is hindered and human horizons of creativity strictly limited. The same problem confronts all new movements, including especially religious movements: How to sustain the original spontaneity and creativity of the founding generation rather than lapsing into dogma? In the beginning commedia dell'arte was promising, but in the end its purpose was entertainment, not therapy. "Working within the framework of the legitimate theater and without a system of spontaneity training, the Commedia dell Arte [sic] died a slow death."

## The Parrot

J.L. was deeply disappointed by the reception of his revolutionary theater. Identifying once again with another rejected prophet, he had to admit that he "lost many friends but registered calmly, '*Nemo profeta in sui patria.*'" It was an attitude that served him well over the years. Taking heart, he continued to reflect on the idea of a new psychological drama. Meanwhile, he redoubled his determination to overthrow the traditional concept of performance. The first public performance of the Theater of Spontaneity took place in 1922 in rented rooms near the center of Vienna, with a main hall that seated seventy-five at most. Anticipating much modern improvisational theater, J.L.'s assembled cast put on spontaneous dramas according to themes suggested by the audience. J.L.'s student Elizabeth Bergner occasionally appeared in the troupe, as did actress Anna Hollering, whose father was the director of Vienna's House of Comedies.

The Theater of Spontaneity may not have passed esthetic muster from the standpoint of the critical establishment, but the troupe soldiered on and continued to attract attention in the Vienna theater world, at least some of it more favorable. In 1924 the music historian Paul Stefan wrote about the theater in a Viennese newspaper, *Die Stunde*, indicating a thorough knowledge both of J.L.'s innovative techniques, especially what would later be known as the empty chair and his messianic ideas. "Young actors under the direction of the 'father' (as Dr. Jakob Moreno Levy calls himself in his writings) perform two or three times a week in a hall, Meysedergasse 2. The throng is large, the themes are brought along or suggested by the audience. . . . There is a 'truth chair': whoever sits on this furniture must show himself the way he really is. . . . I assure you this can be more amusing and engaging than the well-respected classics, including Strindberg."

Laszlo Lowenstein/Peter Lorre himself quickly became J.L.'s star actor. According to Lorre's biographer, J.L. suggested his stage name. "The psychodramatist [J.L.] borrowed his friend Peter Altenberg's Christian name, bemusedly recalling the actor's resemblance to the character of *Sturwwelpeter*, an unruly young man in German children's literature 'whose hair and nails grew to unreasonably lengths.' For a surname Moreno suggested Lorre, which means 'parrot' in German." J.L.'s suggestion of parrot/Lorre might have been inspired by the young actor's talent for mimicry. One of his routines was "How to Catch a Louse," an exceptionally engaging warm-up to the play. As J.L. remembered it, "[h]e used to go into the audience and look for lice infesting the heads of affluent Viennese intellectuals. He made all sorts of grabbing motions, to the delight of everyone. It was a big drama. Suddenly he would get his louse!"

Lorre said that the spontaneity theater was the perfect training ground. "Years later," his biographer writes, "Lorre remembered it as an 'ideal school of acting.' Instead of focusing on linear time, the actors discovered a collection of moments that 'aroused the subject to an adequate reenactment of the lived and unlived out dimensions' of their private worlds. In this way, he [Lorre] pointed out, they could commit 'dramatic suicide,' if they were so inclined, and rid themselves of psychic complexes at the same time." Unfortunately for Lorre, as an acting school the Theater of

Spontaneity was too perfect. "After watching him repeat his best lines and movements—he had already developed the 'peculiar grin' he later trademarked in Hollywood—Moreno cautioned him to 'de-conserve' his 'mimic behavior.'" Sadly for Lorre, J.L. was right. The creepy character Lorre developed ultimately trapped him as the paradigmatic victim of typecasting. By the 1950s the Lorre persona was so stereotyped that a cartoon character "performed" with Bugs Bunny.

One of Lorre's talents was his ability to get underneath the skin of another person's being. The idea of role reversal, of taking the role of the other, was already one that J.L. was conceptualizing as both an opportunity for dramatic training and for its healing effects. Because of its dual function as described by Lorre, the Theater of Spontaneity was also called the Therapeutic Theater ("*Therapeutisches Theater*"). In 1924 J.L. tried to explain the concept of his new form of theater in a little book called *The Theater of Spontaneity*. The book is an excellent example of the way that ideas flowed in prodigious and enthusiastic quantity from J.L.'s mind. Though to today's reader they seem disorderly and undisciplined, the ideas in the book are redolent of the expressionist esthetic of the time. In essence he conceived of four forms of revolutionary theater in one: the theater of conflict wherein the audience challenges the actors to see the truth; the theater of spontaneity later known as Impromptu Theater; the therapeutic theater in which those present play themselves; and the theater of the creator in which every one of us is a self-creator or self-actualizer, living life to its fullest in the manner of Jesus or perhaps Nietzsche's Overman. This was one example of J.L.'s lifelong tendency to develop new categorizations and expressions of his ideas as his fulsome intuitions moved him, making it hard to organize his thoughts into a static framework that could be easily taught and transmitted. True to his idea of spontaneity, he was constantly reframing his ideas.

Despite J.L.'s best efforts, audiences resisted abandoning their expectations of some form of traditional theater, and so did his actors themselves. "The worst difficulty I had was that I saw my best pupils flirting with the cliché even when acting extemporaneously. Finally they turned away from the theater of spontaneity and went to the legitimate stage or became movie actors. Peter Lorre was one of them, though he had a remarkable gift for spontaneous acting." To enhance spontaneity they sometimes performed what J.L. called the "Dramatized Newspaper," later the "Living Newspaper." Cast members would reenact events that had taken place in the city that day, often at the last minute to combat the audience's suspicion that the performances were secretly scripted.

## THE RUSSIANS

The living newspaper was also performed as early as 1923 by the Blue Blouse Theater, a Russian group, but their performances were usually scripted and they had a practical purpose: to bring news to illiterate peasants. The Blue Blouse players were inspired by the Russian Futurist movement of the 1910s, artists who wanted to challenge their audiences and obliterate the art of the past. J.L. certainly knew about developments in the Russian theater world, which his friend Robert Muller had written about. He might well have run into them when he took his spontaneity theater troupe on the road to places like Berlin. Another Russian who was working in a similar spirit was the playwright Nikolai Evreinov. Ten years J.L.'s senior, Evreinov started writing plays in 1902. In 1927 he published a book called *The Theatre in Life* in English, based on his 1915–17 Russian works collected under the title *The Theatre for Oneself*, where "[p]eople will play themselves, and for themselves, needing neither actors nor spectators." And in a passage that sounds remarkably similar to J.L.'s declaration about spontaneity, "*Theatrum extra habitum mea sponte!* . . . [E]very artist of 'the theatre for oneself' must be his own playwright. It is exactly in the free improvisation that lies one of the greatest attractions of this institution. . . . [D]o not be afraid of creating, of improvising." He also wrote of "theatrotherapy," the therapeutic effect of the drama and of the Godhead in a way that was similar to J.L.'s view of the theater as a divine instrument.

Evreinov was well known in the 1910s for his play *The Gay Death* and for his 1920 mass reenactment of a key moment in the Bolshevik Revolution, the storming of the Winter Palace, in which he used eight thousand performers. These were J.L.'s formative years. The possibility that he was influenced by Evreinov is too great to dismiss, especially because Evreinov occasionally visited Vienna and they both arrived in New York within a year of each other, where Evreinov had a briefly successful career on Broadway. J.L. only refers to Evreinov once, and then only in footnote in the 1947 English edition of *The Theater of Spontaneity*. There were certainly many potential points of contact between the two in the small world of New York theater in the 1930s. For example, the actor and director Harold Clurman performed in Evreinov's play *The Chief Thing* and was also part of the Group Theater where J.L. was well known.

Not only spontaneous theater, but also early feints toward the use of theater in therapy were in the early twentieth-century air. A Ukrainian named Vladimir Iljine was a pioneer of the use of drama therapy with psychiatric patients in Kiev. His Therapeutic Theater was influenced by Stanislavsky, the pioneer of method acting. Iljine published a book called *Improvising Theatre Play in the Treatment of Mood Disorders* in 1910 and translated J.L.'s *Theatre of Spontaneity* into Russian, finally meeting him in Paris in 1964. At an international meeting of psychoanalysts in 1920, the Hungarian psychoanalyst Sandor Ferenczi reported a case of a woman who was unable to sing a song as well as her sister, who usually accompanied her. Only after he encouraged her to repeat the song exactly as her sister would have did she capture the melody. "It was astonishing how favourably this little interlude affected the work," Ferenczi recalled. "Presently memories of her early childhood, of which she had never spoken, occurred to her. . . ." But Ferenczi did not pursue his "active technique" further than that. Less notable figures also had the idea of using theater techniques in therapy, like the New York physician S.E. Jelliffe who wrote an article about psychotherapy and drama in 1916. The late nineteenth-century dramatist Richard von Meerheimb wrote a set of short plays he called "psychodramen."

But no one pursued the idea of psychological drama as persistently as J.L., nor did any of the dramatists stick so closely to his no-script principle of theater, including Evreinov and all the other activists and critics of the theater in Russia and Vienna at that time. Two historians of the commedia dell'arte have concluded that despite its novelty, it too, "was not truly spontaneous; it was not devised wholly impromptu and off-the-cuff while the players were actually on stage and in performance." Besides the Living Newspaper, J.L.'s spontaneity theater players can be credited with other innovations, like taking suggestions for scenes from the audience, and inviting audience members to join the actors on stage whenever they were moved to do so. According to American improvisational theater expert Keith Sawyer, J.L.'s group "may have been the first professional theater to perform without a script, improvising dialogue on stage in front of a paying audience."

## "BARBARA"

Finally, in light of his audience's resistance and skepticism about spontaneity, J.L. turned to therapeutic theater. "It was easier to advocate 100 percent spontaneity in a therapeutic theater. The esthetic imperfections of an actor on stage could not be forgiven by his audience," he wrote, "but the imperfections and incongruities a mental patient shows on the psychodrama stage are not only more easily tolerated, but unexpected, and, often, warmly welcomed." Thus the source of J.L.'s most famous creation, the psychodrama, was partly as a solution to a problem he faced in inducing both actors and audiences to accept the idea of true spontaneity. It emerged easily from the idea of "psychological drama" that was very much in the Viennese air among the modernists and the theater directors in J.L.'s social network. Using the drama as a site of psychological exploration was another approach to the goal of more honest and open human relationships. The explicitly therapeutic potential of the psychological drama impressed J.L. in a particular experience with one of the actors in the spontaneity theater. In his frequent descriptions of the case, he protected their identities by calling them George and Barbara, though "Barbara" was Anna Hollering, one of the actresses in his regular troupe, who was skilled at playing ingénues in romantic roles. "George" was George Kulka, a contributor to *Daimon*. A romance developed between her and George, a young poet and playwright who always sat in the front row and took obvious delight in her performances. One day they announced their marriage. All was well until one day when George approached J.L., "his usual gay eyes greatly disturbed."

> "What happened?" I asked him. "Oh, doctor, I cannot bear it." "Bear what?" I looked at him, investigating. "That sweet, angel-like being whom you all admire, acts like a bedeviled creature when she is alone with me. She speaks the most abusive language and when I get angry at her, as I did last night, she hits me with her fists." "Wait," I said. "You come to the theatre as usual, I will try a remedy."

That night J.L. told her that as wonderful as her work had been, she was getting stale, that audiences wanted to see her portraying "the rawness of human nature, its vulgarity and stupidity, its cynical reality, people not only as they are, but worse than they are. . . ." Barbara agreed immediately. She herself was getting tired of the same old character. It happened that a streetwalker had been killed by a stranger in a seedy section of Vienna. Barbara was to play that role in a Living Newspaper performance, and an actor J.L. called Richard (perhaps Peter Lorre), was put in the role of a man leaving a café with her in the midst of a heated argument about money. "Suddenly Barbara changed to a manner of acting totally unexpected from her. She swore like a trooper, punching at the man, kicking him in the leg repeatedly." George started to rise from his usual seat to defend her as the attacker took a prop knife from his jacket pocket and chased her in circles, slashing her repeatedly. The audience shouted "Stop it! Stop it!" but before long she was "murdered" on the stage. After the play the two went home in ecstasy, as though her demons had been released. George reported that her temper at home was lessened and that while they were fighting they would sometimes both laugh, as though they saw themselves in a "psychological mirror."

J.L. put Barbara in a variety of roles as George continued to observe the performances, each of which was followed by J.L.'s analysis of the action. George said he became less impatient with Barbara, more tolerant of her personality. Gradually, he became part of the plays as they enacted their actual life at home, then scenes from their childhoods and projections about their dreams for the future. Not only were the two actors affected (now properly called protagonists in their own dramas), but the audiences seemed to be deeply moved by these Barbara–George scenes. They had progressed from the sociodrama of the Living Newspaper to the psychodrama of emotional problems, in which the group experiences a catharsis along with the protagonists. It was exactly what J.L. had understood about the nature of catharsis from his reading of Aristotle.

## Theater or Therapy?

The psychological approach had an enormous impact on twentieth-century theater. Reinhardt and other psychological theater experimentalists used the play to explore human nature from new psychological perspectives unhindered by staid conventions; for all that, however, they were still clearly working within the boundaries of theater even while rebelling against it. As psychodrama emerged, there was a core ambiguity that became yet another obstacle in the acceptance of J.L.'s ideas: Was it theater or was it therapy? The question remains critically important, for in practical terms the two domains are claimed and validated by two different social sectors, either the theater fraternity or that of the clinicians. The ambiguity had enormous ramifications. Upon it turned the legitimacy of the method and its social acceptability, as well as legal and ethical questions. There has never been a question about the emotional power of the therapeutic theater or its ability to evoke strong feelings from participants. This, too, has exacerbated questions about its adoption and the credentials required for its use.

The cultural resistance to theater as therapy never made sense to J.L. In this respect and in others, he was both worldly and a bit naïve. For him the question, "Which is it?" was a simple one: Of course, it is both. That is the very core of the idea of the drama in the Western tradition, one invoked by Aristotle, frequently cited by J.L.: "A tragedy, then, is the imitation of an action that is serious . . . in a dramatic, not in a narrative form; with incidents arousing pity and fear, with which to accomplish its catharsis of such emotions. . . ." The idea that catharsis was an antidote to repressed emotions was popularized by Freud's collaborator, Josef Breuer, in his famous case of Anna O., who suffered from a variety of ailments including paralysis and hallucinations. Freud seemed to believe that her ailments were symptoms of hysteria, which was in turn a result of her repressed anger toward her father for the illnesses that led to his death. Breuer used hypnosis and free association to help bring Anna's actual mental operations to full consciousness. Freud was deeply impressed by Breuer's experience, which became a cornerstone of psychoanalysis, though a controversy has ensued over the ultimate benefit of the treatment to Anna O. and even whether she was correctly diagnosed.

J.L. believed that Breuer and Freud were on the right track, but that Freud's "talking cure" did not go far enough. Why not apply the cathartic element of theater, which is both one of the most familiar in Western thought and the most evident in the experience of theater-goers since time immemorial? The therapeutic setting is unavoidably a theatrical one, though the couch of classical psychoanalysis failed to exploit that fact for therapeutic purposes. As compared to the "passive and retrospective" approach of free association, "the patient actor is like a refugee who suddenly shows new strength because he has set foot into a freer and broader world." Considering J.L.'s experience with refugees in World War I and his later struggle to establish himself in America, the reference is poignant.

Their psychodramatic experiences did not preserve the marriage of Barbara/Anna and George, as they ultimately separated and George took his life five years later. In an interview with J.L.'s biographer, Anna's sister suggested that J.L. was so emotionally involved with the case that he might have overlooked George's own problems. This incident and a second on-stage couples' therapy experience deeply disturbed J.L. The second case involved another *Daimon* expressionist writer, Robert Muller, a friend with whom J.L. had long talks about new theater movements in Europe and who was an enthusiastic supporter of the spontaneity theater. Muller shot himself in the chest in 1924, the day after a psychodrama with his girlfriend Diora. J.L. took Muller's suicide hard, yet it may have had nothing to do with his relationship or the therapy. The founder of his own publishing house that had gone into bankruptcy, Muller seems to have been besieged by creditors. As J.L.'s biographer notes, Muller's death occurred while J.L. was going through many problems of his own. It caused him to reexamine his diagnostic skills and might have contributed to his decision to leave Austria less than two years later.

Like George Kulka, Robert Muller found his muse on J.L.'s spontaneity theater stage. In 1923, while still observing the object of his affection from his front-row seat, Muller wrote about "(a)n unusually great talent, natural and entirely uncut, but with extraordinary organic qualities, could be observed in a blonde young girl who name is Diora. She should be remembered."

## The Stage

For the Theater of Spontaneity J.L. wanted a special kind of stage, one that reflected both horizontal and vertical dimensions, one of breadth and height in which all could be part of the action and there was no spatial distinction between audience and actors. In *The Theater of Spontaneity* he included a diagram of his ideal stage, a multilevel affair with a circular central stage surrounded by several smaller round stages in a distinctive rosette pattern, and an outer circle composed of still more round stages—fourteen in all. Each level of the stage complex represented a different level of action, from warm-up to growth to action to the level of the messiah, a balcony. No audience member could escape being on stage, even at the outermost ring. Freud, too, was quite meticulous in managing the setting of the consulting room, appreciating its effect on the analysis. But J.L. dismissed its formality and artificiality, as well as the studied detachment of the analyst. "The couch isn't even a real bed," he once said to me, and the classical psychoanalytic relationship is at best a poor shadow of a real human relationship. To him, the esthetic of the Freudian consulting room was as impoverished and disdainful of the innate human capacity for spontaneity and creativity as was psychoanalytic theory itself.

A scandal erupted when J.L. entered his model stage at The International Exhibition of New Theatre Techniques in Vienna in 1924. Another stage design attracted more attention. It was created by Frederick Kiesler, a tiny man who was often called the "Viennese Bohemian," known to J.L. from the cafés and sometimes a participant in J.L.'s theater. J.L. had made sketches of a railway theater with an architect named Honigfeld, plans that were apparently circulated and influenced the design of the Bauhaus stage. Kiesler had his own improvisational theater (also called the Theater of Spontaneity), that aimed to blur the boundaries between performers and audience and he, too, was working with the architect Honigfeld on a round stage design. When Kiesler published a catalogue of his stage sketches he quoted J.L. at the beginning, but not in connection with the stage.

The situation came to a head at the stage exhibition. As director of the exhibition Kiesler was able to have his stage built. At the gala opening ceremony, attended by the mayor, J.L. made a scene, loudly accusing Kiesler of plagiarism. "When Fred was called upon and the mayor stretched out his hand to shake Fred's, I stopped the proceedings. I spoke out, calling him a thief. The mayor stopped the ceremony and everyone, delegates and spectators, rose to their feet, astounded at my action. The police entered and I left the auditorium." J.L. might also have been annoyed that Kiesler had higher social status as a member of the Jewish upper class, giving him a political advantage that resulted in the construction of his stage for the exhibition rather than J.L.'s. Kiesler's well-placed family included his cousin, the actress Hedy Lamarr, a Max Reinhardt protégé who was both stunningly beautiful and a talented engineer: During World War II she patented a radio-guided torpedo for the United States Navy.

Kiesler sued J.L. for libel in January 1925. As it involved two colorful figures, the case was widely covered in the newspapers complete with caricatures. One depicted the antagonists as boxers at the top of a multilevel series of circular stages.

Figure 1. J.L. and Kiesler having it out on Kiesler's stage, October 3, 1924.

After a theater critic in the newspaper *Die Stunde* took Kiesler's side, declaring that the two men's stages resembled each other as much as a radio resembles a crocodile, another cartoon depicted J.L. and Kiesler in front of a judge, with J.L. holding a radio and a crocodile.

For the rest of their lives both claimed that they had been vindicated, but Austrian trial records are destroyed after thirty years so the actual outcome remains a mystery. It is not at all clear the Kiesler stage concept was an infringement on J.L.'s, though it was certainly not as radical. Nor were their visions quite as original as either man might have wanted to think, and not only in the wake of Max Reinhardt's innovations. Excitement about stage engineering was an international phenomenon. In 1914, an American named Hiram Motherwell wrote that "[t]he last ten years have brought to the service of the theatre a new figure. His coming we can regard as symbolic. It stands to us as a sign that the theatre of the future can choose what it needs, instead of taking what it can get. . . . This demand is being met in the modern theatre

Figure 2. J.L. and Kiesler before the judge,
with J.L. holding a crocodile and a radio, January 1925.

by three stage devices the revolving stage, the wagon stage, and the sliding stage." Motherwell cited examples in Vienna, Munich, and New York.

Whatever the equities involved, the conflict did no credit to either man. The incident might have imprinted J.L. with the determination to vigorously protect his ideas, a conviction that later made him seem so self-involved that he struck observers as nearly paranoid. By coincidence, both J.L. and Kiesler immigrated to America in 1926 and settled in New York, though they seem to have had no further contact. Kiesler became a professor of architecture at Columbia University. Today the Kiesler Foundation Vienna sustains his memory by supporting innovative projects in architecture, visual arts, design, and theater. Like J.L. when Kiesler left Vienna he hoped to find more opportunity in the New World, but J.L. had more reasons than that to find a place to begin again.

## THE WONDER DOCTOR

In 1921 a wealthy but depressed man sought J.L.'s help in an assisted suicide, even offering to make J.L. his heir. Citing his Hippocratic obligations,

J.L. explained that he could not help the man die, but he offered a different kind of treatment. He had him check into a hotel in Voslau, the small resort town where J.L. was the district physician. For many weeks, with Marianne's help playing various roles of important people in the man's life, they rehearsed his proposed death, including preparing his will. Feeling as though it might be his last meal, the patient's appetite improved as they engaged in vivid enactments of his suicide. This model of residential treatment with systematic enactments was one J.L. institutionalized in his sanitarium beginning in the 1930s.

Along with his experience with Barbara and George's difficulties, putting the therapeutic side of the spontaneity theater to work for a case of clinical depression planted in J.L.'s mind the seed of a new approach to psychotherapy. In psychodramatic terms, the man had an "act hunger" that needed to be sated. J.L. also engaged in a kind of family therapy by entering homes and exploring troubling situations through reenactments. These exercises in group therapy moved beyond the discussions he held in the House of the Encounter to resolve problems among the families of displaced persons. Gradually, the power of the group itself as a therapeutic tool was becoming apparent.

However, his unconventional style and charisma created confusion in the small town, where it was also known that he traveled regularly to Vienna to consort with odd characters who sometimes also came to visit him. Confounding the locals even more, often he refused to charge for his services. Having little patience for bureaucracy and no business sense whatsoever, he was known to prescribe medications without following the usual procedures. When some in town accused him of practicing without a license, he displayed his medical diploma outside his office. He was also beginning to have direct personal experience with anti-Semitism. Marianne, his lover and muse, was Roman Catholic. Even though J.L. had developed a reputation as a "wonder doctor" for some well-publicized successful treatments of prominent locals, his scandalous cohabitation with Marianne nonetheless caused resentment. The couple often felt physically threatened, even in the daylight. On one occasion J.L. had a fistfight with some local proto-Nazi youth at the rail station. For all his bravado, the tensions in Voslau, the libel lawsuit brought against him by Fred Kiesler over the theater stage design, and the suicides of his friends Kulka and Muller must have been disconcerting.

These societal and personal tensions were among the various reasons that in 1925 J.L. pondered his next move. Politically astute friends like Franz Werfel predicted the continued decline of the old central European culture. The treaty that concluded the Great War had left multiple political issues unresolved and created some new ones, especially horrific financial instability, characterized especially by episodes of galloping inflation. Soviet Russia was an option; in his circle both political and theater people were excited about the new society supposedly being created in the Bolshevik workers' paradise. But J.L. hesitated. "The East of Europe was dominated by Soviet communism which was, by 1924, firmly entrenched," he wrote nearly fifty years later. "It offered little hope for any new ideas unless I was willing to accept the given structure of Soviet society and bore from within." Encouraged by business opportunities in North America, his astute younger brother William was preparing to leave Austria. William convinced him that the West would be a more promising platform for the dissemination of his ideas and the new adventures for which he longed.

CHAPTER FOUR

# IMPROMPTU

J.L. around 1925, before he left for New York.

*The present traditional theatre is defended by its apologists*
*who claim its productions are in themselves unique, and works of art.*
*The written drama is subordinated to the machinery of the theatre.*

J.L. Moreno, 1931

O N AUGUST 9, 1925, THE *New York Times* published a story head-
lined, "A Steel Band Called Radiofilm Makes Record of Broadcasts." Reporting that "[t]wo Viennese Inventors, Dr. Moreno-Levy and
Franz Lornitzo have built a new device in an attempt to solve the problem
of making radio listeners independent of the time of broadcasting," the
*Times* gave examples of the usefulness of the invention. "For example, if
President Coolidge broadcasts a radio set owner can adjust his receiver

to make a permanent record of his talk." Radio-film used several extant inventions as its platform, but added several improvements that kept the magnetized steel band from tangling and allowed the listener to mark out segments of the program he wanted recorded. Still more remarkable, the device could also be used to solve "the problem of television." Radio-film relied on sounds to generate electrical current, but if instead it used light, those currents could be received to generate a ten-by-ten centimeter moving picture. It seemed that the "two Viennese inventors," who were still in Austria, were on the verge of great wealth.

## RADIO-FILM

J.L. said he started out making a big splash and had to keep on splashing. At age 35 he had been a children's story teller, a published author, the founder and editor of a literary journal, the founder and administrator of a refugee home, the founder and director of an experimental theater group, an army medic in charge of a refugee camp, had made his first forays into psychodrama therapy, and was a practicing physician. By the early 1920s his life in and around cultural circles in Vienna had unfolded largely with one success after another. But not all was well. He was disappointed with the reception of *The Words of the Father* in the German-speaking world, experienced the loss of two friends and collaborators to suicide, and was about to hit some financial roadblocks. With Kiesler he had also become embroiled in the first of several very public quarrels over his long professional life, controversies that he sometimes initiated when he believed that others took his ideas without acknowledgment. He always saw his position as proceeding from moral principle, but right or wrong this pattern tended to undermine his reputation, as he came to be seen in some circles as a controversialist.

J.L. was also a dreamer. In his autobiography he claimed that several years before he left Vienna he had a dream that he was riding in a car down a grand avenue in a large city past skyscrapers. In the dense traffic each car has a loudspeaker instead of a horn.

"The fastest passenger line to the U.S.A. is the Mauretania." "Buy Camel cigarettes" blared from the window of a skyscraper. "When I woke up from that dream it was as if the dream had said to me, "You have expressed so many nasty thoughts about machines, but here is a machine which will help you to get out of Europe and come to the U.S.A., where you will be able to attain the fulfillment of your ideas."

As happened so often in his life, the timing of J.L.'s dream was lucky. By 1925 he had put himself in an awkward financial position. To expand his medical practice, he had invested in an expensive X-ray machine, for which his girlfriend Marianne's brother, Franz, who was also the co-inventor of radio-film, was to be the operator. However, in another example of his poor business sense, it turned out that J.L. lacked the appropriate licensure to use the device. He and Franz needed another way to make money. J.L. brought the idea that came to him in that dream to Franz, who developed a design. They acquired an Austrian patent for their radio-film. The early reaction to radio-film could hardly have been more auspicious, even leading to J.L.'s first appearance in the *New York Times* months before he arrived in America. It appeared that one machine would rescue J.L. from the ill-considered investment in another.

## WELCOME TO AMERICA

Whether the tale of J.L.'s dream is accurate or not, the *Times* article surely gave J.L. and Franz ample reason to think that radio-film would find many interested investors in America. The company that showed the most interest was General Phonograph, which had offices in New York City and Cleveland, Ohio, and a factory in Elyria, Ohio. The founder of General Phonograph was Otto Heineman, himself a German immigrant. Apparently J.L. had established a relationship with Heineman while he was on a business trip to Europe. In a November 1925 letter from J.L. to his brother William in America, he reported that "Heineman is paying for my trip to New York starting in Southampton, first class [on the] 'Mauretania' Cunard Line (=263 dollars)," and that Heineman would pay him several hundred dollars more on arrival. The plan was for J.L. and Heineman to travel to New York together and Franz to come later. In the letter J.L. also stresses the need to make sure Franz is taken care of and present in the United States. "The main reason why we need Lornitzo here is that in case of a demonstration we need a technician and it would certainly be dangerous to work with an unfamiliar technician. I am certainly able to do the demonstration myself [a bit of conceit on J.L.'s part, as he was in fact mechanically incompetent], but it could quite easily happen that a cog on the device is not working properly then we might have to rely on an unfamiliar technician. Furthermore Lornitzo has for several months made such an effort in this matter that I very much would like to share the success with him." To J.L. it was more than coincidence that this opportunity arose just as his situation called for a spontaneous and creative act, but evidence of his destiny. He was, he liked to say, a special case with God.

Finally though, God seemed to have other plans for him. Like so many initially promising business prospects, radio-film didn't go far. Unfortunately for J.L., there were hundreds of sound recording ideas in the mid-1920s. General Phonograph was in the process of being acquired by Columbia Records in 1926. Heineman was also busy developing his own record label, Okeh, which came to be well-known for hot jazz recordings, and was then switching over to the new electric microphones. Considering the management and technical changes, along with the fact that there were superior recording systems in the works, it is not surprising that J.L. and Franz's efforts with the company failed. The Austrian patent for radio-film was never registered in the United States. On the other hand, with first-class accommodations on a fine cruise ship the radio-film adventure did bring J.L. to the New World in high style. More important, it signaled his persistent interest in the possibilities of technology, especially film, which he came to see as a way of engaging large numbers of people in the psychodrama experience.

Notwithstanding his first-class ticket, J.L. disembarked on a Hudson pier in January 1926 as a penniless thirty-six-year-old immigrant armed with an Austrian patent for radio-film, his clever younger brother's support, and a few contacts from his former life. For an accomplished man who had achieved a degree of local celebrity and enjoyed being part of the era's most intense cultural center, J.L.'s entrance to America must have been intensely disappointing and frustrating. His story is emblematic of the obstacles that even ambitious, talented, and well-connected immigrants confronted, especially those who had fantasies of get-rich-quick schemes in America. Besides having to contend with the usual problems like a new language, alien culture, and obtaining resident status, his attempts to sell radio-film that at first seemed promising ultimately floundered.

On the personal side, the demise of the radio-film project complicated

J.L.'s relationship with Marianne. Her brother Franz and his family were surely let down by the failure of the business venture; no doubt J.L. had made confident predictions about his impending conquest of America. Further aggravating tensions, over the next few years J.L. insisted that she continue to pay rent on J.L.'s house in Voslau with funds he occasionally sent her. In his letters J.L. assured Marianne that he would either return or bring her to America. Those promises and the letters gradually trailed off. I visited Voslau in 1984 with Grete Leutz, the German physician and psychodramatist. With no previous appointment we went to see the mayor, who welcomed us; like everyone else in town he knew about the illustrious Moreno's history in the town. After a flurry of phone calls we learned that Marianne had died just six months before, but her younger sister was still living and would meet us with her daughter, Marianne's niece. The family's resentment about the relationship lived on through the decades, though Marianne's younger sister did not seem to share it. She recalled her crush on her older sister's boyfriend, his colorful friends, and the amusing stories about his Godplaying in Vienna. In later years Marianne was very close to her niece, to whom she told the tales about her adventurous romance with J.L. His rather shoddy treatment notwithstanding, she bore no ill will toward him. Marianne had a long and happy marriage, but no children. She said she had experienced such a complete relationship with J.L. that she was satisfied with a local man and a simple life.

## IMMIGRATION

The period following World War I was not an auspicious one for would-be American immigrants. Unions feared cheap workers, and the government was watchful for anarchists and criminals. Postwar isolationism led to the Quota Act of 1921 and strict limits were imposed on the numbers of new entrants and their countries of origin. The Act favored northern Europeans but not Jews, whose previous influx many deemed threatening to native Americanism. On top of all that, relations between the United States government and the new Republic of Austria following the Empire's defeat in the war were rocky, and J.L. was traveling on an Austrian passport. At least once he went to the Austrian consulate in Montreal to renew his temporary visa. Of these machinations J.L. had little to say and was somewhat mysterious. "I was on the point of going back to Europe, of getting myself involved in another scheme to change my immigration status, when another opportunity offered itself. I did go to Canada for a few days to have my visa extended. I visited the American consul and money changed hands, but I was unable to have my status changed permanently." Letters between J.L. and his brother William in those days suggest that they were also dealing with a corrupt official who was subject to bribery.

Somehow his visa was extended, but he also needed to generate some income and establish professional contacts in New York. Not long after J.L. arrived in New York he called on a friend from Vienna named Bela Schick. The Hungarian-born Schick had been on the University of Vienna medical faculty while J.L. was a student and became famous for developing the Schick test for children's susceptibility to diphtheria. Schick was appointed chairman of Mount Sinai Hospital's pediatrics department just a couple of years before J.L. came to New York. He invited J.L. to conduct a demonstration of his work with children at Mount Sinai, perhaps the first time that drama therapy was used with pediatric patients in a hospital setting. Today drama therapy and other creative arts therapies are well established in Child Life programs for young patients in hospitals all over the world. These programs make the hospital setting more child-friendly and lessen the anxiety and stress of hospitalization for both the children and their parents. Another Mount Sinai pediatrician also befriended J.L. Ira S. Wile was an activist in the birth control movement and a close associate of Margaret Sanger, founder of the organization that became Planned Parenthood. He began to work with Wile in the hospital's "mental hygiene" clinic. J.L's knack with spontaneous children's theater and his therapy work provided him with some modest income while he went through the application process for his medical license.

Just what techniques J.L. used with the children at Mount Sinai or in the psychology clinic can't be known with certainty; neither he nor the other therapists seem to have written about them, and there are no records in the hospital archives. However, one can imagine that J.L. experimented with ideas about lessening the children's anxiety by enacting situations associated with their medical care. For example, he might well have had the children play the role of their doctors, explaining to them what needed to be done to make them get better. Or he might have put them into the role of a favorite nurse caring for them. And he could have asked them to imagine themselves leaving the hospital, going back to school, and reuniting with their friends. It's impossible to know for sure, but creative enactments like these would have been the seedbeds for ideas that have become part of action therapies, like role reversal (in this case, becoming the doctor or the nurse), or future projection (leaving the hospital), all for the sake of reassuring the children. (J.L.'s friend Alfred Adler also did group counseling with children, encouraging group members to participate in the session. Adler, who was on the editorial board of the *Daimon* journal, arrived in New York from Vienna a year after J.L. Though Adler was a psychoanalyst who became known for his concept of the inferiority complex they remained on good terms, perhaps because they both had a dim view of Freud, and Adler referred some of his patients to J.L.)

J.L. must also have used his Mount Sinai experience to continue exploring an idea he began to develop with his Theater of Spontaneity actors in Vienna, the spontaneity test. J.L. believed that children are most able to respond to situations in new ways between the ages of two and six; compared with most adults, children are much better at drawing upon an infinite store of creativity, the source of which is spontaneity. By putting a person in a new situation one can test their ability to draw on that reserve. In general, children do not need to be trained to act spontaneously the way older people do. J.L. believed that psychodramatic techniques can help facilitate spontaneity, that there is nothing paradoxical about the idea of spontaneity training.

Finally in 1927, after Marianne arranged to have documents sent from Vienna and he passed the New York State medical examination, J.L. received his license to practice medicine. But permanent status in the United States was still a problem. And according to letters he wrote to his brother in 1927 and 1928 while William was working in Canada, he was rather desperate for money, waiting for patients to pay their bills. In the end J.L. achieved American citizenship, through the time-honored method of a marriage of convenience. Fitting J.L.'s ambitions, this was not just any marriage, but a formal union with one of the most famous and controversial American families of the nineteenth century: the Beechers. Among those impressed by his work with children at Mount Sinai was a child psychologist named Beatrice Beecher, the granddaughter of the evangelist and abolitionist Henry Ward Beecher. Her great aunt was Harriet Beecher Stowe, author of the antislavery novel, *Uncle Tom's Cabin*. It seems that Beatrice spent her whole life in Brooklyn, where she was born, and where her illustrious grandfather preached in his Plymouth Congregational Church. At Beecher's suggestion the two were married in 1928 as a solution to his immigration problem. "I was saved by a saintly woman," he said. During their platonic six-year marriage J.L. and Beatrice were both close friends and professional colleagues. But it seems that when it ended they never had any further contact. J.L. reported that they remained on good terms until she died of tuberculosis shortly after they divorced, but—in what seems to be another example of his surplus reality—publicly available death records indicate that one Beatrice Beecher died in 1972.

## Impromptu

Besides her work at Mount Sinai Hospital, Beecher was also active in the institute that was associated with the church, a settlement house that was somewhat in the mold of Hull House in Chicago, founded by the pioneering social worker Jane Addams. J.L. must have been reminded of his earlier experience in the refugee camps and the House of the Encounter. Beecher arranged for demonstrations of his theater techniques at the church, probably starting sometime in 1927. A 1928 flyer for the "Impromptu School by J.L. Moreno" locates it at the church's Plymouth Institute. Compared to their early foray into vocational training, the two were more successful in reestablishing J.L.'s spontaneity theater. Unlike spontaneity, a word that J.L. helped to popularize but that still seems somewhat highbrow, in the 1920s the word impromptu was in the air. J.L.'s friend Robert Muller referred to J.L.'s "impromptu theatre for the intellectuals of Vienna" in 1923, and Hans Kafka (no relation to Franz), wrote about J.L.'s theater in a 1923 article called "Impromptu Express." That same year an American novelist and later Hollywood screenwriter named Eliot Paul published his novel, *Impromptu*. Paul was one of the young Americans who inhabited the Montparnasse neighborhood after military service in World War I, becoming a close friend of James Joyce and an enthusiast of the jazz-inspired writings of Gertrude Stein. *Impromptu* was also the title of a 1932 comedy short.

Several of the Impromptu cast members were familiar figures in New York so the word about the new theater spread quickly. On February 3, 1929, the *New York Times* ran an article on the work at the church, head-lined "Impromptu Plan Used in Education; Children in New Brooklyn School Are Taught to Exercise Their Spontaneity Rather Than to Depend on Standardized Habits." J.J. Robbins was both an actor in the Impromptu Theater and the managing editor and a contributor to J.L.'s short-lived journal *Impromptu*. Robbins brought with him an excellent network in the experimental theater communities in both New York and in Moscow, where he had been assistant to the great Russian theater director Konstantin Stanislavsky, and was the translator of Stanislavsky's autobiography. He and J.L. shared an acquaintance with the lively experimental theater scene emanating from Russia to the rest of Europe in the 1920s, including the Blue Blouse groups. Along with his other talents, as former head of the translation department at the Jewish *Daily Forward* Robbins possessed editorial skills that J.L. needed, especially as he was becoming accustomed to working in English. Robbins was a crucial part of J.L.'s circle of important relationships; it was another case of the good fortune that followed the struggles of his first years in America.

Besides his theater, by 1929 J.L. had given a number of psychodrama demonstrations in schools, churches, and universities, thus gaining a modest foothold in the academic world. Taken together—drama games for children followed by an improvisational theater for adults, then innovations in science and social reform—the pattern resembled his evolution in Vienna. Nonetheless, America was a much bigger pond than Austria and J.L. wanted to reach a wider audience. Beecher helped him with the English translation of J.L.'s book on *The Theater of Spontaneity*, but finding a publisher was another matter. In a letter to his brother William in February 1928, J.L. excitedly reported that Viking Press was interested in the manuscript, and that they would arrange the usual book tour and paid lectures, as well as royalties. "The book should be available commercially at the very latest at the beginning of spring (simultaneously with a small theatre)." He believed he had some serious financial backers. "These people are enthusiastic and are keen to promote a religious movement all over the country. Two men of the group are New York businessmen. . . ." The situation was far different from that with radio-film. "This time I will not make a mistake," he wrote. "In case it goes wrong it will be all my own fault. This time we will prevail: On this occasion there is not a technical device in question; this time it is me who is in question but with all my tremendous energy." Despite his "tremendous energy" there was no deal with Viking. It would be another twenty years before *The Theatre of Spontaneity* was final published by Beacon House, the publishing company that J.L. founded to produce his books and journals.

## MACY'S

Beatrice Beecher's extensive social network included William H. Bridge, a Hunter College speech and literature professor who later became the director of the Martha Graham Dance Company. J.L. recalled that when they met in 1927 Bridge "was on the point of being fired from Hunter [at that time Hunter was a women's college] because he had kissed one of his students." Bridge was enough of a public personage for the incident to be reported in the *Brooklyn Daily Eagle* on November 30, 1929. "Cause of the trustees' investigation was described by Mr. Bridge as 'a perfectly legitimate friendship' with a girl in one of his classes.' A 'false interpretation' was given this friendship by the girl's parents, the rector–professor added. All this, Mr. Bridge contends, was done with the full consent of Mrs. Bridge, herself an instructor at Hunter." Whatever the real story J.L. was quite taken by Bridge, whom he described as "a handsome, dashing English gentleman, a cavalier. We made a good pair."

One of their first joint projects was to bring J.L.'s ideas about training in spontaneity to Macy's department store. In 1929 the local Putnam County, New York, newspaper reported on a presentation of their work at a community center with the stately name "the Homestead at Crafts." Bridge and J.L. described a "vocational training" program that R.H. Macy & Co. had adopted. Pursuing a pet theory of J.L.'s (and of many others), Bridge argued that technology was making us weaker. "Prof. Bridge pointed out that our senses of hearing, sight, smell, etc., are not anywhere near as keen as those of animals and primitive races," the newspaper explained. "Because of our increased reliance upon machines to do the work which human beings originally did for themselves, we are relinquishing our obligation as human beings to be creative, for says Prof. Bridge, the thing that distinguishes us from animals is that we are creators."

J.L. and Bridge shared a prevalent romantic view that technology undermines human strengths, though in his Putnam County lecture Bridge might have taken J.L.'s views a bit further than J.L. would have done. The idea is at first plausible—think of "labor-saving devices" and, in our own time, childhood obesity. But the logic of the idea runs into a paradox: If we're becoming less creative how are we able to create all those remarkable machines, and more and more of them? And have our senses lost their sharpness only since the Industrial Revolution? That's not much time in which to deteriorate as a species, especially our basic physiology like the five senses, which took millennia to develop. Some of the same assumptions about evolution and acquired characteristics were made by the eugenicists of that period, who believed that biology could be used to improve the species and that human racial quality is in decline because of our reliance on modern technology.

But logic and evidence didn't stand in the way of the intrepid pair's argument that "[i]n the performance of our daily tasks, we do not act spontaneously and impromptu but act as cultural automata." So the work at Macy's involved "placing a person in a given situation" that challenged his creativity, which J.L. called a "Spontaneity Test." According to the newspaper article, after Bridge's talk J.L. took the floor to describe the origins of his spontaneity theater in Vienna, but the reporter's account highlighted Bridge's remarks about "what we can do in a machine age to preserve the integrity of the human personality." How and why J.L. and Bridge happened to give their presentation in a small rural Hudson Valley community is unknown, as is any further information about the work at Macy's. Nonetheless, theirs must have been one of the first attempts to incorporate group dynamics training into corporate America, a movement that really took off after World War II.

The Putnam County appearance demonstrates J.L.'s desire to bring his ideas into the community and the workplace. No doubt he also enjoyed spending time with his new friend, the dashing William Bridge. Just an hour north of New York City, Putnam County has long been a convenient location for the country estates of affluent New Yorkers. Nonetheless, J.L. and Bridge would have been an exotic pair to even the most sophisticated American audience in 1929. Here were a theatrical Brit and an Austrian, each sporting a suitable accent and Old World manners. The trip to the country with Bridge was also one of J.L.'s first glimpses of the lush Hudson

Valley, which reminded him of Voslau and the Valley of the May, and where he established his home and workplace a few years later.

## THE LIVING NEWSPAPER

As he had in Vienna, when J.L. couldn't make a fully spontaneous theater generally acceptable he turned to the idea of the living or "dramatized" newspaper, a subset of impromptu theater. The April 6, 1931 edition of the *New York Times* called it "a newspaper drama. . . ." In the words of the *New York Evening World Telegram* on March 28, 1931, "[t]o obviate the suspicion of previous rehearsals Dr. Moreno's troupe will dramatise news events of the day." The *New York Morning Telegraph* for April 7, 1931 announced that "[t]he impromptu players will present a spontaneous dramatisation of a newspaper. . . ."

J.L.'s was not the only living newspaper project in New York, but the others had a more political mission. Bertold Brecht protégé Mike Gold tried to set up a workers' theater in the later 1920s. Several theater groups were allied with the labor movement in the early 1930s: the Rebel Players in Los Angeles, the Vanguard Group in Philadelphia, the Jack London Group in Newark, and the Solidarity Players in Boston. There was even a Boston Blue Blouse, directly taking the mantle of the Moscow-based Blue Blouse. One of President Franklin Roosevelt's depression-era government programs was the Federal Theatre Project, aimed at keeping unemployed actors, writers, and other artists on the job. Predictably, J.L. criticized the Federal Theatre Project as insufficiently spontaneous and a distortion of his spontaneous dramatics. He was sure that the Project had been inspired by his work. He might have been right, but then J.L. saw all subsequent work as a challenge to his originality and as a turning away from the purity of his ideas. In this case, the Vassar College professor who directed the Federal Theatre Project, Hallie Flanagan, had visited Moscow in 1927 to see the Blue Blouse Players. Nonetheless, drama therapy historian John Casson notes that "as Moreno worked with actors in Vienna and New York, his influence cannot be entirely ruled out."

Beginning in 1935 the Federal Theatre Project mounted live performances on sensitive issues like the spread of syphilis, the American Medical Association's campaign against "socialized medicine," and race relations, often with a progressive slant. Among the alumni of the Federal Theatre were Orson Welles, Arthur Miller, and John Houseman. Finally, the Project unnerved the State Department when it performed a living newspaper production called Ethiopia about the North African nation's popular struggle against Mussolini's invasion. Members of Congress like the influential right-winger Martin Dies accused the Project of subversive communist sympathies. Having become a thorn in the side of the Roosevelt administration, it was shut down in 1939.

The prestigious site of the first public production of J.L.'s Impromptu Theatre on April 5, 1931, was Carnegie Hall, just up the street from J.L.'s new haunt, the Russian Tea Room. Opened in 1927, the Tea Room was a gathering place for the theater crowd and was where J.L., his friend Alfred Adler (who had also been a medic for Austria-Hungary during the war), and other intellectuals from central Europe were able to recreate a modicum of their old café life. Like his Theater of Spontaneity in Vienna, Carnegie Hall was strategically located both in the center of the city and its cultural institutions, where his Impromptu performances were sure to attract attention. And attention they got, but not always the sort for which J.L. had wished.

The mainstream theater critics in New York received J.L.'s efforts in much the same way as their counterparts did in Vienna. A scathing review appeared in the *New York Times* the morning after the first public performance. "From their atelier in Carnegie Hall, where rumors have been rife for weeks of seismic alterations impending in the American drama, Dr. J.L. Moreno and his Impromptu players came last night to the Guild Theatre for their first appearance in public. The occasion was manifestly serious. Dr. Moreno, who has delved into these impulsive theatricals in several foreign capitals, presented the idea in a somewhat impassioned introductory speech as 'not only a theatrical venture but the protest of man as a biological being against the robots.'" Understandably, J.L.'s throwaway line about robots eluded the reviewer. He often peppered his discourse with somewhat opaque references to his philosophical views without providing context, partly because he was overflowing with ideas and partly because he overestimated their transparency. This was one of those times. J.L.'s point would have been more obvious a few years later, when Charlie Chaplain's film *Modern Times* captured the depression generation's thinking about the perils of industrialization.

The *New York Times* reviewers' judgment of the Impromptu Theater went from bad to worse. "The first play, like the ones that followed, turned out to be a dab of dialogue uneasily rendered by its hapless players. Although the impromptu scheme called upon them to burn with fires of creation, they appeared lucky to remember a few of the phrases of the melodramatic cant, and when the dialogue was not witless or absurd it was patently looking for the nearest 'out' or curtain line. . . . Demanding wit above all else, the Moreno players lacked that essential as fully as the premeditation on which they frown so heartily. The legitimate theatre, it can be reported this morning, is just about where it was early last evening." From this establishment reaction, J.L. drew much the same contrarian conclusion as he did in Vienna: that it only proved his point. "The theatre of 'one hundred percent spontaneity' met with the greatest resistance from the public and the press. They were used to depend on 'cultural conserves' of the drama and not to trust spontaneous creativity. . . . We lost the interest of the public and it became difficult to maintain the financial stability of the theatre." Again, total spontaneity was more acceptable in the "therapeutic theatre."

J.L.'s Impromptu Theater did receive at least one favorable review by A.B.W. Smith, identified as a "dramatic critic" in J.L.'s journal *Impromptu*, which published only two issues, both in 1931. As in Vienna, J.L. followed the strategy of simultaneously running a theater company and editing a journal that could help explain the rationale for his theater. Smith's remarks are most notable for his description of the integration of the actors with the audience, an arrangement that would be thoroughly familiar to anyone who has attended a modern improvisational performance. "The initial point of difference between the Impromptu and all other theatres is the fact that the pleasant young lady who meets you at the door and introduces you to others in the audience, later turns out to be one of the actresses. And you are even more surprised as the evening wears on to find that your neighbours in the audience suddenly leave their seats, disappear, and then reappear on the stage *as* actors in the plays. The entire audience is activated. There is a sense of kinship between it and the stage that *is* entirely absent in the legitimate theatre" (emphasis in original). Another contributor to the *Impromptu* journal offered a less elevated account of his attraction to J.L.'s productions: "First of all it is a hell of a lot of fun. Maybe it can increase American culture.

Maybe it can release inhibitions that Mr. Freud never even thought of; but the only inhibitions I am interested in releasing are those of person-able members of the opposite sex."

## THE GROUP

Though J.L.'s ambition to become the impresario for a new kind of American theater was frustrated, even as his Impromptu venture was failing, he became involved with one of the most influential theater companies in history, the Group Theatre, which was founded at the same time as J.L.'s impromptu project. The Group Theatre's immediate predecessor was Eva Le Gallienne's Civic Repertory Theatre, where in 1930 J.L. conducted spontaneity exercises. There he met theater greats Elia Kazan and Stella and Luther Adler. Seventy-five years later, Gilbert Laurence recalled his experience with J.L., whom he met while apprenticing at the Civic Rep:

> Moreno's group met regularly in a studio at the back of Carnegie Hall. Moreno had some wealthy sponsors who paid the expenses and some-times held fund-raiser affairs at their luxurious homes. I remember one woman who lived in a house on Sutton Place with a living room ceiling which had been painted by John Barrymore when he had lived there. Again there was no money for those of us who performed the "impromptu" sketches taken from the daily newspapers. Dr. Moreno would speak to us individually, explain what our character was and how we were to interact with the other characters. When he was fin-ished he would leave the small stage and we would proceed. Some-times the result would be a dramatic illumination of the synopses the Dr. had given us; other times the sketch would be short and lacking in any dynamic contact. But at no time was a psychiatric interpre-tation presented by Moreno. Some of the actors were professionals and it was decided to present a Sunday evening demonstration of what was billed as the "Impromptu Theatre". The theater used was the "Guild Theatre", then operated by "The Theatre Guild". Being one of the cast I don't remember who were in the audience. Among the Civic Rep actors with whom J.L. worked were Harold Clurman and John Garfield, all of whom went on to the Group Theatre in 1931. The Group Theatre was based on the principles of the Russian Konstantin

Stanislavsky, who trained his actors in the Moscow Art Theater to appeal to their own memories to recreate emotion.

So effective were the Group Theater players at recreating the emotions of real life that sometimes the results resembled those of the encounter groups that emerged several decades later. After a performance of a Clifford Odets play *Waiting for Lefty*, about a corrupt union leader, the feelings raised both on and off stage were so intense that when the cast members left the building on Fourteenth Street they found "clusters of people still gathered outside, laughing, crying, hugging each other, clapping their hands." As described by Wendy Smith in her book about the Group, "[n]o one wanted to go home. Sleep was out of the question. Most of the Group went to an all-night restaurant—no one can remember now which one—and tried to eat. Odets sat alone, pale, withdrawn, not talking at all. Everyone was too dazed to have much to say. It was dawn before they could bring themselves to separate, to admit that the miracle was over . . . *Waiting for Lefty* changed people's idea of what theatre was. More than an evening's entertainment, more even than a serious examination of the contemporary scene by a thoughtful writer, theatre at its best could be a living embodiment of communal values and aspirations." Here was an American version of what 1920s Vienna understood about the power of drama. But J.L. believed that the possibilities for social transformation could be still greater if the players themselves were the playwrights and the border between them and the audience melted away. Here, too, was an example of the difficulty of drawing emotional boundaries between theater and the "real world." As a zealous Aristotelian it was a phenomenon of which J.L. enthusiastically approved, sought to exploit, and believed was in any case finally inevitable.

Riven by interpersonal conflicts, financial problems, and the complications of impending war, the Group Theatre closed in 1941. Its spiritual descendent, the Actors Studio, was founded in 1947 and adopted the Group Theatre's philosophy, which came to be known as "method acting." "The method" bears obvious similarities to J.L.'s psychodrama in its attempt to relive previous experiences, at least at an emotional level. Scholars of the innovative theater scene of the era agree that J.L.'s influence on the Group Theater and the Actor's Studio was substantial. Group

Theater member and Actor's Studio cofounder Elia Kazan, who directed such classics as *A Streetcar Named Desire, Death of a Salesman,* and *On the Waterfront,* is said to have used psychodrama in his rehearsals. In 1947, J.L. demonstrated psychodrama at the White Barn Theater in Westport, Connecticut, with Group founders Stella Adler and Harold Clurman in the audience. Theater historian Keith Sawyer argues that J.L.'s spontaneity theater in Vienna and his Impromptu Theater in New York "had an indirect but nonetheless pervasive effect on twentieth-century theater." J.L. felt a special affinity with actors, with whom he remained popular for the rest of his life, some observing psychodrama, some becoming his students, some seeking psychiatric care, and some all three at once.

J.L.'s Impromptu Theater and the Group Theater were getting under way just as another important American theater experiment was ending. The Provincetown Players came together in Provincetown, Massachusetts at Cape Cod in the summer of 1915. They were a certifiably bohemian group. Among the early Players were John Reed, a journalist and author of the famous first-person account of the Bolshevik Revolution, *Ten Days that Shook the World,* and arts patron Mabel Dodge. Their leader was the charismatic George Cram "Jig" Cook, a Grecophile who wanted to start a "beloved community" of actors to mount plays that would challenge their audiences. After a few years the Players found a site on Washington Square in New York City. The performances were scripted, but invited the audiences to be part of the theater-space. In his history of the Provincetown Players, Robert Sarlos writes that "the plays were first thought of as a therapeutic party-game for a small, close-knit group," remarkably similar to the Theater of Spontaneity. "About the time when the Provincetown Players experimented with works of art that grew from creative group dynamics, a young psychiatrist in Vienna [J.L.] detected apparent parallels between God-to-man and man-to-man relationships, and perceived them as the root of social adjustment problems as well as solutions."

Sarlos finds numerous points of ideological kinship between Jig Cook's healing collective and J.L's psychodrama, including the idea that human beings are only truly complete in the group. "They recognized how crucial trust and interdependence, spontaneity and release were in an increasingly mechanized and impersonal world." Both placed theater in a quasi-religious role. Referring to the "encounterculture" that wended its way from the spontaneity theater to Impromptu through Chicago improv, existentialism, group therapy, social network analysis, Esalen and the Living Theater, Sarlos concludes that Jig Cook and J.L. were among the precursors of this revolution of "collectivity and spontaneity," and that J.L. had "a probable impact on founders of the Group Theatre whose theatre he shared."

## SOMETHING WONDERFUL

The question of how much spontaneity is required to qualify as true improvisational theater was another implicit challenge presented by J.L.'s radical views to other theater groups. Already in Vienna his purist approach had set him apart from the Blue Blouse troupes that emerged from Russia. That issue became important in the organization of improv from the 1930s on. One of them was Viola Spolin's Chicago-based "theater games" movement, dating to 1938, earning her the title of "Mother of American Improvisational Theater." Spolin was a student of Neva Boyd. Boyd was a pioneer of group games and dramatic arts for children at Hull House in Chicago in the 1920s and a Northwestern University professor. The Frenchman Jacques Copeau had introduced improvisation theater games in the 1910s for theater rehearsals before Boyd used them for problem-solving exercises. But Spolin was certainly the most powerful direct force in innovative theater games that led to today's improvisational theater. Improv historian Keith Sawyer writes that Spolin "acknowledged the influence of Moreno on her work, once using Moreno's term sociodrama. Spolin's original goals for her exercises were explicitly therapeutic rather than dramatic. She drew on Moreno's innovation of basing improvisations on audience suggestions, and through her, this technique became a hallmark of Chicago improv," especially the famous Second City company.

However, the actor and director Andrew Harmon, a Spolin protégé, told me that she regarded her approach to theater as therapeutic, but not as therapy. Spolin certainly saw the value of theater as training in spontaneity in much the way J.L. did. In his oral history of Chicago Improv, *Something Wonderful Right Away*, Jeffrey Sweet writes that "Spolin's rationale was that if you put someone onstage (particularly a child since she worked most frequently with children) and tell him how to 'act,' he will feel inhibited and self-conscious, but if you transform the situation into a game, the actor, in concentrating his energies on playing the game, will lose his self-consciousness and perform naturally and spontaneously."

Because Spolin's games were too short for stage performances, she started an acting workshop in 1955 with her son Paul Sills that combined a series of scenes, as suggested by their friend David Shepherd. This "scenario" concept caught on in performances at the University of Chicago. Also in 1955, Shepherd and Sills founded The Compass Players, often beginning with a living newspaper followed by a scenario. Although the scenarios were written, the dialogue within each scene was improvised. The Compass only lasted a year and a half, reorganizing in St. Louis with Shepherd's approval, but Elaine May abandoned the scenario concept in favor of scripted scenes, which finally became the Second City style when it opened in 1959, once again with Spolin as the driving force. May teamed up with Mike Nichols for an enthusiastically received run in New York. Shepherd and Sills were unhappy with the largely scripted orientation of Second City, though Spolin continued to work with the Second City performers in rehearsals.

Other than Spolin, were the founders of Second City aware of J.L. and psychodrama? In a revealing interview, Paul Sills remembered that in the early 1950s his Playwrights Theater performed *La Ronde*, the sexy play by Viennese modernist Arthur Schnitzler that so shocked the Viennese powers-that-were. Then he created The Compass Players, which he said was radically different not only from anything that had been done in Chicago before, "[o]r anywhere else. I would like to know where else. This was the first improvisational theater. People say it happened in Zurich back when or something. I don't know. But I think as a theater with a place on the street and a continuous history, it started with The Compass back on 55th Street." Although Sills' pride in his originality is understandable, he must have been aware of the commedia dell'arte. The otherwise inexplicable offhand reference to Zurich might have been an unconscious association to odd bits of information he got from his mother about Vienna and J.L. Sills was also a devotee of Martin Buber's "I–thou" philosophy, thus he had a specific but indirect exposure to J.L.'s idea of the encounter. He might also have known about psychodrama from the clinical psychologist James Sacks, a backstage observer of The Compass, Elaine May's boyfriend, and later one of J.L.'s favorite students when he was part of the core group of psychodramatists in New York. Sacks brought Spolin's theater games to his psychodrama work, and in at least one instance inspired a sketch based on his experience with psychiatric patients. Another young psychodramatist, Marcia Karp, participated in improv groups in the Bay Area in the mid-1960s, taking audience suggestions in the style of Second City.

As the director Andrew Harmon pointed out to me, the dilemma that J.L. faced with his spontaneity theater and Impromptu was also faced by Spolin, and led to the break between The Compass and Second City styles, and is implicit in the art form: If the performance is truly spontaneous audiences often find that it lacks a compelling narrative arc, but if it unfolds in traditional dramatic fashion audiences don't believe it's truly unscripted. The cofounders of the Second City, Del Close and Bernie Sahlins, had a decades-long argument about true improv, with Close defending it and Sahlins concluding that "[i]mprov never was a presentational form," "[t]o do it night after night in a theater setting is impossible." In the end Sahlins might have been right. For J.L. the answer was clear. To avoid compromising about the aesthetic he wanted to achieve, and because the truly spontaneous theater did not seem to be able to support itself financially, he turned more and more to psychodrama, psychiatric practice, and social science.

Reaching his fortieth birthday in 1929, J.L. must have felt he had found his footing in America. During the following two frenetic and intensely creative decades, he reached the pinnacle of fame and influence. His personal style was largely set, a combination of mystic, dramaturge, impresario, therapist, Svengali, and maestro. As his attraction to the dashing Hunter College literature professor William Bridge suggests, with his Viennese accent, sandy hair, deep blue eyes, and flamboyant theatrical manner J.L. was something of a bon vivant among Americans, an image he was happy to cultivate with journalists for the rest of his life. He was a ball of energy, excited and excitable, a style that was more Austrian eccentric than American academic scientist, many of whom found it more disconcerting than charming. In truth, he was temperamentally better suited to the actors he gathered about him in both the Old and the New Worlds than he was to the academics in either. Although J.L. clearly enjoyed his years with the New York City theater crowd, he hardly ever spoke about that period of his life with me or with my mother, who met him in 1941. It was his way of moving on to a new chapter.

## GOD IN *STATUS NASCENDI*

J.L. arranged his endeavors and established his relationships in New York in much the same way he had in Vienna; the simultaneous production of a theater and a journal was a pattern he repeated several times in his career. Although it published only two issues, the 1931 *Impromptu* journal gave J.L. a vehicle for introducing his ideas into the English language and to the American intelligentsia while he was conducting his psychodrama performances at Carnegie Hall. The very first item in the first issue of *Impromptu* is J.L.'s brief theological piece "Ave Creatore," culled from his 1914–1915 writings. J.L. observes that deists, agnostics, and atheists all attribute various positive and negative qualities to God, but not His quality as the creator before creation itself. As he had written in his younger days, "More important than the creation is the creator." Once God created the universe and all its creatures He could be evaluated based on His creations, but what about assessing God as He was in the midst of the creative act itself? "He had become susceptible of analysis because he was already delivered of the child. All the affirmations and denials of God, all His images, have revolved around this, the God of the second status, the God Who [sic] had reached recognition in the affairs of the universe, so to speak. . . . But there is another status of God, which even as a symbol has been neglected, that is the status of God before the Sabbath, from the moment of conception, during the process of creating and evolving the worlds and Himself."

We humans may be judged based on what kind of life we've created. Is it one of cruelty or kindness? Are we destroying the planet or stewarding its resources wisely? Our creations reflect on us. Parents often feel that way about their children, that how they turn out indicates their own qualities, that their children are a reflection on them. This tendency is the source of countless and sometimes irremediable conflicts between parents and children. The same is true of the way we normally judge God. Like human beings, once God became a creator He can be judged by admirers and by critics based on that which He created, the "conserve." Only then does the existence of evil in the world become a matter of debate about the nature of God, either to see Him as a sadist or as setting up a series of challenges for us.

But what can we say of God *in status nascendi*, God in the act of creation? No matter how paradoxical it may sound, J.L. argues that the creative moment in God's career is much closer to mankind's own experience, as a mother is closer to her child during pregnancy than after separation from it, because while in the act of creating God is not the perfected unreachable existence that is painted before our eyes, but a growing, fermenting, actively forming, imperfect being, striving towards perfection and completion. In plain words, God is a lover.

Here J.L. expresses the underlying rationale for the spontaneous theater. Human beings have become so impressed with their creations—"[t]he last stage of a work, the books in the libraries, the finished paintings and sculptures in the galleries and museums, the mercantile products of inventive ideas, the rigid standards, the ethical, psychological and physical formulae"—that they have forgotten the glories of the creative act itself. All of these items are "conserves," now dead stuff that are the products of life in its essence, but they are not living. "Who can tell what a self-satisfied Philistine Dante became after the creative moments of the *Divine Comedy* were over? . . . Our world needs a corrective, a glorification of the creative act, an asylum for the creator. . . ."

His emphasis on creativity put J.L. on all fours with an Anglo-American philosophical movement often called process philosophy. In contrast with classical Western philosophy, which understands reality as timeless, the process philosophers emphasized becoming over being, viewing reality as a process of emergence rather than a static thing. The European philosopher who came closest to this metaphysics of process was the Frenchman Henri Bergson, who argued that philosophers had not taken seriously enough the immediate intuition of change or flux, which he referred to as *duree*, or duration. Bergson was wildly popular in Europe during J.L.'s university years, winning the Nobel Prize for literature in 1927. When J.L. arrived in America, he studied the important English-language process philosophers, especially the American Charles Sanders Peirce and the Briton Alfred North Whitehead.

The fact that there was a strong American philosophical movement that fit so well with his conception of creativity helped J.L. identify with the intellectual side of his new country. Some of the process school also shared his interest in the philosophy of religion. Of the later important process philosophers the most prominent was Charles Hartshorne, who spent much of his career at the University of Chicago and the University of Texas, where he retired. In 1978, I was a fledgling philosophy professor at Texas and was delighted to be assigned an office right next to Hartshorne's, who was by then a mere eighty-one years old (he lived to 103), and we often went to lunch together. When we were first introduced, Hartshorne asked me if I was related to J.L., whose lectures he had attended at Chicago. In September 1978, I found myself walking down the long hallway in the University of Texas philosophy department alongside the tiny, wiry, illustrious professor with a high-pitched voice. "Your father once said that creativity is the most important idea of the 20th century. I agree with that!"

## LINCOLN

In 1931, just as J.L.'s involvement in the New York theater scene was cresting, he made his initial foray into the politics of American psychiatry in a characteristically large way: by taking on the prominent American psychoanalyst and principle translator of Freud's works into English, A.A. Brill. The stage was the 1931 American Psychiatric Association annual meeting in Toronto, and the subject of their disagreement was no less a personage than Abraham Lincoln, with J.L. casting himself as the Great Emancipator's defender. In the course of the incident, he became famous for the first time as a psychiatrist rather than as a theatrical innovator. The episode won him instant fame among the general public as well, generating sympathy in the press as a recent and colorful immigrant scientist who embraced American values, but J.L.'s new notoriety came at a professional cost. As J.L.'s biographer points out, after this incident "most psychoanalysts turned against Moreno."

The Austrian-born Brill trained in medicine at Columbia University, lectured and practiced at Columbia and New York University, returned to Vienna to study under Freud, and was the past president of the American Psychoanalytic Association and honorary president of the New York Psychoanalytic Society. By 1931 he was the very embodiment and unchallenged leader of the American psychoanalytic establishment. On this occasion

Brill chose to deliver an innocuously titled talk (and one that he never published) on the psychology of the great American president, "Abraham Lincoln as a Humorist," in the spirit of Freud's 1905 book, *Jokes and Their Relation to the Unconscious*. It was perhaps the most controversial paper ever delivered at a meeting of North American psychiatrists, drawing enormous media attention. With headlines like "Lincoln Analyzed by Psychiatrist" and "Savants Clash Over Lincoln's Vulgar Stories," the confrontation between Brill and the upstart J.L. was covered in every major and most minor newspapers and was the subject of a movie theater newsreel. The day after the session the *New York Times* ran a story headlined, "Dr. Brill Describes Lincoln as 'Manic'—Dr. Moreno is Skeptical."

In the paper Brill diagnosed Lincoln as a "manic schizoid personality" whose depressive moods stopped short of mental illness. According to an Associated Press report that appeared in dozens of newspapers, Brill argued that Lincoln's schizoid or "split" personality was due to "his conflicting inheritances from his mother and father." The window to Lincoln's unconscious was his off-color humor. "What is very peculiar about Lincoln's stories and jokes," said Brill, "his own and those he appropriated from others is that many if not most are of an aggressive and algogenic nature, treating of pain, suffering and death, and that a great many of them were so frankly sexual as to be classed as obscene." Despite the many privations and struggles of his life, including a cruel father, deep poverty, an unrequited love affair, and a troubled marriage, "he attained the highest ambition of any American. Nevertheless thruout [sic] his life he was unable to disburden himself of his depressive moods."

Lincoln's psychology has long been an object of fascination among Americans, but the interpretation of his dark and dour frame of mind has shifted. In the decades following his death Lincoln's melancholy was widely recognized; Lincoln himself described his notorious, sometimes scatological storytelling as necessary for his emotional survival. But then modern psychology applied itself to an attempt to understand the great man's inner demons. "Inspired by Freud himself," one historian has written, "psychoanalysts eagerly put Lincoln on the couch, examining his life through the lens of childhood traumas and sexual conflicts." In our time, popular histories like Doris Kearns Goodwin's *Team of Rivals* and films like Stephen Spielberg's *Lincoln* understand him as a tortured but deeply philosophical soul who bore the nation's pain as his own and still could see further in our national story than anyone else. His humorous asides and off-color stories seem less shocking as Victorian attitudes recede in the public mind, viewed as windows into his deep insights about human nature rather than evidence of psychosexual conflicts.

In his formal response to Brill's paper, J.L. made the most of his first moment at the center of the American psychiatric community. Only six years before he had arrived in the United States with little but ambition and intellectual brilliance; now he had the opportunity to speak to a powerful group of scientists on behalf of the greatest moral hero the nation had produced. Like Lincoln, he appealed to moral principle as well as to the ethics of psychiatry. "It is not fair to psychoanalyse [sic] the personality of a man now dead, as you have to do it without his consent. . . . Dr. Brill's conclusions are based on the statements of friends and contemporaries who may have had all kinds of motives to relate all kinds of stories about Lincoln. Had a contemporary psychiatrist made a study of Lincoln, Dr. Brill would have been justified to some extent in accepting the findings. But as no scientific study of the great American emancipator has been made during his life-time there was no justification for any attempt to analyze his personality from what is related by laymen." J.L. went on to turn the tables on Brill by psychoanalyzing his need to attack Lincoln. He suggested that Brill had developed a "transference" to Lincoln, the psychoanalytic term for unconsciously redirecting feelings about one person to another. Brill, he argued, "was building himself up to appear before the world, the American public, in a great role, the role of the psychoanalytic emancipator and liberator. Seeing him in action, I could not help comparing him with Lincoln, the object of his analysis. He is little more than five feet tall. Lincoln was a giant, way above six feet. Both have a beard and both have the first name, Abe. . . . Brill had waited patiently for a chance to measure up to that other Abe today, in this hall, before all of us, he had this opportunity—the President of the American Psychoanalytic Society versus the President of the United States."

A 2003 historical note in *Psychiatric News* said that "Moreno tore apart Brill's paper as being based on unproven and unsubstantiated conclusions." Yet Brill himself had chosen J.L. to respond to his paper. Why choose someone known to be an outspoken critic of psychoanalysis? Writing years later, J.L. suggested that this decision was an expression of Brill's internal conflict.

He wasn't confident that psychoanalysis could analyze a genius of Lincoln's caliber, or that he himself could stand up to the American idol. Brill was unsure if the American people would accept him, an immigrant, in the place of Lincoln. "He felt guilty. Freud was not around to help him, and in a masochistic mood, with a brazen gesture, he called upon the very man whose ways of production and presentation should have been as mysterious to him as those of Abraham Lincoln. He called upon myself. Like the dying Hamlet he called Fortinbras to take over." In his 1937 book *Moses and Monotheism* Freud suggested that Moses was not a Jew, a claim that subsequent scholars have argued was a manifestation of Freud's own desire to replace Moses the liberator, or even to be seen as the messiah himself. In something like this way J.L. claimed that Brill had an unconscious need to feel superior to Lincoln; otherwise why choose such an iconic figure for analysis?

Freud must have known about this harsh attack on his favored American protégé, but at least publicly he said nothing. Brill and his many allies surely regarded J.L.'s response as at the very least ungentlemanly, and at the worst egomania, opportunism, and self-promotion, especially in light of the fact that Brill himself had offered the discussant's role to him; the references to Brill's physical appearance verged on the ad hominem, though psychoanalysis commonly cites insecurities about personal characteristics in explaining neurotic complexes. Brill was furious. "In a histrionic manner Dr. Moreno tries to show that we don't know anything about anybody who is dead," he said after J.L.'s response. "We know a lot about Lincoln. If his friends and contemporaries tell us about him we have a right to accept what they say as facts." Yet it cannot be denied that J.L. also demonstrated adeptness in psychoanalytic discourse, including its potential to be turned upon the analyst easily, and in that sense its self-referential and unscientific nature. These rhetorical skills, too, must have infuriated the analysts. As the author of J.L.'s academic biography writes, J.L.'s real target was not Brill but Freud and psychoanalysis itself. His career in psychiatry was from then on marked by a continual hectoring of psychoanalysis, and the analysts reacted in kind.

Even before J.L.'s remarks, the lecture itself was delivered in an atmosphere of expectation. A Brooklyn psychiatrist, Edward E. Hicks, filed a protest about Brill's speech with the association president Walter M. English after he saw an advance abstract. According to the Associated Press story Hicks described Brill's statements about Lincoln as "insulting to right thinking Americans and to the memory of one of the two greatest presidents of this republic." In the event, Brill went on a bit longer than the time granted him; the official minutes of the meeting record that the president had to cut him off: "[T]his was such an interesting paper that I was loath to ask Dr. Brill to stop." In the face of Hicks' protest, perhaps Brill wanted to expand on his account in self-defense, or he might have stumbled a bit over his text in anxiety. Then, in a transparent attempt at diplomacy, President English added, "[i]t is now before you for discussion. From its presentation, I see nothing of which we can complain."

J.L. was by no means alone in his criticism. A number of established psychiatrists also thought that Brill's assertions were inappropriate and threw an unfavorable light on American psychiatry and psychoanalysis. Among the most outspoken were L. Pierce Clark of Manhattan State Hospital, who planned to write his own book defending Lincoln, Frederick Peterson of Columbia, and Chicago psychiatrist Francis Gerry. Even the politicians got into the act. A New York State senator named William L. Love arranged for the state legislature to formerly censure Brill for his unpatriotic act and threatened to introduce a bill to ban psychoanalysis from the state as a fraud "akin to hypnotism."

Beyond the questions of personality and politics, what is most important about the Brill–J.L. squabble is that it helped establish a line between psychoanalysis and nonpsychoanalytic forms of psychotherapy. Distinguishing J.L. from the other critics was the fact that he had his own comprehensive alternative to psychoanalytic therapy: the psychodrama. The next quarter century would lay the groundwork for new therapies under the banner of existential and "humanistic" labels, often called the third force in psychology, with psychoanalysis as the first force and behaviorism as the second. For a brief moment in the early 1930s J.L. was in a position to establish himself as the unquestioned leader of the alternative movement to psychoanalysis and behaviorism, but new figures, philosophical systems, and events in the world beyond psychology, as well as J.L.'s own foibles, put obstacles in his path.

## CHAPTER FIVE:

# THE SOCIAL NETWORK

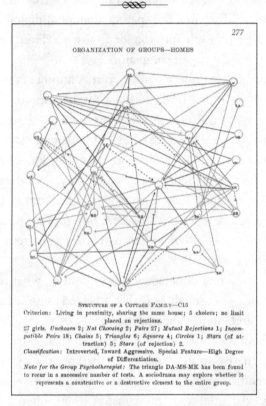

ORGANIZATION OF GROUPS—HOMES

STRUCTURE OF A COTTAGE FAMILY—C15

Criterion: Living in proximity, sharing the same house; 5 choices; no limit placed on rejections.

27 girls. *Unchosen* 2; *Not Choosing* 2; *Pairs* 27; *Mutual Rejections* 1; *Incompatible Pairs* 18; *Chains* 5; *Triangles* 6; *Squares* 4; *Circles* 1; *Stars* (of attraction) 5; *Stars* (of rejection) 2.

*Classification*: Introverted, Inward Aggressive. Special Feature—High Degree of Differentiation.

*Note for the Group Psychotherapist:* The triangle DA-MS-MK has been found to recur in a successive number of tests. A sociodrama may explore whether it represents a constructive or a destructive element to the entire group.

The sociogram of a residential cottage in the State Training School for Girls in Hudson, New York, 1934.

*There are certain structural processes observable in the groups studied which are best explained if it is assumed that networks exist.*

J.L. Moreno, 1934

ALTHOUGH IT DIDN'T MAKE THE HEADLINES, a second event at the Toronto psychiatric meetings in 1931 turned out to be far more significant for the history of psychology and for J.L.'s career than the

Lincoln controversy, one that made him one of the most influential and unconventional social scientists of the twentieth century. This event also marked the real beginning of social network analysis. E. Stagg Whitin, an expert on prison reform and a Columbia University instructor, organized a roundtable to appeal to psychiatrists for new ideas about applying their skills to prison management. "Your kind reception of my request," Whitin said, addressing the psychiatrists in Philadelphia a year later, "led to a general discussion which was followed by the volunteering of Dr. Jacob L. Moreno to give us a concrete answer. Moreno was a stranger to me, and I was surprised as well as pleased by his audacity in daring to come forward with an answer. His answer was put in writing. Experiments have been made at Sing Sing, in a public school in Brooklyn, The Riverdale Country Day School and at the New York State Training School for Girls under Moreno's direction."

The "experiments" Whitin referred to took place mainly between 1928 and 1933 at schools, a prison, and what was then called a reformatory for delinquent girls. They were the first attempts at what is now known as social network analysis, which J.L. called "sociometry," the science of measuring the relationships between members of a group. Rejecting the distinction between research and application, as a matter of principle J.L. believed that the results should always be the basis for intervening in the life of the group to improve the lives of its members. J.L. acknowledged a number of influences on sociometry, including famous sociologists like C.H. Cooley, George Herbert Mead, W.I. Thomas, and the philosopher John Dewey, as well as the earlier German philosopher–sociologist Georg Simmel. But he said that he "went a step ahead and defined experimentally the interpersonal situation and developed interpersonal measurement."

In the case of the experiment at the famous Hudson River prison Sing Sing, the question was how to classify prisoners for processing and assignment to living and working situations while incarcerated. J.L. believed that the standard psychiatric classifications were too individualistic for institutional change, that they failed to take into account the social nature of the human being, even one who would be assigned a psychiatric diagnosis or who was a hardened criminal. The underlying, often invisible social networks in which people actually lived, or those in which they preferred to live, needed to be charted to improve social conditions. It is hard to overstate the importance of these pioneering projects. The authors of a 2009 paper in the prestigious journal *Science* began their review of network analysis social science with a description of J.L.'s experiments in the 1930s. They are the ancestors of social media like Facebook and Twitter (more about social media in the last chapter), and for organizational assessments in government, industry, the military, and civil society. "Network research is 'hot' today," the authors of the *Science* paper wrote, and because of tools made possible by the Internet it's getting hotter: Three times as many papers were published on "social networks" in 2009 as in 1999.

J.L.'s mastery of his own social networks opened the doors for his pioneering work on social dynamics. The school and prison work were made possible by several important friendships. A young Columbia University graduate student named Helen Hall Jennings joined his impromptu theater group at Carnegie Hall. The brilliant young sociologist introduced J.L. to her mentor at Columbia, Gardner Murphy. Six years younger than J.L., Murphy was already a prominent social psychologist and also an exponent of psychical research, especially telepathy. Murphy was in the proud American tradition of the Harvard philosopher and psychologist William James, older brother of the novelist Henry and a founder of the American Society for Psychical Research. Anticipating later humanistic psychologists like Stanley Krippner, Murphy thought that creativity had its wellspring in parapsychological phenomena, putting human beings in touch with their greater potential. Thus he had a natural intellectual connection with J.L.'s mystical side. Murphy's writing style often rambled and was full of jargon (another characteristic they shared), but his 1958 book, *Human Potentialities* was important in the later development of humanistic psychology. Murphy used his academic perch at Columbia to introduce J.L. to some of his most important collaborators in the 1930s and 1940s, including such famous social scientists as Kurt Lewin, Gordon Allport, and Robert S. Lynd, coauthor with his wife of the famous sociological study of "Middletown."

But in the early days of J.L.'s social reform experiments no collaborator was more important to him than Helen Jennings, one of the great, unsung heroes of American social science. Much like other women in the history of science she has been overlooked. As J.L. admitted, it was Jennings who did the dry work of collecting data, doing the computations, and organizing the material into charts that J.L. called "sociograms," work that today can be done at the stroke of a few keys using free software like Pajek. He described Jennings as "brilliant and ambitious," and "one of the most talented social scientists I have ever met." During her long career at Brooklyn College, which maintains a scholarship in her name, she published several books on sociometry as it applied to personality, leadership, race relations, and the classroom. But today Jennings and her contributions are hardly ever noted.

Though Jennings was married briefly, she had no children and is remembered in our family lore as a lonely person. During the 1950s and early 1960s, she got some press attention as an expert on psychology, including a stint as a consultant for a rather mawkish daytime TV show called *Chance for Romance*. The host of the show was the newsreader and game show personality John Cameron Swayze, who was perhaps most famous as the spokesman for Timex Watches ("It takes a licking and keeps on ticking"). Anticipating by twenty years far more successful programs like *The Dating Game*, the premise was that a panel of experts, including Jennings, would decide which members of the audience should date each other. An Associated Press story about the short-lived program (it lasted one season, in 1958), called it "an absolutely awful show in which various people, for unfathomable reasons, parade their private lives before the public on the chance of finding romance with another lonely mortal." For better or for worse, the "parade of private lives" on television that was offensive in the 1950s is routine today. Jennings defended the program as "absolutely honest. It seeks mature people. . . . Singleness is often due to a lack of opportunity of meeting others. A mature person does not spend his time running around looking for someone who will be a friend or marriage partner." The remarks were poignant considering Jennings' unfulfilled private life. Her participation in the program also reflected her and J.L.'s earnest conviction that it is possible to "read" implicit emotional connections in a group.

## Social Networks

Often the greatest ideas are the simplest, most obvious ones. One of J.L.'s premier insights was what he called the "sociodynamic effect." Consider any community. The choices people make about with whom to associate always vary from randomness; that is the sociodynamic effect. For example, whenever I enter a newly assembled group, as in the case of a college class or a committee, I note the gender arrangements of the seating. Those arrangements are virtually never simply "boy–girl, boy–girl, boy–girl." In every culture I have experienced, there is a tendency for males to sit next to one another and females to sit next to other females, especially if the group is a new one meeting for the first time. If those choices are not random, then there must both be a reason for them and a social structure that can be studied. This is a trivial example, but the fact that there is an implicit structure within any group creates tremendous opportunities for research.

One of the few exceptions to the nonrandom nature of group structure among humans is the community of infants in a nursery, but even there, J.L., Helen Jennings, and their coworkers made interesting findings. In this study, which seems to have taken place in the late 1920s, they assembled groups of babies from birth to forty-two weeks and arranged their cribs near one another. Infants of up to about twenty weeks did not show outward signs of response to the babies in the cribs next to them, but from twenty weeks up to about twenty-eight weeks of age they showed signs of developing the ability for social interaction. Infants at forty-two weeks or so could be observed looking at each other or looking in response to being looked at, crying when another cried, smiling at another baby or smiling in response, trying to grasp another baby, and touching another baby. By the time the babies were around forty to forty-two weeks old a "map" or sociogram of their relationships could be drawn based upon measuring these initiated or responsive behaviors, as shown in Figure 1. Each circle is a baby. The one-way arrows represent behaviors that are not reciprocated, those crossed with a perpendicular line indicate a mutual response. The sociogram is a summation of the patterns of their responses to one another.

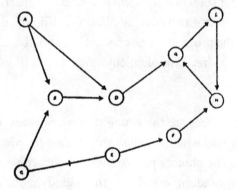

Figure 1. Interpersonal "choices" of babies in a nursery.

By modern standards the methods of this study were crude. For example, in J.L.'s brief report there is no way of knowing whether those recording the interactions were noting the same or equivalent behaviors, a concept called *inter-rater reliability*. On the other hand, making the study somewhat more valid, there was a control group of babies who were placed near dolls. At first, the results were similar as the infants showed signs of attempted interaction with the dolls, but as they grew older the chance influence of the dolls to the babies seemed to decrease compared to the experimental group.

It seems that the babies were in many cases long-term residents of a nursery, almost certainly at Mount Sinai Hospital in New York City where J.L. and Beatrice knew the distinguished pediatrician Bela Schick and could have been given access to the nursery. J.L.'s report states that as some were discharged new babies were introduced into the study. The fact that they were in a nursery suggests that they were too small or too ill to go home with their mothers or had problems related to low birth weight. In those days before newborn intensive care units it was not unusual for babies to be kept in nurseries for weeks though if they were seriously ill there was little that pediatricians could do. J.L. didn't say anything about their health status, but if the babies were not very sick at the time of the study that might have influenced the results. Nonetheless, J.L. and Helen were able to show that some rough measurements of a baby group's formation could be made and that the potential for internal group structure based on responses to physical proximity emerges early in life. More important was their pioneering attempt to graph human relationships. According to a standard textbook, "[b]efore Moreno, people had spoken of 'webs' of connections, the 'social fabric' and, on occasion, of 'networks' of relationships, but no one had attempted to systematize this metaphor into an analytic diagram."

J.L. and colleagues undertook another study of children's groups, this time at PS 181 in Brooklyn, where again Beatrice Beecher would have had good contacts. They observed relationships in a kindergarten class and then in classes through the eighth grade. The children's interpersonal choices were recorded based on whom they chose to sit next to while studying or playing. Triangles were used to signify boys and circles for girls, with their initials in the middle. What is remarkable is the way that the sociograms progressively illustrate more and more self-organized and integrated social systems as they move up the age cohort. In the kindergarten sociogram there are very few reciprocal choices; that is, hardly any children chose each other by their actions to form a couple of "dyads," and there are no mutually selected groups of three or "triads." In general, according to J.L.'s social network theory, the fewer dyads and triads there are in a group the less organized it is. The most highly organized group is a collection of triads all linked to one another, much like a three-dimensional crystalline structure. In theory, a group that is a series of linked triads would also be the most integrated and stable group, as well as the most difficult to infiltrate. There is also no obvious social differentiation by gender in the kindergarten group, as boys choose girls and girls choose boys seemingly at random.

In the first through third grades there is noticeable division between the boys and the girls. This segregation by gender is so striking that by the fourth grade there is only one unreciprocated choice of a boy for a girl. Also notable by the fourth grade is the increasingly organized internal structure, defined by the emergence of dyads and a few triads. The fourth graders also include certain often-chosen individuals or "stars," another indication of growing sophistication in the network. And there is an isolated female dyad, which could be a sign of trouble ahead among the girls. The dyad seems both to reject and to be rejected by the rest of

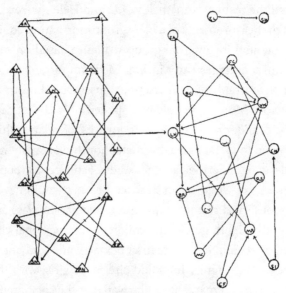

Figure 2. The structure of a fourth-grade class,
with boys as triangles and girls as circles.

the girls. By eighth grade, one observes a far higher frequency of dyads and triads and a single conspicuous male–female dyad. The Italian computer scientist Massimo Franceschetti writes that for all the popularity of social networks, "[f]ew know, however, that the first example of social network is attributed to psychiatrist Jacob Moreno, a hand-drawn image depicting friendship patterns between the boys and the girls in a class of schoolchildren, presented at a medical conference in New York in 1933. Moreno used the term sociogram to refer to a social network and laid the foundation of sociometry, modern social network analysis."

J.L. and his team followed up the kindergarten through eighth grade study in the public school with a project in an elite private high school, the Riverdale Country School in the Bronx. At that time only boys attended Riverdale. (Just before J.L. started his work the students included the three Kennedy brothers, Joe, John, and Bobby.) The sociometrists examined relationships between new students and continuing students as the school year progressed and charted the way the boys' social positions changed. Based on the evolving number and pattern of choices received from other boys, J.L. found that the students who boarded at the school became better adjusted more quickly than the boys who only attended the day school, and that the boarding students received on the whole more choices than the day students. He attributed this result to both more intimate frequent social contacts within the group of boys who were boarders and a certain mystique their group had among the nonboarders.

## Hudson

J.L. and Helen Jennings were able to show that human groups evolve in their complexity as the members grow from infancy to early adolescence. The study of school-age children also suggested that teachers and other school personnel could benefit from understanding the structure of classroom groups, both for educational and social psychological reasons. Over the next several decades a wave of sociometric studies and texts were aimed at school teachers, counselors, and administrators who worked in conventional school districts. But what about larger groups of adolescents who were considered to be "offenders"? Could their relationships be understood in a way that could make their behavior more manageable and socially acceptable, in a word, to rehabilitate them?

The opportunity to answer this question came when E. Stagg Whitin introduced J.L. to another remarkable woman, Fannie French Morse, superintendent of the New York State Training School for Girls in Hudson, New York. Beginning in 1923, Morse set about transforming the school, known simply as "Hudson," from an old fashioned punitive "reformatory" into a center for rehabilitation. She was one of a generation of female social reformers and activists, "progressives" who found in Eleanor Roosevelt the very embodiment of their spirit of social action. The first edition of J.L.'s classic account of his sociometric philosophy and theory, *Who Shall Survive* (1935), was dedicated to Morse, "Educator and Liberator of Youth." At its height Hudson housed as many as five hundred "incorrigible" twelve- to sixteen-year-old girls referred by the state courts, mostly for minor offenses like truancy. It was closed in 1975 along with many other "asylums" as part of the international movement known as deinstitutionalization.

J.L. could hardly believe his good fortune in having Morse's total support (though as he discovered not that of other power centers in the school), in attempting to realize his twenty-year-old dream of constructing a model society according to sociometric principles. With sixteen residential cottages, a chapel, a school, a factory, a laundry, and a farm, Hudson was what the sociologist Erving Goffman later called a "total institution." Obvious aspects of its social organization when J.L. arrived were its housemother system, the fact that the girls all had jobs in the various functional parts of the school (as waitresses, cooks, laundresses, etc.), and that the "colored" girls were housed in separate cottages. One of his important findings was that the school's invisible social currents were greatly influenced by the attractions and repulsions of the white and African–American girls.

The data J.L. used in his experimental sociology at Hudson was the collection of the girls' choices of whom they would like to live with in their cottage, as compared with those with whom they actually lived. The structures of these "cottage families" were complicated enough in themselves, though at least they could be reduced to various kinds of graphs on a single page; the overall task was made more tedious by the need to prepare an aggregate sociogram for hundreds of girls in all sixteen cottages. Although today the task of mapping a social network can be accomplished in a split second using social media software, in the 1930s the arduous work had to be done by hand. In later editions of *Who Shall Survive?* a fold-out sociogram of the entire Hudson community is included, taking up the equivalent of nearly ten pages in physical size.

Yet the results were worth the effort as all sorts of interesting observations flowed from the data. It was as though a new continent was being exposed, beneath the apparent forms of human relations and social systems. For example, the cottages could be ranked based on the percentage of attractions and repulsions within each cottage group. In this ranking cottage two had 85.36 percent of attractions, while at the other end of the scale cottage four had only 48.41 percent of attractions. Could these numbers predict the degree of harmony in each cottage? To some extent the answer to that question depended on more specific structural factors. Various typical patterns appeared, such as pairs of mutual attraction or repulsion; pairs in which one is attracted to the other but the other rejects the first; a chain of attracted triads or three individual who reject one another; a "star" in which several individuals are attracted to the same person, but not to one another; and an individual who is actively rejected by several others.

It is easy to understand why these sociometric observations were tremendously exciting to social scientists and social workers in the 1930s. They laid bare a largely invisible social system that could be studied by skilled workers, graphically illustrated and even characterized in arithmetic terms. In writing about the reciprocal feelings that individuals may have for one another J.L. develops his concept of "tele," a sort of mutual empathy that allows us to enter into one another's private worlds. Unlike the psychoanalytic idea of transference, which refers to the projection of, say, one's feelings toward a parent upon the analyst, tele is an authentic "feeling into" the psyche of the other person.

The school experiments made J.L. one of the most famous social scientists of the 1930s, as journalists followed his innovations with interest. In April 1933 the *New York Times* reported on J.L.'s "new science of psychological geography." (It was typical of J.L. to change the names of his creations as it suited him, and somewhat maddening for his followers.) At a meeting of the New York State Medical Society he described the way he had mapped the school communities. The *Times* writer expressed fascination at the seven thousand lines needed to map relationships at Hudson. "A mere glance at the chart shows the strange human currents that flow in all directions from each individual in the group toward other individuals, from group to group, and from the entire group to the individuals." It was something like the shock that microbial communities must have given the earliest users of the microscope.

The newspaper also reported on J.L.'s estimate of the proportion and absolute number of isolated people in the United States. For example, 16 percent of the girls at Hudson were unchosen by any other girls. J.L. theorized that there were about ten million to fifteen million socially and emotionally isolated people in the country. Their suffering, and that of the communities they affect, could be treated by addressing their loneliness. In a characteristic bit of excess enthusiasm, J.L. told the *Times* that he had "completed plans to chart a map of the psychological geography of New York City." Such a map never materialized, but a small sociometric study was conducted with fifty-two individuals between the ages of eighteen and twenty-five in New York City. It turned out that 12.2 percent of the men and 13 percent of the women were unchosen by others in their neighborhood. Compared to modern social science these kinds of studies seem primitive. They certainly lack the statistical "power" that would be required for a valid study today. Yet their pioneering role in social survey research is undeniable. J.L. believed that he had hit upon a world-changing insight. "Until we have at least determined the nature of these fundamental structures which form the [social] networks, we are working blindly in a hit or miss effort to solve problems which are caused by group attraction, repulsion, and indifference," he told the *Times*. Sociometry could provide guidance to the design of healthier and more satisfying communities.

Just as J.L.'s sociometic studies were getting under way in 1929, Robert and Helen Lynd published their first landmark study of a place they called "Middletown," where they note that radios and automobiles had reduced interest in cultural organizations like book discussion groups, a form of civic life that has recently undergone something of a revival. Social isolation has continued to be a hot topic in sociology, as in influential works like David Riesman's classic *The Lonely Crowd* (1950), and Robert Putnam's *Bowling Alone* (2000). Riesman argues that our society is dominated by "other-directed" persons, leading to inadequate use of human potential, while a half century later Putnam claimed to have found a decline in American participation in civic life. The idea that social alienation is a common experience, especially widespread in our large cities as J.L. suggests, is now familiar, but would have been a far more disconcerting revelation in the 1930s.

## RACE

The role of race at Hudson receives quite a bit of attention in *Who Shall Survive?* More than thirty years before the modern civil rights movement, race relations were a largely repressed fact of life in America, though one that was rapidly becoming impossible to set aside. Between 1910 and 1930 six million African Americans moved away from the South in what has been called The Great Migration. Northern cities and towns were experiencing an unfamiliar presence that often created social friction and sometimes outbursts of violence. White Americans resented and felt threatened by the influx and black Americans encountered what was in some ways at least as harsh as, if more subtle than, the racism they had experienced for generations in the South. At Hudson, J.L. noticed that the proportion of minority girls in a group was related to the hostility directed toward them, evidence of a racial "saturation" point. J.L. pointed out that a single African American or "Indian" (i.e., Native American) child in a group of whites produces "interest and sympathy," while several African American girls in a group of twenty or so is more likely to be accompanied by a negative change of attitude toward them. At a certain point, a minority turns from a curiosity into a threat.

J.L. and his coworkers were among the first social scientists to be sensitive to the race issue and to attempt to ameliorate racial tensions, once again using Hudson as a laboratory. Attractions and repulsions based on race at Hudson were observed grossly in the ways the two "colored" cottages were sociometrically situated (relatively isolated, they are placed on the extreme left of the aggregate sociogram of all the relationships in the community), and more particularly in the girls' selections and rejections. Keeping in mind principles like numerical balance, J.L. theorized that with sociometric guidance an integrated cottage could be designed and even sketched one out in a sociogram based on attractions and repulsions among dozens of white and African American girls.

The sociometric reorganization of the girls' cottages and work groups were only one form of intervention. Through J.L. believed that in general people should be able to choose with whom they wanted to associate, that any good society would enable its actual social structures to comport with the tele of its members for one another, he also recognized that prejudices could create false and dangerous divisions. Simply allowing people to organize into groups without establishing genuine telic relationships might only reinforce racial, ethnic, or tribal conflicts. These conflicts or potential conflicts had to be dealt with in sociodramas, especially in role reversals, so that people could understand one another from their different points of view. This was part of the meaning of the idea of training spontaneity. For example, the sociogram of a steam laundry at Hudson displayed racial tensions. In a "Note for the Group Therapist" appended to the sociogram we learn that later on there was a race riot. "A sociodrama at the psychological moment in which all workers at the laundry and the white management would participate, might have prevented the racial riot which took place a few weeks after this sociogram was made." That is why J.L. always refused to separate sociometry from his group therapy method, which is precisely what happened when his sociometry was adapted by social scientists as social network analysis after World War II.

Indeed, sociometry without social therapy can be a dead end (J.L. called it "cold sociometry"), or worse. In the 1950s, many school districts adopted sociometry in efforts to improve student behavior and the educational environment. But in 1972 the sociologist Kurt W. Back wrote that "[i]nstitutions using the sociometric test in earnest have often been suspected of using it as a backhanded way for introducing segregation, which would be the outcome of many sociometric tests. In fact the 'freedom of choice' plan of Southern school districts is in effect a sociometric test." J.L. would have seen this as a horrid distortion of his ideas. It was one hazard of sociometry without social intervention. He advocated psychodrama techniques like role reversal to help the oppressors take the point of view of the oppressed. Decades before the civil rights movement began in earnest, J.L. took special pains in his studies at Hudson to note ways that his sociograms suggested that the black and white residents could be integrated.

An important metric J.L. used for improvement at Hudson was a marked reduction in the number of runaway incidents. The initial sociometric assignments began on February 22, 1933. As the reassignments became evident the number of runaways from July 1, 1933, to March 1, 1934, "was unprecedentedly low, a total of six," J.L. reported, "which would be equally unusual for an open population outside the institution, consisting of an equal number of adolescents." Confidence in this data would require knowing more about what counted as a "runaway" and, despite the assertion that the number of such incidents was "unprecedentedly low," one would want to know the specific baseline comparison number. J.L. argues that no other variables could account for the reduction of runaways. Other behavior changes are anecdotally observed. In an explanatory note accompanying one of the sociograms of a cottage after the reassignment, we are told that the housemother reported "a considerable change in the behavior of the girls; the number of temper tantrums, stolen articles, secret dates, passing of incriminating letters, had decreased to about one half of the former frequency." As noted in the text, another challenge is the fact that during the sociometric data gathering the community was not stable, as girls were always being admitted and discharged.

One white girl whose complex relationships were taken as a case study and who participated in spontaneity, role-playing exercises, was named Elsa. Among Elsa's interesting social characteristics was her choice of a "colored girl" as part of a life that was largely unknown among others in her circle. Her friend Maud, also white, shared the attraction to the African American girl, putting them both in a unique alliance and also pitting them against the dominant currents of the community. Apart from these observations, J.L. and his team didn't note any other adverse conditions for the African American girls, though the relatively isolated and controversial nature of their cottages must surely have alerted them to the possibility that the situation was fraught with risks for them. More recent information suggests that J.L. and his team might not have noted—or at least did not describe—an important and disturbing factor in the situation at Hudson.

## ELLA

After her death, the great American jazz singer Ella Fitzgerald was revealed to have been a resident of Hudson for about a year until 1934. It was a part of her life that she refused to talk about in public, but to friends she confided that the African American girls were subjected to beatings by the white guards. Like many of the other girls, Ella was sent to Hudson for foster care as an orphan. The last director of Hudson told the *New York*

*Times* that she rebuffed him when he invited Fitzgerald and other former residents to a reunion: "She hated the place. She had been held in the basement of one of the cottages once and all but tortured. She was damned if she was going to come back." A retired English teacher remembered her as a model student. "I can even visualize her handwriting—she was a perfectionist." Though known to have a wonderful voice, Fitzgerald reportedly was barred from the all-white choir, a fact that contradicts J.L.'s statement that although the cottages were segregated "in education and social activities white and colored mix freely."

The initials "E.F." do not appear in any of the circles representing the individual girls in the sociograms, so it appears that Fitzgerald was not a resident at Hudson at the exact moment that the data from her cottage was collected, or perhaps during the days her cottage was being surveyed. Perhaps there was an error in transcription, or her admission followed completion of J.L.'s data collection. In any case, there is no reason to doubt Fitzgerald's recollections. But they raise troubling questions about the social diagnosis at Hudson. Were the sociometrists or the distinguished Hudson director Fannie French Morse aware of the physical abuse? It is a fair question why the intensive collection of interpersonal data and individual interviews did not turn up reports of the beatings or what have since been described as the especially poor conditions in the African American cottages; and if they did turn up, one wonders whether any interventions were attempted or proposed. These are questions that may never be answered: The records of Hudson have been destroyed by the State of New York.

Despite their efforts at identifying opportunities to improve race relations at Hudson, in retrospect J.L. and his team did not seem to have identified all the institution's troubles. Although J.L. notes that "[t]he 'emotional currents' radiating from the white and colored girls, and vice versa, have to be ascertained in detail, their causes determined, and their effects estimated," similar attention was not paid to the power of the guards over the girls as it was to the girls' interpersonal dynamics. It may be that the "several bottlenecks" J.L said he encountered when he entered Hudson to do his work included some that were never known to him or his coworkers, such as the suppression of information or suspicions about physical abuse of the African American girls. In fairness, during the decades following the civil rights movement any social intervention in a closed society like

Hudson would naturally pay more attention to this possibility than would have been the case in the 1930s. And our collective expectations of the quality of large asylums and the professionalism of employees are much higher than they were before World War II, though the apparent failure to identify rampant abuse cannot be waved aside.

## SAVING DEMOCRACY

J.L.'s experimental sociology came along at a sensitive time in the international political climate. In the early 1930s there was good reason to think that liberal democracy had run its course. The United States and much of the capitalist world were mired in depression. The Bolshevik Revolution seemed to be bearing fruit in the Soviet Union, reducing levels of poverty and fostering industrialization and modernization. Fascist and militaristic movements were on the rise and also seemed a plausible, if not inevitable, alternative to the liberal state. In 1932, just as J.L. was doing his work at Hudson, the fascist Italian journalist Benito Mussolini declared that liberal democracy was in its death throes. But J.L.'s sociometry was both a democratic social science, basing its data on individuals' actual social preferences (he called it "the sociology of, by and for the people"), and also provided a basis for a democratic reconstruction of society, or at least of the functional units within the larger society. In the sociometric approach everyone is equal in the sense that one person's attractions, repulsions, or neutrality are worth as much as anyone else's. For example, the true leaders of groups could be identified in this way, and not only those who achieved their status through inherited position, wealth, intimidation, or violence. Thus leadership studies became popular among sociologists, for whom sociometry offered the twin advantages of being both empirical and experimental.

J.L.'s work provided reassurance that democratic institutions can be studied and improved. The minister of President Franklin Roosevelt's church had read *Who Shall Survive?* and used it as the basis of a Sunday sermon. In 1934 the White House called J.L. asking him to meet President Roosevelt at his Hyde Park estate. Roosevelt was looking for new ideas to wrest the demoralized country from the torpor of the Great Depression. Displaced workers and farmers were one of his problems. "The attempt of technocracy to save the country from unemployment had failed," J.L.

wrote recalling the meeting. "The President sat in the first row of pews. I sat in the last and when the religious ceremony was over Mr. Roosevelt had to pass my seat. Suddenly he stopped and said, 'Hello, Dr. Moreno,' as if he would know me. He invited me into his car; on his lap he had a copy of *Who Shall Survive?* He opened it and pointed at one of the sociograms. 'This looks like progressive sociology,' he said, and added pensively, 'if I had not taken my present course this is what I would like to do.' He further stated, 'When I am back in Washington I will see where your ideas can be put to use.'"

FDR was true to his word. Within the next year social scientists in the US Department of Agriculture Resettlement Administration applied J.L.'s ideas about sociometric organization to homestead projects for the families who had been devastated by the depression and drought in midwestern farming communities. A settlement for about two hundred fifty urban workers, small farmers, and their families, planned along sociometric lines, was created in the Midwest. Called "Centerville" in government reports, it was one of dozens of such planned communities created during the New Deal. A paper published in J.L.'s journal in 1937 described the Centerville project as "a new form of domestic colonization, designed to provide a measure of economic security for its families." AP's Howard Blakeslee described J.L.'s concept in a 1938 story called "Neighbors for New Communities May Be Lined Up By 'Sociometry.'" The story was accompanied by a sociogram of a community. Before being assigned to their new homes the prospective residents of Centerville were brought together for a series of face-to-face meetings, their preferences mapped in sociograms, then so far as was practicable they were housed according to their mutual choice of neighbors. The complex, multistage process was supervised by a new breed of social expert called Family Selection Specialists. One of the government officials involved in the project was Charles P. Loomis, who remembered that "all of us in the Department of Agriculture formed an early alliance with J.L. Moreno, the sociometrician. He came to Washington often because he knew that we were doing these studies for the Resettlement Administration, and we did sociometric analyses. Some of the earliest that were done on villages were those that we did." Although the World War I refugee camps in which J.L. worked sprang from different circumstances than those of the dislocated American farmers, the underlying social challenges of resettlement were the same.

The idea of sociometry as a democratic social science continued to grow in importance during the crisis decades of depression and world war, reaching the height of its appeal as a scientific examination of democracy in the 1930s. But if sociometric methods were a form of social diagnosis, what benefits did they actually yield? It might seem intuitive that a community's morale is improved when people live and work with those with whom they want to live and work, but what social problems are actually solved by these methods, considering their expense? The agriculture department's Loomis said that in the farm resettlement colonies "[y]ou could note from the sociometric chart the relationships of all of those people who moved away, and all of those people who stayed. You can see that they did this in groups."

## "Social Engineering"

Twenty years later Centerville would be used to attack J.L. and his methods as evidence of insidious attempts by New Deal liberals to undermine American freedom through centralized planning, not to enhance it by implementing democratic choice. J.L.'s sociometry happened to coalesce with the New Deal framework that favored action-oriented government and later caused him to be associated with those who loathed anything and everything about F.D.R.-style liberalism. In 1958, the conservative magazine *Human Events* published a McCarthyite screed that all but accused J.L. of communist sympathies. Notwithstanding his sophistication about philosophical and psychological matters J.L. was something of a naïf about ideological politics. He thought he could transcend ideology by appealing to the "here and now" and warming people up to an authentic encounter. (In 1965 he wrote President Lyndon Johnson, offering to conduct a psychodramatic role reversal between the president and North Vietnamese leader Ho Chi Minh, a suggestion that was met with an icy reply by presidential press secretary Bill Moyers). But in the hothouse atmosphere of the 1950s Red Scare that kind of earnest notion got little traction. In the *Human Events* article "Social Engineering for 1984," its author called J.L. "the most influential of the 'social engineers'" who used his sociograms and psychodrama to channel the behavior of human groups that he and other "pseudo-liberals" like anthropologist Margaret Mead thought best. Describing J.L.'s friend at Mt. Sinai, the physician Bela Schick as "a chief instrument of the communist party," the author used the standard tactics of belittling language, innuendo, and guilt-by-association of the far-right bullies of that era.

Being called out for communist sympathies was no joke in the 1950s, when many social scientists found their loyalty suspect. The case of psychologist Goodwin Watson was well known. An authority on morale and propaganda, Watson had been denounced by the House Un-American Activities Committee as a communist as early as 1941, forced out of his position at the Federal Communications Commission (FCC), and hounded for much of the rest of his career. Like so many others in science and the arts, Watson was certainly a leftist, but he was no communist. That distinction didn't matter as pretty much anyone who specialized in the study of "group dynamics" was subject to suspicion. In January 1959 J.L. sent a copy of the *Human Events* article to a number of colleagues soliciting their advice on an appropriate response, writing that the article "has been distributed widely and may be harmful to the liberal cause." The responses revealed uncertainty among some of the country's leading thinkers about whether to ignore such attacks or to challenge them. One of the organizations mentioned in the *Human Events* article was Children's International Summer Villages, founded by J.L.'s friend Doris Twitchell Allen. In her reply to J.L., Twitchell Allen said that a lawyer told her there was "a good case for court action" though later she concluded that the time and money weren't worth the trouble. Harvard psychologist Gordon Allport wrote "I have no idea how to combat this type of frightened ignorance [of social science]. It is similar, I suppose, to the abuse heaped on Galileo, Pasteur, Darwin, and every progressive human movement since the beginning of time." Sociologist Howard Becker offered to be a witness in a libel suit, believing J.L. would win, while theologian Paul Tillich urged him to ignore the matter. Sociologist David Riesman said "[o]ne course which I used to think about a good deal and have since discarded is libel action." In her long and detailed letter to J.L., Margaret Mead advised against responding as that would only play into the critics' hands.

## SING SING

Although not as extensive or as famous as the project at Hudson, perhaps the most provocative of the social network experiments in the early 1930s was the one at the Sing Sing maximum security prison in Tarrytown, New York on the Hudson River. Named after a Native American nation, Sing Sing, now called the Ossining Correctional Facility, occupies an important place in American history. In 1831, five years after it was opened, the young Frenchman Alexis de Tocqueville visited Sing Sing to view a model New World institution. But by the 1910s, like so many other large settings for social deviants, Sing Sing had deteriorated into a sink of corruption. An imaginative warden, Lewis Lawes, turned Sing Sing around during the 1920s. Lawes' book *Twenty Thousand Years in Sing Sing*, was made into a movie with Spencer Tracy. Lawes was a progressive but he was no soft touch, as he oversaw more than three hundred executions during his years as warden. Even with Lawes's improvements, penologists believed that American prisons could be improved, especially in reducing recidivism rates. National prison expert J. Stagg Whitin brokered a visit for J.L. to Lawes at Sing Sing. Though Lawes started out as a skeptic when he saw J.L.'s sociograms he decided it was worth giving the idea a try.

J.L. and Helen must have worked fast. With the copyright held by the National Committee on Prisons and Prison Labor, their official report was dated August 1931 and presented to the psychiatric association in June 1932. They had had to get oriented to the prison, gather their data, conduct their analysis, and write it up within a few months. Clearly, they didn't want to let this opportunity to introduce their work into a major social system pass them by. Although the booklet lists J.L. as the sole author it acknowledges that "This investigation has been made with the assistance of Helen H. Jennings, M.A." J.L. and Helen were already a well-oiled team following their studies in the nursery and the school. Nonetheless, Sing Sing presented a different set of challenges. In the words of the objective they set themselves, "how it would be possible to transform the promiscuous, unorganized prison system into a socialized community through a method of assignment of prisoners to prison groups."

In the text of his report to the national prison office, J.L. refers to "experiments which we have made since 1911" with adults and children in the community, as described in his book on the spontaneity theatre, admitting that work in a prison is a different matter. He doesn't mention the concerns he had about the arbitrary assignment of families to housing in the Mittern-dorf refugee camp, though that was the most relevant analogy to Sing Sing in J.L.'s experience, even if still some distance from a prison filled with violent thugs and ingenious swindlers. The continuity of his thinking, ranging from improvisational theater to social systems, is evident in his use of spontane-ity testing with the prisoners. It's hard to imagine, but these hardened 1930s convicts were successfully instructed to take part in role plays to evaluate their personalities. The results were often startling, not at all what one would expect given their histories as offenders or their usual behavior. "And they, too, committed in the various situations assigned to them often the most bewildering acts, although in the realm of fiction, which seemed unrelated to their individual selves when we saw them in daily life." In other words, beneath their tough exterior these criminals were able to exercise creative imaginations in the theater games J.L. organized. Not surprisingly, some prisoners enjoyed being given new assignments in each play, while others preferred to repeat their roles in situations and could not perform very well spontaneously, but had good memories for scripts.

The prisoners who performed well when assigned roles in unfamiliar situations were judged superior in their spontaneity. J.L. claimed that the spontaneity test was an important supplement for the IQ test of the day. Developed by Alfred Binet in 1905 to help assess struggling students, by 1930 the intelligence test was used in many large organizations, including the military and prisons. But J.L. expressed skepticism about its cultural bias. "[W]hen entire race groups (Negro, Mongolian, etc.) and entire nationality groups (Italian, Russian, Polish, etc.) are judged by the mental tests such as the Binet to be appreciably lower in intelligence than some nationality groups of northern Europe and the United States, we have good reason to suspect that the measuring instrument itself is incom-plete." At a time that eugenics and race classification were the rage, J.L.'s was a rare dissenting voice from the assumption of intellectual differ-ences among ethnic and racial groups.

The title of J.L.'s official report for the prison experts was one that wouldn't pass political muster today: "Plan and Technique of Developing a Prison into a Socialized Community." Within two decades "socialized" would be a dirty word in the America, especially as applied to medicine. But here it meant only taking social factors into account in organizing the prison. One of these factors was the cohesion of the group in its domestic, labor, and social activities. Prisoners were assigned to units based on "mental type, sexual characteristics, racial traits, former performances, criminal record, actual observations of behavior in prison, and so forth." Then, like the sociometric studies they had already done, J.L. and Helen considered attraction, rejection, and neutral feelings toward a unit leader. The selection of a leader for each unit was to be determined based on the prisoner's "father-qualities," intelligence, similar "social kinship" with most of his men, some kind of previous success in business or family, and outgoing nature.

The report was sprinkled with other terms and concepts J.L. had developed, including "impromptu" to refer to the unexpected behaviors that often emerge in the course of a spontaneity test, the idea of "warming up" to a spontaneous state (which would become the first phase of a psychodrama session), and even the use of a "talking machine" to record interviews with subjects so that their reactions can be systematically recorded. As in so many of J.L.'s writings the philosophical observations, categories, and concepts flow so prodigiously that they can overwhelm the reader. Apparently, Helen would not or could not edit his grammar, which showed signs of being written by a native German speaker. The impatient reader can easily lose track of the essential idea, that personality types and classification for living and working assignments could be achieved based on the prisoners' reactions to impromptu situations. Nevertheless, there are clarifying examples of recommendations for matching men to groups and charts of their "reaction types" and relationships within the group.

## REACTING TO SING SING

Introducing the 1932 Philadelphia psychiatric conference session on J.L.'s Sing Sing report, the psychiatrist William Alanson White said that "[t]hroughout all society's dealings with the criminal, both in court and elsewhere, the act has always been considered rather than the actor. At best this is a very imperfect method. And even when the psychiatrist comes to understand why the criminal did commit the particular act, this is also insufficient. He again must consider the doer of this act and his inter-relations with other people." By contrast, instead of concentrating on diagnosing individuals, the groups within which they function should be analyzed and prison life reorganized according to insights obtained from that analysis. "Moreno calls this approach, 'Group Psychotherapy.' As I looked over the portion of Dr. Moreno's monograph which deals with the structure of social groups, I was interested in the charts illustrating them. They look like formulas in a book on chemistry. They reveal how strange and complicated are human inter-relations and also how much we can profit from the study of these structures in the successive stages of their development." J.L., who thought of himself as a social scientist whose ideas about group structure revealed something universal in nature, would have been pleased with White's analogizing of his social network graphs with chemical formulae.

Among those in attendance at the meeting, reactions to J.L.'s plan were generally favorable, at least as an experiment worthy of pursuit. New York prison official C.V Branham, said that the plan

> [C]ombines the individual with the biological, the psychiatric with the sociological, urged by the aim to transform the prison into a cohesive, integrated, socialized community. . . . [M]an lives neither as an individual for himself nor in a mass, but in small coteries in which he attracts or repels and it is through his relation to these men that his personality is developed. This is the starting point of Dr. Moreno's plan. The question put forward is: Is it possible to form coteries of this sort synthetically? To answer this question he analyzes the inter-relations of men to one another and places them into groups as appears to their best advantage. Out of this attempt an analysis of inter-relations and a system of scoring grew which even in its beginnings contains a promising direction for research and the germ of a workable method for social organization. A new principle of approach confronts us and I am convinced that it will lead to a change in our outlook and our procedure.

The several dozen mental health experts and penologists at the 1932 Philadelphia meeting had varied reactions to J.L.'s proposal. Sing Sing prison's own "director of classification," Amos Baker, was circumspect. Baker had also been in practice at Matteawan State Hospital for the Criminally Insane in Beacon, New York (another institution named for a Native American tribe), where J.L. would buy an estate for his mental hospital a few years later. Baker wasn't so ready to deemphasize individual psychology in assigning prisoners to living and working groups. "In respect to the classification of the men into groups, I would place greater emphasis upon the prognosis of each of the men. Symptomatology, diagnosis and prognosis are the three principles upon which group classification should be based."

Fannie French Morse, the Hudson school's director, rose to J.L.'s defense. She had already committed herself to introducing his approach at Hudson despite the bureaucratic obstacles. In her remarks she adopted both J.L.'s concepts and his terminology. "For years I have protested against the mechanical measuring of the child," she began. "For a long time I arranged the cottages [at Hudson] according to psychological measurements. But I have never gone back to it. Something higher is needed. The social fitness is the real criterion. More and more I am releasing the child, her spontaneous life. And I must say, it seems to work. Why does one child choose another? It is not because they are the same in intelligence or in some other factor because there is something in one which appeals to the other. This 'socializing' process is the great point in developing human beings." A middle view was expressed by a New Jersey official, William J. Ellis who worried that J.L.'s method was too labor-intensive for prisons given their limited funding and inadequately trained personnel. At least for the time being he saw it as more applicable to the school setting.

Prison reformer Whitin, who was in effect J.L.'s sponsor for the project, argued that analyzing prisoners' social networks was at least a plausible response to what he saw as a grave social crisis. Under the pressure of the social disruptions associated with the Great Depression, between 1930 and 1940 the federal prison system alone swelled from fourteen facilities to twenty-four and the prison population from thirteen thousand to more than twenty-four thousand, a process that penologists seem to have anticipated. "Moreno has made an honest attempt to give an answer [to the problem of applying psychiatric work to prisons]. If this is not an answer, who has got one? Hundreds of thousands of men are being poured back into society from our institutions worse than when they went in. These disordered minds have developed a crime situation which threatens our civilization."

At the end of the session J.L. was given an opportunity to respond to the comments on his report. Of course, he started out, he could not do justice to his hundred-page paper or all the comments on it in just a few minutes, nor did he have the advantage of being able to show what he had done by taking those present on a tour of the prison. So, to illustrate his method, he proposed to focus on the "here and now," that he and the dozens of experts with him in the room should take themselves as an example of an impromptu group in action. Consider the leadership factor. How different might the speeches have been if someone other than Dr. White, a father figure, had been the chair of the session? What if the chair had been more critical or, like Whitin, more openly supportive? The responses of the group would have been different. Individual psychology alone could not account for these differences but must be seen as the products of interpersonal attraction, rejection or indifference. The group dynamic is always at work; who happens to occupy the leadership role is especially important for the way the group functions. For example (turning on his Viennese charm), "the ladies who were so excellently represented by Mrs. Morse, Miss Jaffray, Mrs. White, Miss Jennings, Dr. Potter, Mrs. Johnson, might have received less opportunity to speak if we had a moderator less gallant" than Dr. White.

> Last but not least we must find—besides the most desired individuals, solitaires [solitary or isolated group members], mutual pairs, dissatisfied aggressives, gangs, etc.—still another condition which illustrates the psychology of grouping. There is an individual who is in a similar situation to that of Dr. White, only in the opposite sense. He is also a center, but maybe the center of resentments and repulsions, not of attractions. He is undesired like a solitaire, but he has a certain distinction: he is the prototype of the unwanted individual who attempts to impose something upon a group that is, by its very nature critical and suspicious towards him as towards anyone who assumes authority before the reason for it is fully demonstrated. This person is, you have already guessed, myself.

In his brief remarks, J.L. weaved in oblique references to the here and now, the encounter, and his ideas about social networks. He even managed to cite "a teacher greater than Socrates," Jesus, who inspired therapeutic groupings known as monasteries. During his discourse on the history of monasteries the prison officials in the room might have wondered at the analogy, though his point was that though families are not formed by deliberate choice other institutions can be shaped by what he called sociometry, "an exact science of group organization." If not exactly Pericles's funeral oration, it was nevertheless a dramatic performance that showed J.L.'s classical education, his mysticism, and what would commonly be known among his critics as his "bombastic" personality.

Considering the attention J.L.'s ideas received among the psychiatrists, public officials, and social workers in 1931 and 1932, just as the obstacles to his spontaneity theater were repeating themselves in New York, it was not difficult for him to decide which path to pursue. The doors of the scientific establishment were thrown open to him in those years and he walked through them. But he retained the personal style of a mystic and an impresario, characteristics that were to prove both provocative and troublesome in the years ahead. One of his modern critics, the sociologist Linton Freeman, typifies the reaction and puzzlement of the later social science establishment to J.L's. rise to prominence and his personality.

> By the mid 1930s these books [on sociometry], along with public support from Jennings, Murphy and the prominent psychiatrist, William Allison [sic] White, turned Moreno into something of a social science celebrity. He started a journal, the *Sociometric Review*, in 1936. But a year later he dropped that publication and started another journal, *Sociometry*. By the late 1930s he could count among those who were involved in his work such notables as Franz Alexander, Gordon W. Allport, Read Bain, Howard Becker, Franz Boas, Emory S. Bogardus, Jerome S. Bruner, Hadley Cantril, F. Stuart Chapin, Leonard S. Cottrell, Stuart C. Dodd, Paul Lazarsfeld, Kurt Lewin, Charles P. Loomis, George A. Lundberg, Robert S. Lynd, Margaret Mead, Karl Menninger, George Peter Murdock, Gardner Murphy, Theodore M. Newcomb, William H. Sewell, Pitirim Sorokin and Samuel Stouffer. These names are a virtual Who's Who in American sociology and psychology at the time.

Though he finds J.L.'s appeal to all these important people somewhat puzzling, Freeman nonetheless affirms that J.L. "was—at least for a short time—a major intellectual force." But Freeman notes J.L.'s lack of mathematical training that is crucial in modern network analysis, and (no doubt accurately) he attributes much of his successful pursuit of sociometry to his intellectual partnership with Helen Jennings, who he says, was briefly able

> to "clean up his act" and present him to the world as a creative social scientist who was capable of conducting systematic research. But she was unable to suppress the fundamental flaws in his character. So although Jennings introduced us to Moreno as Dr. Jeckyll, as time went on, Mr. Hyde kept reappearing. . . . [H]is commitment to mysticism, his bombastic personal style and his megalomania drove most of his early supporters away. These features of Moreno's persona were too much for regular members of the academic community to bear. They simply could not be accommodated in the day-to-day academic or scientific world. . . . Most people simply backed off from Moreno the man, and in so doing they refused to recognize the importance and generality of Moreno's approach.

J.L.'s allies, and no doubt J.L. himself, would have said that the fault was not his, but the social science establishment's lack of imagination. Though earlier work on small groups like that of Georg Simmel must be acknowledged, it was J.L. the "bombast and megalomaniac" to whom even Freeman attributed pioneering status in recognizing the potential for the structural analysis of groups, not the social scientists of the day. Yet there is no doubt that J.L.'s refusal to restrain his mysticism, theatricality, and ironic sense of humor annoyed many in the post-World War II generation of social scientists. "My own memories of Moreno date from the 1950s when he was still presenting his work at annual sociology meetings," Freeman says. "Those presentations always took the form of demonstrations of impromptu theater. His style was bombastic and overbearing but his theater was always entertaining. Although Moreno's dramas might have provided entertainment, they seemed to me to lack serious intellectual content—they failed to cast any light on sociological questions." J.L.'s powerful insights about social networks were adopted by the social scientists, but at the cost of separating working with groups in action from measuring their internal structure. It was the first of many ways in which his ideas were adopted without the philosophy that made sense of their unity.

CHAPTER SIX

# THE GROUP AND THE SELF

J.L around 1940.

*There is no controversy about my ideas, they are universally accepted.*
*<u>I am the controversy</u>.*

J.L. Moreno, 1953

ANTICIPATING THE 1960S ENTHUSIASM for "therapy for all," J.L. argued that a new field is needed, a "sociatry," that "treats the pathological syndromes of normal society, of interrelated individuals and of interrelated groups." Not only mental patients have emotional problems that need to be treated. We all need the love and support of those around us, and the freedom to explore the troubles that are part of life. J.L. wanted to integrate a science of group structure and process with

145

therapeutic change of social institutions like schools, prisons, and asylums. Ever since his experience as a doctor in the refugee camps during World War I, J.L. was interested in reforming institutions based on the study of people's actual preferences. He thought that at work, at school, at play, or in dormitories, institutions would work better if social arrangements were based on the choices we make about whom we would like to be with. Creativity takes place in groups, he thought, but the spontaneity required for it to flow depended on satisfactory relationships, which could be facilitated through sociometric means.

J.L. basked in the attention his prison monograph received at the Philadelphia meetings. The moderator of the session on his work was William Alanson White, at that time director of the famous Washington, DC psychiatric hospital, St. Elizabeths (by tradition there was no apostrophe in the name). A former president of both the psychiatric and psychoanalytic associations, White is today remembered as one of the great icons of American psychiatry. Erich Fromm and other famous psychologists named their Manhattan psychoanalytic training institute in White's honor, and he would play a crucial role in introducing J.L.'s ideas into asylums in the 1930s.

## GROUP THERAPY

Near the end of his report on the Sing Sing experiment at the psychiatric meeting, J.L. asserted that coordinating the men with one another in the ways he describes can be useful in "group therapy." Standard psychological treatment "copies the relationship of the physician and patient," which is not an ideal arrangement for men in prison who are already suspicious of the system. "In the group situation once the assignment is accomplished, the groups function for themselves and the therapeutic process streams through their mutual inter-relationships." Still more fundamentally, J.L. intended his focus on the group as part of a shift away from what he took to be Freud's assumption that individual mental health could be secured independently of life with others. Because human psychology is inextricably linked to social experience psychotherapy must be a social therapy.

Credit for coining the terms *group therapy* and *group psychotherapy* was of great emotional and symbolic importance to J.L. Sensing that his place in history might well rest on being the first to introduce the vital importance of the group in psychology in a systematic way, he rose repeatedly and somewhat defensively to defend his priority. When he was recognized it was often grudging. In 1959 a book review in the *American Journal of Psychiatry* noted that "Moreno claims for himself the first coinage of the term 'group psychotherapy' (1932), without, however, substantiating his claim, although he cites many 'witnesses' for his testimony, such as William Alanson White, Winifred Overholser, Pierre Renouvier, S.H. Foulkes," all distinguished psychiatrists of the 1930s and 1940s. Strangely, the reviewer seemed to depreciate J.L.'s claim to priority while also acknowledging that some of the top psychiatrists in the world agreed with it. The situation was frustrating and galling to J.L. In a letter to the editor of the journal he pointed out that his 1932 monograph on the Sing Sing experiment included a section with the title "Concerning Group Therapy." No doubt his history of self-promotion alienated the establishment. Nonetheless, the book reviewer's language seemed designed to leave room for doubt about J.L.'s claim to priority.

The more interesting debate focuses on the origins of the practice of group therapy itself. For many years it was common for histories of group therapy to begin with a Boston physician named J.J. Pratt, who believed that the treatment of patients with tuberculosis should involve good hygiene, a healthy diet, and fresh air. In 1907 he held weekly meetings of fifteen to twenty-five patients to record and discuss their progress. These mutual support groups have become an important part of the modern treatment of addictions, especially of substance abuse, crystallizing in a global movement of "therapeutic communities" starting in the late 1940s with a few British psychiatrists who had worked on group therapy with soldiers during World War II. Alcoholics Anonymous is the most famous example of a "TC," though many are residential treatment settings and not only regular group meetings.

This history raises many further questions. Were Pratt's meetings with TB patients the forerunner of group therapy? J.L.'s organization of prostitutes in Vienna a few years later was also a self-help effort. The later therapeutic community movement sometimes involved various explicit therapeutic techniques, but sometimes it was a rather straightforward opportunity for troubled people to share their problems and find succor in one another. J.L. agreed that the important practical point is the power of the group. But to him group support systems alone would not have counted as group psychotherapy; mutually beneficial group meetings alone lack the methods he believed could enhance spontaneity and creativity and therefore better prepare group members for life's challenges. The mutual support was fine in itself, but short-lived. Nor did these group meetings utilize the internal social structure of the group to understand and improve its function, as was possible using his social network analysis.

For J.L. an accurate accounting of the history was of course a matter of personal pride and of his professional stature, but it also shaped the question of how group therapy is to be practiced, and in light of what philosophy and psychological theory. Some group therapy textbooks cite the Frenchman Gustav LeBon. In the 1890s LeBon published books about "group mind" and the implications of the unconscious for shaping crowd psychology, the "herd mentality." His ideas about the ability of the media to influence the mass mind have influenced fascist politicians like Hitler and Mussolini, progressives like Theodore Roosevelt, the founders of group psychoanalysis in Britain, and even modern media commentators like the American conservative Ann Coulter. LeBon's ideas represented a burgeoning interest in the science of groups at the turn of the century in both Europe and the United States, culminating in the recognition of sociology and social psychology as distinct fields of study. Writing under the emerging shadow of European fascism, Freud, too, contributed to the application of psychology to group theory in his book, *Group Psychology and the Analysis of the Ego* (1922). Also influenced by LeBon, Freud saw groups as almost inevitably overtaken by the aims of a strong leader. Still others in the 1920s, like Trigant Burrow and Louis Wender in the United States, started doing group work within the rubric of psychoanalytic theory. Burrow in particular saw the need to conduct psychoanalysis in the group setting and is credited with the term group analysis in his 1927 book, *The Social Basis of Consciousness*. Wender, another New Yorker, published papers in J.L.'s journal.

Although he admired Burrow's recognition of the need for the analyst to engage in a role reversal with his patient (and though Burrow is sometimes said to have anticipated group therapy), J.L. never accepted the notion that psychoanalytic theory could be made compatible with his vision of group therapy. Beginning in the 1940s many group analysts adopted the therapeutic techniques he developed in psychodrama, but for J.L. psychoanalysis was inherently individualistic and efforts to shoe-horn it into a group theory required contortions that distorted its original concept. Rather, he viewed group psychotherapy as part of a disciplinary triad with psychodrama and sociometry in the service of enhancing and training spontaneity and creativity. This was one of the reasons underlying his stubborn, lifelong insistence that the critical demarcation of group psychotherapy from mutual aid groups and broad group psychological and sociological theories came with his 1932 monograph that sought to meet the prison reformers' challenge. Nor could group therapy simply be attributed to sociologists like Comte, Emile Durkheim, or even the fascinating studies of the social effects of group size by the sociologist George Simmel. "It is farfetched to trace the origins of group psychotherapy to European sociologists," he wrote in 1959. "One could equally quote American sociologists. Every new idea has forerunners but the moment of emergence of the scientific group psychotherapy movement into scientific history, its *kairos*, was the year 1932, within the fold of the American Psychiatric Association."

J.L. claimed that William Alanson White, who championed his group work, told him after the Brill paper, "[f]irst you will get the sociologists, then the social psychologists, then the general practitioners, then the plain people. But you will never live to see the day when psychiatrists will accept group psychotherapy." However, J.L. was nothing if not stubbornly confident in his own genius and that his ideas would ultimately prevail. In fact, the more stubborn the resistance the more intransigent he became. Though admirable in some respects, over the decades J.L. became so accustomed to rejection, especially in the science establishment, that he sometimes turned aside even reasoned criticism.

## BEACON

Living on New York's East Side near Fifth Avenue, J.L. enjoyed the social life of a single man who was a rising and well-connected intellectual star. As he recalled in his autobiography, "[a]ctresses, chorus girls, writers, psychologists, rebels: many tried to seduce me. Many succeeded." It was, after all, the Great Depression and joy was in short supply. The Bohemian life associated with his Impromptu Theatre activities was appealing, but the work itself was stalled. As in Vienna, J.L. could not find an aesthetic for the spontaneity theater that appealed to the mainstream theatergoer. Yet, paradoxically, within the science establishment his star was rising. The reaction to his work from the world of asylums—mental hospitals, reform schools, and prisons—was gratifying and brought an income. Between his Sing Sing and Hudson projects, J.L. had spent a lot of time in New York's Hudson Valley. With a $2,000 loan from a grateful patient's daughter, he purchased an estate in Beacon, New York, overlooking the Hudson River. The place was formerly a boys' school owned and operated by Woodrow Wilson's nephew. J.L. converted the main building into a mental hospital, the Beacon Hill Sanitarium. The lovely, rural setting reminded him of his previous home in the Valley of May outside Vienna. Through the 1970s the small city of Beacon might have boasted the largest number of psychiatric patients per capita in the world. Besides J.L.'s modest operation there was a large state hospital for the "criminally insane" called Matteawan, and a well-appointed hospital for wealthy patients called Craig House, which at one time or another cared for John F. Kennedy's sister Rosemary, Zelda Fitzgerald, Henry Fonda's wife Frances Ford Seymour, and Judy Garland, all with utmost discretion. There was a direct train line to New York City, an important consideration because he was often commuting to Manhattan and J.L. never learned how to drive. Beacon provided him with a haven, a sanctuary over which he could rule and actualize his theories about spontaneity, the encounter, and the group. But the purpose would be psychotherapy, not reforming the theater.

J.L. had a handsome and well-furnished hospital building; all he needed was patients. Securing even a few residents would determine Beacon Hill's financial viability. In those days, people diagnosed with psychiatric disorders could be expected to be in residence for a few months to many years, but unless they had some independent means they were consigned to large state institutions. Again, an angel in the form of a remarkable woman appeared. Gertrude Franchot Tone was the wife of a wealthy Rochester industrialist. An alcoholic, she was nevertheless an avid follower of social science who had read *Who Shall Survive?* Tone became J.L.'s patient, student, and patron, donating the funds for the first theater of psychodrama adjoining the hospital building in what had been the school gymnasium. Far simpler than the stage he had designed for the Vienna exhibition, it was nonetheless innovative: a round, three-level affair with a balcony. The stage quickly became iconic. J.L. dedicated his theater of psychodrama to Mrs. Tone. Renowned by then for combining theater with therapy, J.L.'s connections to famous actors and directors continued. Gertrude Tone's son was the Group Theater actor and leading man, Franchot Tone, who was married to movie star Joan Crawford.

Though Beacon Hill (later the Moreno Sanitarium) superficially resembled the typical, quiet respite for troubled minds that was then common in the Europe and the United States, J.L.'s philosophical orientation made it unique. With its reliance on group therapy, Beacon Hill in some respects anticipated the milieu therapy in the therapeutic communities for drug abusers that emerged in the 1940s. It also tapped into an older and distinguished chapter in America's psychiatric care, the moral treatment movement. This compassionate response to "lunatics" that began in the early nineteenth century aimed to provide an intimate, supportive, and structured environment. But as America industrialized the moral treatment asylums were overwhelmed and underfunded. Many of them became the massive, public mental hospitals of highly varied quality that were finally emptied out in the 1960s and 1970s under the policy known as deinstitutionalization. Long-term incarceration of the mentally ill was supposed to be replaced by new drug treatment and community mental health centers, but the record has been mixed, at best.

As Beacon Hill's treatment centered on psychodrama therapy, it also gave J.L. the opportunity to apply in an intensely therapeutic setting the various psychological theater techniques he had used since the 1910s. The most famous of these was the empty chair, but several others also became instruments of group therapy and 1960s encounter groups: role reversal, in which one assumes the point of view of the other person as in J.L.'s early encounter philosophy; the auxiliary ego, in which the roles of important persons in one's life are represented by others; the double, when another person attempts to articulate thoughts or feelings that the subject of the psychodrama (the protagonist) is for some reason unable to state or even unaware of; and the mirror, in which someone illustrates the way the protagonist's behavior and posture appears to them. Spontaneity was still the key, the quality that allowed patients to achieve new insights, purge themselves of the "act hunger" that drove them to inconvenient fantasies and behavior, and find new and more adequate ways of living. As psychotherapy the psychodrama was no longer a performance, but the therapist was still called a director, managing the exploration of inner psychological space using these external means. At Beacon Hill classical psychodrama therapy came into its own.

As soon as his stage was completed J.L. directed his ideas about sociometry and psychodrama toward a solution for that most mysterious of human experiences, one that had eluded the greatest philosophers and scientists: love. Not only finding love, but also keeping it dominated his thinking after the Beacon psychodrama stage was completed. Couples therapy had been on J.L.'s mind since the Theater of Spontaneity and he again made it a focus of his work. J.L. attracted the attention of Associated Press reporter Howard Blakeslee, the first modern science writer. According to my mother, J.L. helped Blakeslee through the end of his first marriage. For the rest of his career Blakeslee was a devoted promoter of J.L.'s ideas. Blakeslee published a wide-ranging 1941 piece describing J.L.'s theology in *The Words of the Father* ("a unique book"), his theory of spontaneity, and his work with psychodrama and sociometry. Blakeslee's was a rare favorable account of J.L.'s ideas about God.

In 1937 Blakeslee arranged for the publication of two articles about J.L.'s unique approach to matters of the heart. "Public Quarreling On Stage Seen To Be Cure for Marital Rifts" described "[t]he first six months of the use of this theatre for these domestic, and more serious, mental problems. . . ." The piece cited J.L.'s experience with "Robert" and "Ann" in an account that is clearly drawn from his experience with Robert Muller and Ann Hollering in the Theater of Spontaneity, and not in his new psychodrama theater. Though he doesn't say how many truly new cases he had at that time, J.L.'s patients in 1937 did include at least one original case of marriage therapy: When Joan Crawford and Franchot Tone had marital problems they turned to J.L., much like his cases of troubled theater couples in Vienna, trying to work out their conflicts on the psychodrama state in Beacon; they divorced two years later.

Perhaps seeking a woman's touch, Blakeslee assigned a second and somewhat lighter 1937 article to an AP lifestyle reporter, Lillian Genn. Under the headline, "The Odds Against True Love Are . . . . . . . . ?" Genn's elaborate full-page article featured a picture of J.L., a cartoon of men and women partying in elegant formal dress, a street scene from the melting pot of

New York's Lower East Side, and a photograph of a prison workshop— the common theme: throwing all sorts of people together without taking into account their mutual choices, situations that bring about "a disordered mind," personal frustration, and a lack of social harmony. Described by Genn as "an attractive man with merry eyes and a vital, exuberant personality," J.L. argued that the Great Depression alone couldn't be blamed for the problem of finding a partner. "It is surprising to find just how much misery there is which has nothing to do with economic conditions. . . . The air is fairly filled with the unhappy feelings and emotions of people, almost everyone desiring love or friendship—the mutual kind—and being unable to get it. And these people reflect their feelings into the lives of others." He described his observations about conflict between refugees and soldiers in the close quarters of World War I camps for displaced persons and the viral unhappiness that resulted, as well as the social isolation of certain children in the Brooklyn public school that was uncovered by sociometry. Just two years before the outbreak of World War II in Europe, J.L. assessed Hitler as an angry, isolated youth who was rejected from the art school in Vienna. (A few years later the United States government would undertake a secret long-distance personality analysis of Hitler by one of J.L.'s admirers, the Harvard psychologist Henry Murray.) A lifetime of rejection can make for all sorts of social and individual maladjustment, including juvenile delinquency. To choose and to be chosen in return is "[o]ne of the greatest thrills in life," he said, but few experience it. "The great majority of people never experience the thrill of spontaneous mutual love." Channeling the young Karl Marx's critique of capitalism, J.L. claimed that industrialization and mechanization account for some of the ills of the modern family, as men and women have been reduced to minimal economic roles of breadwinner and child bearer.

J.L.'s penchant for broad cultural observations made him a favorite of the popular press. Then as now, "experts" who were willing to address everyday human problems made for a valuable resource for journalists who needed to get their editor's attention. The "true love" article also exemplified J.L.'s willingness to think in sweeping terms, for linking disparate times, places, and situations in sometimes dubious ways, and for reaching conclusions based at least as much on his intuitions as on systematic experiments, objections he would have seen as small-minded. But whether his views were valid or not, J.L pioneered a role in the pre-World War II media twenty years before advice columnists commonly appealed to psychologists for their professional opinion. Surely Helen Jennings had J.L.'s theories about the precious and rare nature of mutual romantic choice on her mind when she worked on the television show for the lovelorn in the late 1950s. As for J.L., the professional success he enjoyed with his new sanitarium and psychodrama theater was shadowed by a void in his personal life. His nominal marriage to Beatrice had ended and he had not yet decided to marry his second wife, a vivacious young woman named Florence Bridge (no relation to his friend from Hunter College William Bridge), an intern during the project at the Hudson girls' reform school. It was a troubled marriage that ended in divorce after seventeen years.

## More Groups

Interest in the therapeutic possibilities of groups grew rapidly in the years before World War II. The psychiatrist Lauretta Bender, who became famous for the Bender–Gestalt test of childhood schizophrenia, also started play therapy groups for emotionally disturbed children at Bellevue Hospital, including the use of puppets. Bender must have been aware of J.L.'s work with children uptown at Mt. Sinai. Chicago psychiatrist Abraham Low graduated from the University of Vienna medical school two years after J.L. He founded an organization called Recovery, Inc. that encouraged former mental patients to form self-help groups. Low published a paper about Recovery, Inc. in J.L.'s journal in 1945. The idea that groups could benefit all sorts of people with problems was attracting wide attention. Alcoholics Anonymous got organized around the same time, in the mid-1930s.

Another group therapist was Samuel Slavson, with whom J.L. would have a long and bitter feud. Slavson was a Ukrainian Jewish immigrant who came to America when he was about fourteen. Although Slavson was trained as an engineer and not as a social scientist, through his work with troubled New York City teenagers he became a noted progressive educator, work that led him to an interest in groups. Slavson's form of group therapy with adolescents dates to 1934, several years after J.L.'s publication for the prison experts. Like J.L., Slavson was an innovator in therapy for children, making use of puppets, for instance, but Slavson was a Freudian. In 1943 he founded and was the first president of the American Group Psychotherapy

Association, a significant honor considering that he was not a psychiatrist, and published a professional journal and a book on group therapy. (The year before J.L. had founded his own organization, the American Society of Group Psychotherapy and Psychodrama.) Slavson's style was more acceptable to many psychiatrists and psychologists, partly because he seemed to take a more scientific approach to group therapy than J.L., and partly because of his embrace of psychoanalytic theory.

In all these activities Slavson ignored J.L. and was considered by many to be the true originator of group therapy, leading to decades of acrimony between the two men and their followers. When Slavson's group therapy association published a brief history of its first twenty-five years, the writers managed to avoid any mention of J.L. among the pioneers or of his original use of the term group therapy. (By then there was little to distinguish Slavson and Satan in our household, though Satan might have had the edge.) These rivalries and counterclaims of originality often descended into the ridiculous. The Columbia University sociologist Robert K. Merton described the J.L.–Slavson feud in his book on the sociology of science in 1973. Merton used their case as an example of the long tradition of scientists claiming priority for their ideas. As Merton notes, while J.L. said that Slavson liked his ideas so much that he took them without quotation, "Slavson, in his turn, retorts that Moreno was not really the inventor of psychodrama and that priority belongs to Karl Joergensen of Sweden, thus following, perhaps unwittingly, the established practice of countering with the claim of a still earlier priority." A single incident might have been the source of Slavson's anger. Sometime in the early 1930s Slavson attended a performance of J.L.'s impromptu theater. For some reason, J.L. chose Slavson for the role of a barber, an assignment that Slavson found demeaning. J.L. was not averse to using his intuitions to push the buttons of those who rubbed him the wrong way, as seems to have been the case with Slavson. If the story is true, it was a slight that Slavson never forgot or forgave and the trigger for a personality conflict that divided the American group therapy world ever since.

## Gestalt

In Germany in the early 1930s, an important movement was taking hold that aimed to base psychology more firmly in the science of physiology, the study of living systems. Mainly working in Berlin until many were forced to leave for America, the Gestaltists opposed introspection as the key to psychology, favoring scientific methods of objective confirmation of results. They advocated observations of higher primates and the incorporation of physiological knowledge into human psychology. In other words, they were interested in the way that our perceptual apparatus organizes its content into a comprehensive view of the world. Sometimes their approach is summarized as "the whole is greater than the sum of its parts." The Gestaltists' point that mental activity supplements sense data is well confirmed in experimental psychology. For example, a common experiment involves presenting a subject with several discrete points of light that flash from left to right in rapid succession. Under certain conditions they are seen as a single moving wave of light. Always trying to order our perceptions, the brain tends to fill what it takes to be the missing elements. The Gestaltists anticipated much of modern cognitive neuroscience and shaped new humanistic theories of personality as well, in which human beings are seen in their totality rather than as a collection of impulses and habits.

The Gestalt notion that the whole is greater than the sum of its parts was not only applicable to sensations and the human personality, when applied to organizations it fit well with J.L.'s observation that the group is more than simply a collection of individuals. Gestalt psychology heavily influenced two other men who were products of Europe in turmoil, both of Jewish origin, who would both become famous in America and figure importantly in J.L.'s life: Kurt Lewin in social network analysis and Fritz Perls in psychotherapy. Lewin started in behaviorism, but allied himself with the Gestalt psychologists in Berlin before coming to America in 1933. Perls was a Berlin native who became a psychoanalyst, emigrated to the South Africa, and then the United States in 1946, where he declared his style of psychotherapy "Gestalt," though the connection to Gestalt psychology is remote.

Lewin played a vital role in transforming and transmitting J.L.'s ideas into America's war effort, into industry, and ultimately into the human potential movement. Although best known as the founder of academic social psychology, Lewin's work had an enormous influence on corporate management theory and thousands of companies. As Art Kleiner writes, though Lewin was never a businessman "[n]early every sincere effort to improve organizations from within can be traced back to him. . . ." Lewin was born in Prussia in 1890, served in the German army in World War I, and received his doctorate in Berlin under the great philosopher and psychologist Carl Stumpf, who influenced both Heidegger's mentor Edmund Husserl and the Gestalt psychologists. Before turning to Gestalt, Lewin was interested in behaviorism. He was also active in the Frankfurt School, a collection of thinkers who applied Marxist analysis to social criticism, and in the Zionist movement, both in Europe and in his new home in America.

The differences between J.L. and Lewin illuminate their personalities and the disparate ways their work is remembered. They were approximately the same age, grew up in similar cultures, and had very similar philosophical approaches to social science and attitudes toward life. Lewin and J.L. shared the conviction that the application of psychology to social life would strengthen democratic forms of organization, which seem to be so imperiled in the 1930s. But Lewin was temperamentally a more traditional and academically oriented social scientist than J.L. During his young adulthood he was immersed in the popular scientific and political movements of his time. Rather than insisting on creating his own institutions, which was always J.L.'s *modus operandi* (with its attendant advantages and limitations), Lewin was willing to work in organizations that he did not necessarily control, creating opportunities for the acceptance of his ideas in institutions, and ultimately a greater likelihood that he would be credited. Lewin threw himself into civic organizations like the American Jewish Congress, of which he was a passionate supporter. By contrast, J.L.'s insistence on unchallenged domination of his professional activities, his irrepressible showmanship, and his megalomania often worked against him, gradually alienating erstwhile supporters.

In the early 1930s, Lewin was known in Europe and America for his work on his concepts of the "life space," the experiences and perceptions that shape a person's behavior and ideas about the world, and the "field force," the social forces that act upon a person. The interaction between person and environment fascinated him. For example, as early as 1920 Lewin thought that workers' morale was important in the success of an organization. Modern management theory owes an incalculable debt to Lewin. In 1933, when Hitler came to power and Lewin was preparing to immigrate to America, he met the British psychoanalyst Eric Trist at London's Tavistock Clinic. Trist was interested in the way human beings perceive and are affected by others and how they might be sensitized to the reactions they provoke in others, an idea that came to be called sensitivity training. The idea gradually matured into "organizational dynamics," which aimed to improve job satisfaction and performance when applied to work sites in much the same spirit as J.L.'s sociometry. As I will explain later, Tavistock played a key role in helping the British Army in World War II, both in its leadership training and in the care of soldiers suffering from emotional trauma. Whether Trist or Lewin were aware of J.L. at this early stage is not known, but like all the Tavistock psychologists Trist quoted J.L. during the wartime work if not before. In 1935, Lewin established the Child Welfare Research Station at the University of Iowa, which would serve as his base for the next decade.

Lewin shared with J.L. the conviction that modern social science (what he called "action research" and later "group dynamics") could rescue the world from the horrors it faced in the late 1930s. Although the details of their meetings are unknown, sometime in this period Lewin and J.L. entered into a highly productive relationship. Lewin found the basic idea of sociometry a promising basis for his interest in a more scientific approach to human relations. A popular handbook of social psychology explains that J.L.'s sociometric approach "found a highly receptive audience in Kurt Lewin, and the journal Moreno founded, *Sociometry*, became the venue for a number of classic studies by Lewin and his colleagues on the social psychology of group behavior. . . . Because Lewin viewed the rigorous, systematic nature of sociometry as a way to illuminate causal relationships through experimental methods, he adopted sociometric techniques for use in his own research." Though J.L. was only one year older than Lewin, he adopted an avuncular attitude toward the more recent immigrant. J.L. told me that he advised him to pronounce his name "Loo-in" rather than the Germanic "Le–veen", as the latter would sound more Jewish to the American ear. The historian Jenna Feltey Alden reports that she heard a story along these lines while doing research for her work on Lewin. If true, the incident says much about the pre-World War II self-consciousness of even the most successful Jewish immigrants. It also illustrates not only J.L.'s influence, but also his wish to be seen as a universal person rather than being tied to any single group, while Lewin was prepared to be publicly identified as an ardent Zionist. In terms of his engagement in civic causes and organizations, Lewin proved to be a more adaptable new American than J.L.

Some of Lewin's young students attended J.L.'s psychodrama sessions, presumably in New York City, and learned about J.L.'s experiments at Hudson and Sing Sing. In 1935, Lewin and Gardner Murphy saw films of J.L.'s work with the girls at the Hudson school at a special presentation at Columbia University's psychology department. Years later, the extent of these interactions became a matter of dispute, a conflict from which J.L.'s relationship with Lewin's followers, and with the field of social psychology that flourished after World War II, never recovered. What is clear is that Lewin's sociometry-inspired work changed the direction of his career and the history of applied psychology. In the words of historian Jenna Alden, "[b]y 1938 Lewin had moved away from his earlier interest in individuals' psychology and zealously embraced the group as the foundation for most human social processes." That year Lewin published a landmark paper in J.L.'s journal about leadership styles among children, showing that democratic leaders were more effective than autocratic leaders or those with a laissez-faire style. "Though first presented as a study of different educational methods," Alden writes, "the Autocracy/Democracy studies predictably emerged as ammunition in the nation's ideological war against Totalitarianism, and also propelled some of the most important developments in industrial management of the 20th century."

## Role-Playing

Lewin's studies of methods for improving employee morale among female workers at a pajama factory in Marion, Virginia, became a legendary success story. Although the women entered their jobs with enthusiasm and were paid better than in their previous work, they had trouble filling quotas. Lewin and his team showed that production could be improved by groups of workers' determining their own production goals. The Lewinites proposed various reforms during the years of the "Harwood Studies," including self-managing teams of workers, from 1939 until his sudden death in 1947. Not only sociometry, but J.L.'s theater-based role-playing techniques were also incorporated into Lewin's work at the Marion factory. One of Lewin's colleagues, social psychologist Jack French "devised a program of leadership training for all levels of supervision. It would include role-playing, 'sociodrama,' problem solving, and other 'action techniques,'" with an emphasis on experiential learning" instead of theoretical lectures. Lewin's colleague French found that a main complaint of the supervisors was that women on the factory floor would often talk too loud. As described by historian Alden, "French devised a role-playing exercise in which two of the supervisors pretended to be workers talking on the job, while another supervisor walked up to them and tried to quiet them. The supervisors approached the task awkwardly at first (Roy: "Well, Viola, if we've got to talk about something, we might as well talk about this idea. What do you think of it, Viola?" French: "No, that's not it. Girls wouldn't talk about that. . .Come on, be girls. Go ahead and talk about what you did last night.") But soon enough, they'd fallen into the rhythms of shop floor conversation and cathartically enacted some realistic confrontations:

> FRANCES, *acting as supervisor*: [In a scolding tone of voice] You girls are making much too much noise.
> ROY, *acting as worker*: We're just talking.
> FRANCES: You're not supposed to talk.
> VIOLA: Why we've got to talk. You can't live without talking.
> FRANCES: You can't talk. It bothers others. Now quit talking.
> VIOLA: If I can't talk, I'm going to kick somebody.
> FRANCES: Okay. Suppose you go tell Mr. Green down in the office.
> VIOLA: Ok, I will!
> Roy: If you're gonna talk that way, I quit!

The women agreed that this drama was an accurate portrayal of the arguments that ensued on the factory floor. The supervisors said that they learned that they were too quick to assert their authority, which only led to more trouble, and decided they needed to be more respectful of the workers, forming groups to explain company policy. "French pointed to these outcomes when he publicized the experiment in [J.L.'s journal] *Sociometry*. He explained that role-playing worked not just because it served as a forum for the discussion of organizational problems, but because it taught foremen social skills and helped them to create a strong, supportive group of their own. Calling it a form of "sensitivity training," French explained that "supervisors (even the women) are often insensitive to both the reactions of their workers and their own methods of leadership." Role-playing simultaneously offered opportunities for cathartic discussion, reflective self-analysis, and the planning of change. The factory owner pronounced role-playing as "one of the more successful techniques used to elicit participation" by the workers in their self-guided reform of their work environment. Social psychologists were doing similar work in British industry, with the goal of recognizing the individual worker as a citizen of a democracy. "[T]hey painted a picture of the worker as a human being, as one who searched for meaning in experience—and hence as someone who should be engaged in adequate structures of communication," write Peter Miller and Nikolas Rose, citing the influence of Lewin and J.L.

Stimulated by his personal experience with anti-Semitism (his mother died in a concentration camp), Lewin's interests also included the psychological problems of minority groups and the possibility that understanding the dynamics of group membership could help alleviate prejudicial social systems and improve interpersonal relations. The end of World War II had brought many African American men home to conditions that were no better, and in some ways worse than when they left. Why had they fought for freedom for others but not found it for themselves? Others who had uprooted themselves from places like rural Louisiana to Oakland, California, were losing wartime production jobs and fell into urban poverty. This period planted the seeds of the modern civil rights movement.

To address these postwar tensions, in 1946 the chairman of the state's race relations commission asked Lewin and his colleagues to conduct a workshop for fifty community leaders from business labor, education, and social work. The goals were to understand the kinds of conflicts that were being seen throughout the state and to help the community representatives to become better at resolving them by experimenting with various leadership styles. According to the business historian Art Kleiner, "Role play was an accepted therapeutic device: a white social worker might play herself, trying to get a thirteen-year-old black girl to come to a mixed race event: 'Did you know we have a folk dancing group every Wednesday night, Nancy?'" "Although Lewin admitted that progress is hard to measure in a situation like this, he argued passionately and perhaps somewhat idealistically, for the pursuit of his concept of action research. "As I watched, during the workshop, the delegates from different towns all over Connecticut transform from a multitude of unrelated individuals, frequently opposed in their outlook and their interests, into cooperative teams not on the basis of sweetness but on the basis of readiness to face difficulties realistically, to apply honest fact-finding, and to work together to overcome them; when I saw the pattern of role-playing emerge; saw the major responsibilities move slowly according to the plan from the faculty to the trainees . . . I could not help but feel that the integration of action, training, and research holds tremendous possibilities for the field of intergroup relations. I would like to pass this feeling on to you."

Twenty-five years before, J.L. had used role-playing at the House of Comedies in Vienna to try to find a new pattern of leadership for the disintegrating postwar Austrian nation. Now Lewin was using role-playing in an attempt to find new ways to lead postwar America through its own intergroup problems. J.L. would have seen Lewin's workshop as a sociodrama, aided by the sociometric study of small groups that he had devised in the 1930s. Lewin's Connecticut project was also an example of what came to be known as sensitivity training. Through role-playing and discussion the participants were made more aware of their own assumptions about one another and the way their conduct affected the impressions they made on others, lessons that were to be taken home to their communities.

The idea of using J.L.'s methods in race relations was not original with Lewin. In 1937, a student of J.L.'s from Columbia University named Joan Criswell published a paper in his *Sociometry* journal called "Racial Cleavage in Negro-White Groups," about using social network analysis in a Brooklyn public school. But by assembling all those representatives of Connecticut cities, towns, and villages and introducing role-playing, Lewin brought action-oriented group work on race relations into the community. Over the next several decades, role-playing was a popular method for exploring race relations, including "rap sessions" between community leaders and police and among civil rights workers to help young African Americans adapt to the assumptions of the white workplace.

## THE NEW SCIENCE

Only a year after his paper on the Connecticut workshops Lewin died suddenly of a heart attack at age fifty-seven. His loss was a tragedy not only for his young band of rising stars in social psychology, but for American social science's ability to adapt its methods to new social problems. Social psychology, and especially the field of social network analysis, arguably did not recover until the 1970s. And Lewin was in some ways a more suitable academic spokesman for the field than J.L., who was handicapped by his eccentric and bombastic manner as the culture of science changed after the war. Lewin introduced many mathematical innovations on the base provided by J.L.'s sociometry. The title of his 1936 book, *Principles of Topological Psychology* (just two years after J.L.'s more philosophical *Who Shall Survive?*), signified his desire to put psychology on a more modern scientific footing, complete with formulae like his "Lewin Equation," $B = f(P, E)$, which states that "behavior is a function of the person and his environment." Though J.L. also was seen as a scientist who introduced objective methods into the study of interpersonal relations, Lewin was more in touch with attempts to make social science still more rigorous and computational. His later writings are full of mathematized language and novel graphic spinoffs of J.L.'s fairly straightforward sociograms that crunch sociometric data in various ways. Nonetheless, J.L. respected Lewin's contribution. After Lewin's death in 1947, J.L. published a monograph under his Beacon House imprint that includes two papers, one by Lewin and the other by Lewin's close friend and student, Ronald Lippitt. The Lewin paper described the Research Center for Group Dynamics at MIT, which he established in 1944. Lewin's fertile mind and advanced thinking are on display in this paper, which lists many ambitious projects on the study of group life that Lewin and his team were undertaking. One study aimed to answer the question of why minority groups tend to adopt the negative attitudes about their own group held by others (called "labeling" in sociology), another was on the way that the physical grouping of houses acts upon group formation. The Lippitt paper paid tribute to Lewin's ability to create an open and critical atmosphere among his research team. It ends with an encomium that captures the progressive attitudes of social scientists of that era and the need for research on groups in a democratic society: "To Kurt Lewin the American culture ideal of the 'self-made man,' of everyone 'standing on his own feet' seemed as tragic a picture as the initiative-destroying dependence on a benevolent despot. He felt and perceived clearly that we all need continuous help from each other, and that this type of interdependence is the greatest challenge to maturity of individual and group functioning."

J.L. admired Lewin, but he thought that he took his scientific approach too far. At the time, Mill's Methods were a popular reference point among philosophers of science. According to the nineteenth-century philosopher John Stuart Mill, to determine causation certain conditions that appear in nature must be experimentally isolated from others. For example, in the experimental setup for Lewin's study of democracy in children's groups, new groups were created from various classrooms according to a system of control based on the popularity of each child in their actual classroom. By contrast, in his Hudson study with Helen Jennings, J.L. tested the existing relationships among the girls in their actual living quarters, classrooms, and workplaces. J.L. believed that in trying to apply Mill's classical experimental method to groups Lewin exaggerated the importance of "controlled" study because it distorts the actual spontaneous structure of groups as they appear in the real world.

It is the sort of criticism one would expect from J.L., who only a few years before had objected to the traditional theater as a mere copy of real human relationships; he wanted both his theater and his social science to capture people as they live in the "here and now." But that was not the direction that science was taking in the late 1930s. In the crucial decade of the late 1930s to the late 1940s, as J.L.'s sociometry was being transformed into modern social network analysis, experimental science was increasingly focused on the Mill-inspired design of experimental environments in which various elements or "variables" could be controlled to understand the interactions of these elements in the real world. In medicine, the "randomized controlled clinical trial" gradually became the gold standard during the 1940s. Nor was J.L. interested in applying advanced mathematical computations to the group structures that his beloved sociograms revealed. In this and other ways over the next forty years, J.L. would find his vision of social science left behind as he clung to a set of idiosyncratic philosophical principles. In 1952, the science writer Martin Gardner published an immensely popular book, *In the Name of Science*, about science fads and fallacies. Gardner allowed that psychodrama "might or might not have scientific merit," but then dismissed it as a cult and *The Words of the Father* as "stale religious platitudes." Gardner sandwiched J.L. between general semantics and vomit therapy. Whether Gardner was right about the value of psychodrama therapy or not, he was certainly wrong that it had "passed the peak of its popularity." The next twenty years would see psychodrama, group therapies, and techniques like the empty chair carried on a wave of enthusiasm about a new, "humanistic" approach to psychology.

## THE BREAK

But that rebellious movement was yet to come. In the 1950s, Gardner represented a postwar attitude that preferred quantifiable science to philosophically driven social reform and personal growth. J.L.'s mystical sensibility and theatrical style were tolerable to colleagues of his genera- tion, those who came to maturity before World War II. His philosophical orientation reflected a way of thinking and mode of expression that were recognizable to them. Thus, in the 1930s and 1940s he could count as close colleagues the core group of prestige social scientists at elite univer- sities like Harvard, including Henry Murray, Samuel Stouffer, and Pitirim Sorokin. Columbia's John Dewey, the country's most prominent philoso- pher who was especially interested in new educational techniques, was on his journal's advisory board, as was Johns Hopkins psychiatrist Adolf Meyer. But as the center of gravity in social science shifted toward a new generation, the generation of Lewin's students, the academic establish- ment's attitude toward J.L changed, especially among the social psycholo- gists; they clearly did not "get" J.L., and the feeling was mutual.

After Lewin's death, tensions developed between J.L. and some of Lewin's students. They included some of the most important social psy- chologists of the mid-twntieth century, including John French, Alvin Zander, Alex Bavelas, Ronald Lippitt, Leland Bradford, and Kenneth Benne. In Lewin they had lost a young leader who had both adapted to new standards for objective socal science and had immersed himself in the problems of the day like race relations. Lewin's style was more "Amer- icanized" than J.L.'s, even though he was a more recent immigrant. By contrast, they found J.L. eccentric and unwilling to harness his impressive output of ideas to more rigorous scientific methods, much less to restrain his theatrical personality. My mother claims that at one meeting in the early 1950s there was juvenile note-passing among some of the younger men while J.L. was speaking, making fun of his excitable demeanor. His feelings and his pride bruised, in 1953 J.L unleashed an ill-considered broadside against some of Lewin's protégés (though specifically not the deceased Lewin himself). The "bright young boys" who attended his psychodrama demonstrations in the late 1930s were to become some of the most important social psychologists of their generation.

The occasion for J.L.'s attack was a new edition of his 1934 book about his sociometry experiments and philosophy, *Who Shall Survive?* Noting that Lewin and many of his students had published in his journals and others since 1938 on topics with which J.L. had been identified, he said that he had been "bombarded" with questions about the relationship between his work and that of the Lewinites, citing a French author as one example. J.L. acknowledged that many ideas are developed independently, that history is replete with cases of simultaneous discovery, but not this time. "It can be shown on the basis of printed records that the leading associates of group dynamics have been in close contact with me. Theirs is not a problem of productivity, theirs is a problem *of interpersonal ethics*" (emphasis in original).

Careful not to blame the deceased Lewin for the actions of this group, he argued that they had dishonestly played both sides of the fence, appearing to be students of Lewin or of his when convenient, and that they had quoted only "those who belong to their clique" in their articles, giving the impression that the ideas they used had been developed independently. "But the imitators sit near the one from whom they steal the eggs; they are parasites. I did not harbor ill feelings toward them, this is the reason I remained silent. I said to myself: Just as there are people who can have no children, so there are people who cannot create any ideas, therefore they adopt them. What matters is whether they fulfill their obligation and bring them up well. *It is unfortunate—and this is why I am breaking my silence now—that these students of group dynamics have not only published distorted versions of my ideas and techniques, but they are practicing them on actual people in so-called research and training laboratories, receiving large fees and research grants without being properly trained for the job*" (emphasis in original). In a footnote, J.L. cited several allegedly offending research sites, including Lewin's center at MIT. Today an allegation of unethical behavior involving federal research grants could bring government regulators down on one's head, or even lead to congressional hearings. J.L.'s student, the criminologist Lewis Yablonsky, told me that J.L. showed him a draft of an even tougher attack, which Yablonsky counseled him not to use, advice that J.L. took. But in the (outwardly) genteel world of 1950s science the use of the word parasites was inflammatory enough, as it would be even today.

In his attack on the Lewinites, J.L. quoted a businessman named Alfred Marrow who later wrote Lewin's biography. In his 1947 obituary for Lewin in J.L.'s journal, Marrow recalled that he had been responsible for introducing Lewin to J.L. and that they quickly found "common ground." Marrow's timeline supports J.L.'s argument that Lewin's turn toward sociometric research was specifically due to his influence. In fact, there were attempts to extend an olive branch to J.L. In their book Lewin's protégés Kenneth Benne and Bozidar Muntyan acknowledged J.L., "who has pioneered in the areas currently referred to as psychodrama, sociodrama, role-playing, action dynamics, warming-up technique, group psychotherapy and sociometry, and who first introduced these terms into the literature. . . . To a great extent, the basic impetus for certain new trends in group and action research can be traced to the work of Moreno and his numerous associates. . . ."

In his obituary for Lewin, Marrow volunteered the information about his role in introducing Lewin and J.L. Yet Marrow's biography of Lewin, published about twenty years after his death, does not mention J.L., psychodrama, or sociometry. The biography leaves the exact circumstances of Lewin's turn from Gestalt psychology to the influence of groups a bit of a mystery. Marrow mentions twice that "group psychotherapy strongly influenced the development of group dynamics," and the book's bibliography of Lewin's work includes his 1938 publication on autocratic and democratic leadership in the *Sociometry* journal, but there is no reference to J.L.

J.L.'s absence from the Lewin biography might be explained by the fact that J.L.'s outburst against Lewin's proteges as "parasites" alienated him further from the world of academic social science. Many thought him paranoid and unstable. In his history of social network analysis, Linton Freeman writes that J.L. "was an enigmatic figure. He was bright—perhaps brilliant—he was wildly creative, he was entertaining and he was blessed with boundless energy. Like many Viennese intellectuals of the early twentieth century he had presence and style. But, at the same time, Moreno had a dark side. He was self-centered, self-serving and by his own description, megalo-maniacal. He admitted hearing voices, he sometimes thought he was God and he was convinced that others were always stealing credit for ideas that were his. Moreno, then, was both a dynamic intellectual innovator and a severely troubled human being. His role in the development of social network analysis can be understood only by considering both facets of his personality."

Although Freeman does not make it clear why he thinks J.L. was "a troubled human being," it is evident that J.L. troubled and puzzled Freeman and many of his academic colleagues, especially those in the younger, postwar generation: How could such a self-involved showman be such a "dynamic intellectual innovator"? How could it be that a psychiatrist, untrained in research methods, was the one who appreciated the internal structure of groups before the social scientists? Freeman speculates that J.L.'s "bizarre behavior" caused the Lewin students' reluctance to be associated with him. Even allowing for J.L.'s eccentricities, this can't be the complete explanation. As even Freeman notes, top sociologists who were not in the Lewin group, like Harvard's George Homans who founded behavioral sociology referred favorably to J.L. In fact J.L.'s vices were also his virtues. Where Freeman and others saw a disconcerting Jekyll and Hyde routine, other saw his mysticism and dramatic style as inextricably linked to his exceptional creativity and originality.

Although impressed with J.L.'s imaginative approach to social problems, social scientists like Freeman were also annoyed by his lack of scientific self-discipline. Even before Lewin took sociograms to new heights of mathematical analysis, both Helen Jennings and Columbia University mathematical sociologist Paul Lazarsfeld (who became a pioneer of public opinion polling and also worked with Lewin), were needed to provide more complex statistics based on J.L.'s work. To J.L. the academics were for the most part boring, unimaginative, and lacked a sense of humor. J.L.'s Godplaying is an example: Freeman is not alone in singling out J.L.'s messianic preoccupation as bizarre, even somewhat unbalanced. Especially as he aged, his Godplaying became a rhetorical habit, a kind of test of the philosophical depth of his audience, of their capacity for irony.

As far as J.L. was concerned, the joke was on them. A British psychiatrist and veteran of the Northfield experiments in group therapy wrote to me, "Moreno, as I remember him, was quite a flamboyant figure and he seemed to have a joke buried in whatever he said." In the early 1950s Lewis Yablonsky, who died in 2014, was a sociology graduate student at New York University and J.L.'s teaching assistant. He remembered working on a manuscript with J.L. at our house in Beacon. Around 3 a.m. they arrived at a passage in which J.L. quoted Karl Marx. "Of course you know," J.L. muttered casually, "I said that first." Yablonsky, exhausted while trying to keep up with the much older man's work habits, simply shrugged as if to say, "sure, you said everything first," and kept on working. Only after a good night's sleep did he realize that he had been the victim of J.L.'s penchant for keeping his tongue planted firmly in his cheek.

## CHAPTER SEVEN

# SENSITIVITY GOES TO WAR

Warming up to a psychodrama, early 1940s.

*The relation of concepts like "Stegreif," "impromptu," and "spontaneity"*
*to the concept of "Blitz" is obvious. In military situations of modern times,*
*a premium is placed upon emotional stability, speed of performance*
*and—above all—split-second judgment in action.*

J.L. Moreno, 1941

WORLD WAR II EXPOSED A WIDE VARIATION in the skills of America's secret agents. When an intelligence operative took the wrong train from Bordeaux to Paris he ended up in a car reserved for German staff officers, sitting across from Field Marshal Erwin Rommel. Somehow he kept his wits about him and passed himself off as a French businessman, engaging in a pleasant conversation with the tank commander known as the Desert Fox. All the while he had his radio transmitter in his suitcase which would have meant certain death if it had been discovered. When the train reached Paris, the American spy calmly shook Rommel's hand as the Field Marshall wished him well. Not all incidents ended so happily. A female agent parachuted into German territory as part of a team, was captured, and sent to Dachau. While she was being raped by a guard she bit off a sizable chunk of his flesh, ensuring that she would be killed. But before that she was tortured, including having all her teeth pulled out.

In contrast with the coolness and courage of these two agents, another one, apparently frustrated at having to hide his identity, mailed a postcard inside the Greater-Reich to Hitler with the message, "Dear Hitler, Fuck you. (Signed) An American captain in GERMANY." Others suffered mental breakdowns. Yet another clandestine operative, stationed in a neutral country, was said to have been so open about his job that whenever he walked into his favorite restaurant the band played "Boo, Boo, I'm a Spy" (According to a 2013 ABC News story the culprit was a station chief in Istanbul, and the restaurant was in the Hotel Park.) These agents' lack of self-control put them and their colleagues in mortal jeopardy. With their system of spycraft moribund for two decades, the American intelligence services were faced with the problem of screening and training people for sensitive and dangerous missions. Part of the answer: incorporate J.L. and Kurt Lewin's innovative ideas about group dynamics training.

The 1960s devotees of encounter groups and human potential would have been surprised to learn that their movement had roots in the United States national security establishment, and that more than one of their founding thinkers was a consultant to the intelligence community. *Bob & Carol & Ted & Alice* had fun with the intense focus on learning how to become more sensitive to others, and on how we are perceived by others that had become so fashionable in the later 1960s. Those were also among the qualities that World War II spymasters looked for in recruits to undercover operations. The ability to be sensitive to one's place in a social system was another quality that was widely thought to be a characteristic of leadership, another concern of war planners. The California canyon road that Bob and Carol drove up to Esalen started at a secret base outside Washington more twenty-five years before, where America's spies and secret operatives went to school.

## LEADERLESS GROUPS

America's total mobilization for World War II included what might be called human social engineering: how modern applied science can help in the understanding and management of the human mind and human behavior, both in individuals and in groups, and in relation to machine technology. Human systems engineering challenges followed two different tracks with some surprising overlaps. One track was Norbert Wiener's cybernetics, the theory of control and communication. Cybernetics posited the similarities between humans and machines that enabled them to work together. Feedback systems based on the flow of information formed the basis for operations on the modern battlefield. After the war, popular fascination with computers took up the idea that ever faster computers could simulate any system, whether a living organism or an organization. Ultimately, "electronic brains" could become "cybernetic organisms" or "cyborgs."

While the cybernetic engineers at MIT were at work on battlefield systems, a second group tried to make use of the new social psychology to screen candidates for clandestine operations, people who would work for the new Office for Strategic Services (OSS) under its first director, "Wild Bill" Donovan, a larger than life character who had won the Medal of Honor for his World War I service. Donovan was tough, brilliant, imaginative, and prepared to push the envelope when jealous bureaucrats, like the FBI's J. Edgar Hoover, got in his way. Donovan also had no prejudices about the kinds of people he needed for his secret service. According to a history of the Service, "[i]ts members were drawn from Wall Street, academia, journalism, the arts, high society (earning the OSS the sobriquet 'Oh So Social.')" The OSS opened its secret Camp S for psychological assessment of spy candidates in 1943, now the site of a shopping center near Dulles Airport in northern Virginia.

Kurt Lewin was one of the members of a team based at the secret OSS camp, where five thousand potential spies were subjected to a wide variety of personality tests to assess variables like emotional stability and leadership skills. The point was to see the individual not simply as a collection of traits but as an organism, quite in line with the philosophy underlying Gestalt psychology, a "humanistic" understanding of the person. As explained by one of the psychologists, "[i]n the beginning it was the lack of specific knowledge that led us to conclude that assessments could not be made of the specific skills of a given candidate for a specific job but rather in each case an assessment of the 'man as a whole,' the general structure of his being, and his strengths and weaknesses for rather generally described environments and situations." At the same time, it could also be seen as the social science version of cybernetics, though in this case the engineering challenge was to shape human populations. Here was the beginning of a complex relationship between cybernetics and humanistic psychology that continues to this day. Feedback itself was one idea that Lewin borrowed from cybernetics and applied to his group work, a way to check out one's perceptions with others. In turn, cybernetics pioneer Norbert Wiener acknowledged that Lewin's expertise in the physiology of perception helped him make the connection between information theory and psychology.

One of the interests that Lewin brought with him to the work for the OSS was an outgrowth of his pre-war work on autocratic, democratic, and laissez-faire forms of leadership. Often it was necessary not only to assess an individual for leadership skills, but also to build teams that could work efficiently, especially behind enemy lines. As described in an article about Lewin's declassified FBI files, operatives had to be trained to work under the most stressful conditions.

> The OSS was training spies to be parachuted into occupied countries and transmit information back to the allies. The spies were either getting killed off or turning into double agents! They asked Lewin and his graduate students if they would figure out how to make it healthier for these spies. Lewin and his group . . . invented team building. They pulled together a group of spies and worked to get them connected so they all saw and felt the same stuff—bonded so they cared about each other. Then they drop one in Italy and another in Denmark, living totally different lives. These men were able to stay with this terrifying mission because they were connected around the mind and heart.

Being "connected around the mind and heart" required total mutual commitment without a leader imposed from above by some distant authority. As well, often previously isolated operatives would have to merge quickly into a functional unit, so the ability to expand what J.L. called one's "social atom" was an important qualification. As described in a standard social psychology textbook from the 1950s, "[i]nvestigations of leaderless groups, stimulated largely by Lewin and Moreno, have thrown much light on the manner in which dominance emerges in a newly formed group. The device of observing behavior under such conditions was used, among others, in the selection of field operatives for the Office of Strategic Services (OSS) during World War II."

Not everyone is sanguine about the utility of these studies. Princeton professor Daniel Kahneman, the only psychologist to have won the Nobel Prize in Economics, recalls evaluating candidates for officer training in the Israeli Defense Force (IDF) in the 1950s. He attributes the IDF's adoption of the "leaderless group challenge" to the World War II-era British Army.

> Eight candidates, strangers to one another, with all insignia of rank removed and only numbered tags to identify them, were instructed to lift a long log from the ground and haul it to a wall about six feet high. There, they were told that the entire group had to get to the other side of the wall without the log touching either the ground or the wall, and without anyone touching the wall. If any of these things happened, they were to acknowledge it and start again.

Unfortunately, Kahneman continues, the predictions made based on these tests didn't turn out so well. "Every few months we had a feedback session in which we could compare our evaluations of future cadets with the judgments of their commanders at the officer-training school. The story was always the same: our ability to predict performance at the school was negligible. Our forecasts were better than blind guesses, but not by much."

Effective or not, the leaderless group tests that Kahneman observed in the Israeli army learned from the British were at least partly originated by Lewin, who had been in close touch with the Tavistock Clinic since the early 1930s. "In October 1943 an OSS official back from London suggested that a program of psychological/psychiatric assessment similar to that in the English War Office Selection Boards (WOSBs) be set up in the OSS." Tavistock was the U.K.'s leading center for the study of group dynamics, focused on assessing soldiers for possible officer training. Although Tavistock was dominated by the psychoanalytic ideas of Wilfred Bion, his junior colleague Eric Trist was enthusiastic about Lewin, especially the idea that individual and group behavior must be understood together. Trist was also familiar with J.L.'s writings on groups, though they had never met. The connection that Trist made between the ideas of the British Freudian psychiatrist Bion and those of the American social psychologists Lewin and J.L. not only helped the allies share ideas about training for war, but also laid the foundation for British group psychoanalysis after the war.

## SITUATION TESTS

Founded in 1941, the OSS (at first called the Office of Coordinator of Information) was charged with "espionage, propaganda, subversion, and related activities," including unconventional warfare. For America's interwar national security agencies, that was an uphill battle. Not only had the country drastically demobilized after World War I, by the outbreak of the next there was not only a minimal and poorly coordinated espionage establishment, but the culture of government was against it. "Gentlemen don't read other gentlemen's mail," was the prevailing attitude, uttered by no less a figure than Henry L. Stimson, who served as Secretary of State under Herbert Hoover and Secretary of War under FDR. Stimson shut down the Army's code-breaking service, the Cipher Bureau. Into this institutional vacuum stepped Donovan and his OSS, but they were bereft of expertise. In the early years, the Americans required the guidance of their British counterparts until they could build their own spy program, including the psychological and social assessments of candidates for sensitive and dangerous assignments.

An obstacle to getting psychology off the ground in the American and the British militaries was an institutional prejudice that favored psychiatrists over psychologists. Remembering the rush to develop some sort of assessment program, psychologist Donald MacKinnon said that "[n]obody knows who would make a good spy or an effective guerrilla fighter. Consequently, large numbers of misfits were recruited from the very beginning, and this might have continued had it not been for several disastrous operations such as one in Italy for which, on the assumption that it takes dirty men to do dirty works, some OSS men were recruited directly from the ranks of Murder, Inc. and the Philadelphia Purple Gang. The need for professional assistance in selection was obvious, but was resisted by many in the organization." During World War I the emphasis was on intelligence testing, not on personality assessment. As the 1930s had been such a fertile period for the development of new social psychological theories there were many new approaches to integrate into national security operations. Even the psychiatrists were in short supply: by 1940 there were only several dozen military psychiatrists in the American armed forces. One immediate problem that forced the US Army to ramp up its attention to both psychiatric and psychological issues was the publicity given to the large numbers of victims of "battle fatigue," as in a famous incident in which General George S. Patton slapped a hospitalized soldier with his gloves. Though personality screening ultimately had little role in preventing what would today be called post-traumatic stress disorder, by 1943 the problem obliged the military to pay greater attention to the ways that both psychology and psychiatry could aid the war effort.

During World War II, leaderless group exercises were one example of the techniques that were used to bring the new social psychology into the spy business. As Americans gathered experience with agents behind enemy lines, they realized that there was a grave need for improved screening and training of agents. Adaptation to new situations was therefore a key concern in screening personnel for sensitive assignments, including potential spies but also soldiers and others who needed to be assessed. In 1941 the Social Science Research Council asked J.L. to comment on ways that the military could test people for their ability to make split-second judgments. He replied that knowledge and skill were not enough. He cited his experience in devising "sociometric and spontaneity procedures for the study of group and individual behavior, respectively." J.L. was critical of intelligence testing alone, partly because of its artificiality and partly because there are forms of personal and interpersonal competence that a simple measure of intelligence cannot capture. In a way, he anticipated more recent appreciation of different forms of intellect, like emotional intelligence and especially social intelligence. Therefore, he proposed "spontaneity" or "situation" tests that could be constructed in the community, as he had already employed with some of the girls at Hudson and even before that with his spontaneity theater group in Vienna. "The situations are either chosen by him (the subject) or suggested to him by the instructor. . . . The students are told to throw themselves into the situations, to live them through, and to enact every detail needed in them as if it were in earnest. . . . One student takes careful record of each performance. A copy of it goes to every student. . . . After each performance, an analysis and discussion of it opens up in which the students as well as the director take part." He argued that these sociometric procedures were superior to psychometrics like the IQ test because they assessed the realities of human life as taking place in groups.

J.L. (who had been exposed to military culture during his medical service in World War I), then applied his proposal to a soldier's relationship to a superior officer, arguing that the degree to which an officer relies on his soldier's statements depends on their sociometric relationship. "We should consider in the present emergency the commonsense, direct sociometric approach in preference to any exercise of power over individuals, based upon sample groups which have been studied and analyzed independent of the actualities of the individuals and groups themselves." The example is poorly expressed, but the idea of situation tests took hold. Performance in a situation test was one of the measures of leadership potential and the ability to keep secrets including undergoing simulated interrogations under stressful conditions. According to an historian of American psychology, "[t]he three-and-one-half-day ordeal included cover stories to disguise personal identity, simulated enemy interrogations, psychodrama improvisations, and a variety of objective and projective psychological tests."

Other assessment tests were described using J.L.'s concept of spontaneity. Late in the second day of assessment, after the candidate had passed the initial physical they "were assigned in pairs to act in Improvisations. These were role-playing situations dreamed up by the staff in sessions referred to as 'brain storms' and tailor-made for each candidate to help resolve doubts which the staff might still have about him." For example, if there were doubts about how well a candidate took criticism he or she might be asked "what they would actually do if confronted with such a situation. . . ." The link to role-playing, spontaneity, and creativity in new situations might have come directly from J.L. through his contacts with the psychologists who were consulting for the OSS, or they might have been transmitted to the Americans by the British psychologists at Tavistock who were following J.L.'s writings and were advising the less experienced Americans. In 1943, Brigadier J.R. Rees, chief consulting psychiatrist to the British Army, told J.L. that a unit for group methods of selection of British officers had been formed that was informally called the "Moreno Brigade." On the American side, one remarkable figure who was deeply involved in adapting the tests was the OSS's chief psychologist, a professor on loan from Harvard named Henry A. Murray.

## THE PERSONALITY

Known to his friends as Harry, Henry Murray was one of the great psychologists and one of the most compelling personalities of the twentieth century. He was, among other things, a pioneer of the very idea of personality and of methods for identifying personality types. The product of a wealthy New York City family, Murray attended all the "right" schools and graduated from Harvard College. He was tall, handsome, athletic (a star of the Harvard crew team), and charismatic; it was said that few women failed to turn their heads when Harry Murray entered the room. He spent most of his career as a senior member of the Harvard Psychological Clinic where he developed the Thematic Apperception Test (TAT), the first "projective test" that used ambiguous pictures of people to evaluate the way the subject projects their fantasies and motives onto others. Based on that work he published the groundbreaking *Explorations in Personality* in 1938. For all his later academic accomplishments, Murray was an indifferent student until he started medical school at Columbia, where his intellectual blossoming really began, and he stayed on for a PhD in biochemistry. Murray's dramatic forty-year affair with Christiana Morgan, carried on with the knowledge of both their spouses, must be one of the few that has stimulated two biographies, one from his point of view (*Love's Story Told* by Forrest Robinson), and one from hers (*Translate This Darkness* by Claire Douglas). Early in their relationship, Murray, confused by his conflicting feelings for his wife and his lover, sought out Carl Jung for psychoanalysis. Murray held Jung in the highest regard for the rest of his life. Obsessed with *Moby Dick*, he wrote an influential commentary that helped popularize Herman Melville. When I was sixteen, I had breakfast with Murray and my parents in a downtown Boston Hotel. He was dapper, charming, and thoughtful. Years later, while I was graduate student, he helped me with some historical research I was doing on a friend of his who had been in the Harvard philosophy department and had gone to Zurich for analysis with

Jung around the same time. In his three-piece suit Henry Murray was the very image of an Ivy League professor of that era.

In the years since his death in 1988 Murray has faded from popular awareness, and history's judgment of him has been complicated by the revelation that he conducted humiliating experiments with Harvard undergraduates in the late 1950s. The experiments were disclosed in a 1999 book by Michael Mello and detailed in a book by Alston Chase that was published in 2003, including the somewhat sensational fact that one of the test subjects was Ted Kaczynski. Known as the "Unabomber" because he sent letter bombs to university scientists and airline officials and passengers, Kaczynski killed three people and injured twenty-three more before he was finally tracked down in a cabin in Montana; the cabin is now on display in the Newseum in Washington, DC. Kaczynski was a University of Michigan-trained mathematician and Berkeley assistant professor before he seemed to undergo a sudden personality change, resigned from his position, and became a recluse, where he formulated a radical anti-technological manifesto. Under a threat to carry out more bombings, the *New York Times* and the *Washington Post* published Kaczynski's dense diatribe, "Industrial Society and Its Future." After his capture his lawyers suggested that at least some of his emotional instability could be traced to the stressful and demeaning interrogations of Harry Murray's experiment, which were similar to the tests that OSS candidates underwent at Camp S.

J.L. and Murray knew each other only by reputation until they met in 1947, when they formed a lifelong friendship. A letter to my mother from Murray in June 1952 is typically charming, flattering, teasing, and playful. "I have just returned from Europe to find your psychodramatic announcement. Are you convinced that Jonathan David is a real human being? Is he perhaps an imaginary alter ego, a divine child of the mind, rather than a flesh and blood Messiah of the future? Perhaps it is a mistake to make any distinction of this sort. He is both flesh and spirit, and it is impossible for his parents to separate their perceptions of him and their psycho-epic fantasies of his unexampled future."

Besides their shared intellectual interests, Murray and J.L. bonded partly because Murray, too, had a difficult relationship with an "establishment." His Harvard colleagues preferred a more rigorous, less philosophical brand of psychology. In his 1952 letter to my mother Murray wrote "[i]n any event, I welcome him [me] to the world, and at the next opportunity will confer upon him all the necessary academic degrees so that it will not be necessary for him to submit to the deadening twenty years of intellectual discipline our culture deems essential. He will," Murrary concluded with a flourish, "be a creative being from the start, and like his father, bubble like a spontaneous fountain all his life." In 1948, Murray and his lover Christiana Morgan attended a psychodrama seminar at J.L.'s sanitarium, after which Murray built a psychodrama stage in his office building at Harvard, though some suspected its main purpose was to block the path to the psychological clinic that had fallen into the hands of a rival. Writing in 1950 to his friend Lewis Mumford, the historian and architecture critic for *The New Yorker*, Murray's shrewd assessment of J.L. could in some respects have applied to himself as well. J.L. had "contributed a lot," he wrote to Mumford. "His methods do not lend themselves to scientific experimentation & verification, and so he is on the periphery—the pioneering periphery—of science, & overlaps, to some extent, the domains of art & religion . . . Moreno says whatever comes into his fertile head—much of which is Grain, the rest Chaff." Chaff notwithstanding, Mumford became a J.L. fan as well. In his award-winning book on the history of the city, Mumford said that he was one of the few sociologists or psychologists to appreciate that one of the principal functions of the city is the opportunity for people to play many different roles, "the making and remaking of selves. . . ."

## Assessment of Men

Murray was one of several academics who were recruited as part of the senior leadership of the assessment team and made a Lieutenant Colonel. In the 1930s, Murray had for years been developing his ideas about personality in the Harvard clinic where he counseled students. Although he was not a psychiatrist nor even formally trained in psychology, Murray's experience with troubled young people was an asset to the OSS. A somewhat facetious description of the ideal OSS candidate was "a PhD who could win a bar fight," but the reality was more complex. As Murray told Congress in 1950, "[t]he whole nature of the functions of OSS were particularly inviting to psychopathic characters; it involved sensation, intrigue, the idea of being a mysterious man with secret knowledge."

Murray was not only the driving force behind the personality assessments of OSS candidates, especially to weed out psychopaths, he also helped recruit some other top experts as consultants, including Lewin. But the American psychologists operated under several handicaps. They were unfamiliar with clandestine operations, and for security reasons they were in the odd position of not knowing the real identities of the people they were assessing. Murray's ultimate view of the experience was less than enthusiastic: "The government uses social science the way a drunk uses a lamppost, for support rather than light." Nonetheless, Murray and his colleagues were able to refine some of their techniques at Camp S, resulting in a multi-authored volume called *Assessment of Men* (1948), which *The Saturday Review* called the "OSS entrance exam."

Some of the situation tests at Camp S involved timeless requirements for successful clandestine operatives. In one of them several experienced questioners subjected the candidate to interrogation under stressful conditions.

> In this situational test a junior staff member plays the role (a standardized one) of an escaped prisoner of war who is interrogated by the candidate. Background material for the interrogation is supplied in the form of a map and some general information about the imprisonment and escape of the prisoner who had served as a tail gunner of a B-29 before its crash landing. Another staff member sits by and rates the candidate's skill in Developing Rapport, Asking Productive Questions, Following Up Leads and Hints by the "Prisoner," etc.

The candidate was supposed to stick to a cover story, but no matter how well he did he was told that he had flunked the test. Then the real test began. The subject was put at ease in another room with a single staff member and asked to review the assessment process from his point of view, a situation designed to induce him to break his cover. The point was to ensure that those selected were emotionally stable and not taken in by suddenly changed circumstances of high and low stress in which they might let down their guard. Another test of leadership and social skills, the "construction test," gave a candidate ten minutes to build a five-foot-square box with various materials, along with two "helpers" who were actually confederates. They were supposed to act stupid so that they actually impeded the task's progress. Could the candidates manage these idiots without blowing his cool? No candidate ever completed the job, but it was so frustrating that sometimes they physically attacked the stooges.

I had the opportunity to talk about his experience with these kinds of personality assessments with Major General John K. Singlaub, now retired from the US Army. General Singlaub was a second lieutenant in 1943 when he was assigned to the OSS, partly due to his fluency in French. After the war, Singlaub went on to be one of the founding members of the CIA. As part of Operation Jedburgh in 1944, the young Singlaub parachuted into Nazi-occupied France to work with local resistance forces. Singlaub recalled that before he was sent into the field he was subjected to about a week of psychological assessment at another OSS camp called Area A at the Congressional Country Club outside of Washington, DC. The men were given various projective tests, like the Rorschach inkblot. They also had to work as part of a group to move a six-foot cube across a stream, with inevitable failure caused by stooges placed in the group to frustrate the mission. "They created a problem for the appointed leader to solve," Singlaub told me. Then he was transferred for further training in northern Scotland where various tests were repeated. In one, the men were given a cover (called a "scheme" by the Brits) and told to memorize the details, then lived under that cover for several days, after which they were told to go relax in a local pub. Also having drinks at the bar were some colleagues who engaged them in conversation, partly about their undercover experience. Under these "relaxed" conditions those men who failed to keep their cover story flunked and were sent away.

Though he acknowledges that it's hard to be sure, Singlaub believes that the personality assessments did lead to superior performance under actual combat conditions. During the war in Vietnam, when he was in charge of Special Forces teams that included both American and indigenous fighters, he found that often the South Vietnamese volunteers for these units were actually trying to evade combat. Recalling the World War II-era personality assessments Singlaub decided it would be wise to implement them to screen those members of the South Vietnamese army who truly wanted to be part of paramilitary operations. After consulting with Army psychiatrists, however, he was convinced that the cultural differences were too great for those tests to be effective. As to the present day, Singlaub told me he thinks the modern United States military has lost an appreciation for the importance of personality measures and group dynamics. "We are too focused on gadgets. Now we think we can solve all our problems by finding a computer program."

## BATTLE FATIGUE

While Murray and his colleagues were using techniques like leaderless groups and situation texts to screen and train spies, the American and British armed forces were struggling with psychologically damaged returning soldiers on a massive scale. The illness described today as post-traumatic stress disorder (PTSD) was then known as "battle fatigue." As in the case of training intelligence operatives, the British were ahead of the Americans. The Tavistock Clinic's Wilfred Bion, an imposing man who was a highly decorated tank commander in World War I, became a psychiatrist and was an early pioneer of leaderless groups in British social science. He also introduced the use of groups in psychoanalysis and led the way in using group therapy to help soldiers cope with their emotional ailments. Believing that their war neuroses were best treated collectively rather than individually, at Northfield Military Hospital in 1942 Bion tried letting the men self-organize into what later would be called a "therapeutic community." The British Army cancelled the experiment after only six weeks, apparently unhappy with the undisciplined character of the community being formed, and Bion was posted elsewhere. "However," write British psychologists Nikolas Rose and Peter Miller, "something more durable had been brought into existence: the understanding that the group and its dynamics could be used to reveal and to transform the individuals who comprised it."

Apparently independently of Bion, another psychiatrist at Northfield, S.H. Foulkes, had written about group therapy and in 1944 established a second group experiment at Northfield for the men with combat neurosis. Foulkes was a neurologist who had trained in psychoanalysis before leaving Vienna for England as a refugee. Again, the idea was to establish a self-governing community where the men could work out their problems as a group. This one seemed to be more organized.

The hospital and training wing were brought together as one unit. The former tasks of the training wing were diversified into all sorts of activities—artistic, entertainment, recreational and educational—so that the desires and urges of the patients could be given expression. Groups of all kinds were encouraged, clubs, billiards, ping pong, etc., and committees were set up to organize all the activity. A newspaper was established and dance band was formed. The hospital was allowed to grow into a self-governing community in which the patients were expected to take a self-responsible part. The ward meetings changed to involve the patients in the administration of the hospital. Representatives for each ward were elected who attended a weekly meeting of ward representatives.

Rather than sitting around in hospital beds the men were engaged in various activities, such as developing a pamphlet to help orient newcomers: "As far as treatment is concerned one might well say that everything we do here is treatment. It is for this reason that our treatment does not consist of bed and rest, or the usual bottle of colored medicine. Besides interviews with our Psychiatrist, we spend much of our time in various forms of exercise and activities." New men were assigned an orientation guide and shown the various activities taking place, including a Hospital Club, a newspaper office, athletic competitions, model making, stage design, furniture carpentry, all organized by the men themselves.

The stage scenery might well have been in connection with a psychodrama performance, as Foulkes built a psychodrama stage at Northfield after a colleague sent him some of J.L.'s papers in 1944. But Foulkes said he gave it up when he found that group psychoanalysis was dramatic enough for his taste. Although Foulkes and J.L. always disagreed about some theoretical details, they became friends and colleagues after the war, with Foulkes enthusiastically supporting J.L. when he founded the International Association of Group Psychotherapy in 1953. A history of the Bion and Foulkes group experiments at Northfield concludes that "... it is clear, on reading the discussions between the psychiatrists at Northfield, how profoundly Moreno's ideas infiltrated the system there. Psychodrama was the most obvious expression of this, but more deep-seated was the continuing attempt to enable individuals to make spontaneous readjustments to their environment." The Northfield experiments were considered a success at improving morale among the men, and the model of the therapeutic community was to have an enormous impact in the treatment of drug addicts in the United States and Europe, with psychodrama a common component of the therapy.

Two American psychiatrists with troops in North Africa developed a treatment for battlefield neurosis that closely resembled psychodrama, but with an added twist. Roy Grinker and John Spiegel gave the soldiers pentathol, a short-acting barbiturate that is used as an anesthetic but in the right dose makes subjects more cooperative, hence its reputation as a "truth serum." They then helped the soldier to reenact the combat scene that led to his present condition. "The therapist plays the role of a fellow soldier, calling out to the patient in an alarmed voice, to duck as the shells come over, or asking him to help with a wounded comrade." With a little effort and with the aid of the drug soldiers experienced an intense emotional catharsis. Grinker and Spiegel's "narcosynthesis" was popular for a while, but later it was observed to leave the patient more anxious than before and the men's pleas while under the drug moved the therapists so much that they promised they would have no more traumatic experiences. So while narcosynthsis went out of favor it might have inspired J.L., who was normally no fan of drugs, to permit a colleague to use LSD with a therapy group at the Beacon Hill Sanitarium in the early 1960s. Some British psychoanalysts like J.L.'s friend Joshua Bierer were hoping that a rapid-onset version of LSD would help disinhibit patients for therapy. But J.L. was disappointed in the results and never gave the green light for LSD therapy again.

In the United States, another practical reason to introduce group methods in treating returning soldiers with emotional problems was their sheer numbers. The few psychiatrists in the United States military at the outset of the war were overwhelmed with cases and clinical training of psychologists only got established after the war. Especially problematic were the soldiers who were held prisoner as candidates for court martial who might also be mentally ill. The US Army's official report was candid about the problem: There simply weren't enough psychiatrists for individual therapy. "We do have, however, the expedient substitute of group psychotherapy—the careful placement of men with similar problems in relatively small groups, with discussion and lecture by the psychiatrist. Group psychotherapy can be very helpful in giving the man a better understanding of his problem, but should not be confused with group 'gripe' sessions, which, while possibly very valuable in moulding opinion, do not necessarily provide insight." One of the better rehabilitation centers was at Fort Knox, Kentucky, where the men were put in charge of their own groups. "The therapy was largely on a superficial level but served as an excellent mental catharsis for prisoners. . . . [T]he men themselves carried on the discussions and were effective in calling each others' failings to the attention of the group, so that group pressure for social adjustment was effectively employed." There were also those who experienced a psychological crisis after a few weeks of basic training. Take away the prison garb and the bars on the windows and someone parachuting in from Esalen twenty years later might have had trouble seeing the difference between these group sessions of candidates for court martial and their own encounter groups.

> Different techniques were developed by the various therapists. In some places, a lecture-discussion method was used, which included series of talks on such subjects as orientation to the hospital, types of nervousness, causes of nervousness, body–mind relations, and the role of dependency, insecurity, and inferiority. In others, a question–answer technique was used. The method most widely adopted was to have patients tell the histories of their illnesses in front of the group and then, to have group discussion of his situation and illness, with some guidance from the therapist. By specific example, it was possible to demonstrate mental mechanisms—the relationship between present symptoms and behavior and emotional patterns which were developed and fixed in childhood. Some therapists undertook analysis of dreams by individuals in front of the group, with good results.

The Army had trouble measuring the effectiveness of the groups for therapy, but they were undeniably popular. "Many commandants, prison officers, guards, and others voluntarily stated that group therapy alleviated friction, disciplinary problems, and resentment. . . . [T]he widespread employment of group therapy and its inclusion in the official training schedule are facts which bear testimony to its acceptance and to the belief by both medical and line personnel that it was beneficial." By the end of the war virtually all Army prisons had adopted group therapy, and the military leaders even took some credit for giving civilian prisons the idea.

## Land, Sea, and Air

Not only group therapy but also the other key branch of group dynamics, sociometry, was well represented in the war effort. From the end of World War II through much of the Cold War, all three branches of the armed forces used J.L.'s sociometrics, souped up with Kurt Lewin's sophisticated mathematical formulations. The general idea was to enhance morale and cooperation among the troops. During World War I the focus of assessment had been on individual I.Q., but experience taught that the quality of relationships among teams of fighters was at least as important as individual qualities. The idea might have been transmitted from the OSS's assessment program as described by Donald MacKinnon, a Henry Murray protégé who went on to study personality assessment at the University of California at Berkeley:

> On the morning of the last full day of assessment, the candidate's opinions of and attitudes toward each other were collected. The Sociometric Questionnaire asked candidates, "With whom would you enjoy continuing your acquaintance?" "Which men expressed the most realistic and convincing opinions in the debate last night?" "If you were a member of a group on a dangerous mission, whom would you prefer to have as your leader?" and other questions of the same sort.

After the war, Lewin protégé Leslie Zeleny studied the "selection of compatible flying partners" in the Air Force using "sociometric tests." Here is his questionnaire:

> To help make the best flying teams, will you kindly indicate how you feel about flying with each of the cadets in your flight? Below is a list of the names of the cadets in your flight.
>
> 1.    If you would like to fly with a particular cadet in a flying team, encircle "Yes" after his name. If you would not like to fly with a particular cadet in a flying team, encircle "No" after his name. If

you do not know how you feel about flying with a cadet, encircle "I" for "indifferent." Remember, your choices may determine with whom you will fly the next few weeks. (Follow the foregoing directions now. Then read on.)

2.   Examine the name of each cadet after which "Yes" has been encircled; place a "I" to the upper right of the "Yes" following the names of the five cadets who are your FIRST FIVE CHOICES as persons with whom to fly. (Do this now. Then read on.)

3.   Examine the name of each cadet after which a "No" or "I" has been encircled; place an "L" to the upper right of the "No" or "I" following the names of the five cadets who are your LAST FIVE CHOICES in your flight as persons with whom to fly.

Zeleny then explained his "compatibility index," expressed in a series of mathematical formulae. He concluded that his system "should give flight instructors and flight surgeons valuable clues to the diagnosis of both stable and unstable emotional conditions among flying cadets, and perhaps other flyers, too." All those returning pilots with "battle fatigue" were worrisome to both commanders and pilots themselves, who made their selections partly in light of judgments about their peers' emotional stability. These are factors that are lost in the random assignment of flight crews. And then there was the familiar problem of leadership potential, which is so hard to assess in the abstract. "It is believed that the general methods outlined in this study are suggestive of further studies that could be made with respect to the determination of leaders and followers in flight crews and, perhaps, small groups of many kinds."

Sponsored by the Office of Naval Research, the US Navy displayed a special interest in situation tests and group dynamics, perhaps because sailors are kept in such close quarters for so long. Cooperation and patience are at a premium during long weeks or even months at sea. A 1951 study by Lewin's associate Robert French found that the more flight accidents, time in sick bay and disciplinary offenses a sailor had, the lower his number of sociometric choices by others. Using sociometrics it was easy to show that poor morale and cliques resulted from poor group cohesion. The same was true of leadership. In 1959 nearly eleven hundred Navy cadets were reviewed for the correlations between their medical condition, psychological attitude, physical aptitude, academic success, and superiors' ratings. The better they did on these scores the higher their sociometric status. Another study sponsored by the Office of Naval Research in 1953 developed "a new status index derived from sociometric analysis," "taking into account *who* chooses as well as *how many* choose." The Army also participated. A widely used handbook on leadership and management acknowledged J.L.'s "seminal studies" in the 1930s. "From World War II onward, peer ratings of esteem by cadets in Officer Candidate School or at West Point have been found to be one of the best single predictors of subsequent success as a regular US Army officer."

There were many such investigations in the years following World War II. By the 1950s the Moreno–Lewin approach to group research was considered to be a key tool in understanding and improving military morale. Neuroscientist and former US Naval officer and aerospace physiologist James Giordano told me that J.L.'s work remains important to military officer selection and training. "That Moreno's work has made a mark on military officer, and certainly aviation officer selection and training, is hard to question. Many of the factors identified in early World War II-era technical and training manuals such as the technical manual, *Notes on Psychology and Personality Studies in Aviation Medicine*, reflect Moreno's concepts of core qualities of leadership, and these were instrumental to some of the constructs of aviator selection. By the end of the 1940s, J.L.'s work was being directly acknowledged and cited as crucial to military leadership. The idea was to create a cadre of officers who could 'lead by being emulated,' and who could form a personnel pool capable of almost seamless coordinated work, anywhere, anytime, with only minimal supplemental training. In essence, it became the foundation for not only aviation officer selection, but officer selection and training in general, and subsequently, much of aircrew coordination and cockpit resource management training that's used to this day, at least in Naval Aviation."

## T-Groups

Like the rest of social science, the interest in group dynamics emerged from the war with enormous momentum, especially because of the United States and British military investment in sociometry and group therapy. From the military standpoint, anything that could enhance unit cohesion was highly desirable, even the kinds of exercises that might be marked by emotional display. In fact World War II commanders noted the correlation between a feeling of emotional closeness and troop morale, as did earlier military theorists. And these observations were widely implemented, including the Tavistock Clinic's Northfield experiments with group therapy techniques for veterans suffering from what we would now call post-traumatic stress disorder and the US Army's group therapy for incarcerated soldiers and others who had emotional problems after they entered the service. As veterans returned to civilian life to take leadership positions, they brought these experiences to the rest of American society.

Kurt Lewin's commitment to improving race relations hit its apex in his important conclave of community representatives from throughout Connecticut in 1946. It seemed that the same ideas that were applied to group dynamics during the war had an important place in civilian life. Lewin believed that group cohesion could be strengthened by focusing on feelings rather than words. This notion of interpersonal communication could be applied to organizational development as well, especially through what were called team-building exercises. Impressed by their collective experience in national security and civilian work, Lewin and his young colleagues decided to establish a training center in Bethel, Maine to pursue their work on group dynamics. Funded by the National Education Association and the Office of Naval Research, they called their center the National Training Laboratory for Group Development, or NTL. NTL became the home of T-groups.

Like the later encounter groups, T-groups had a leader or "facilitator" who was supposed to be skilled in helping members share their emotional reactions to others' actions. According to Bowling Green State University professor Scott Highhouse, "[t]he candidates [for jobs as spies] participated in assessment activities together, spent leisure time together, and revealed much about their personalities as a result of being isolated as a group. The observed effects of this seclusion likely influenced the decision to create a cultural island for the conduct of T-groups." Within less than two decades the same modalities that were used to screen secret agents were being applied at the new "cultural islands," growth centers like Esalen. "Although the history of the T-group is usually traced to Kurt

Lewin and the serendipitous events in New Britain," Highhouse writes, "a number of experiments with group processes preceded the Connecticut workshop. . . . Much earlier, the German psychologist Jacob Moreno had developed the concept of encounter, which emphasized breaking social constraints and dealing honestly with others. Certainly, Moreno's psychodrama techniques were predecessors to the role-play exercises used in the early NTL workshops."

A typical T-group started with the trainer explaining that whatever happened in the group was up to the members themselves. That announcement tended to be followed by an awkward silence, which was taken as a natural step in the groups self-organizing process. Often a collective decision was made for each member to introduce themselves and say what they hoped to get from the group. After that ritual the trainer might challenge the relevance of the introduction process, an intervention that was often met with anger on the part of some participants, irritably deriding the whole business as a waste of time, with others defending the trainer's point and criticizing the dissidents for their impatience and inflexibility. This created an opportunity for the trainer to encourage the members to focus on what was going on in the group at that moment, how they were responding to one another and on what basis. Perhaps they were stereotyping others based on their appearance or how they expressed themselves. The goal was to encourage the members to let go of their usual self-presentations, to "unfreeze," and to become more aware of the way others perceived them. The T-group was supposed to be an opportunity to think and behave in new ways with feedback from others, a "refreezing" process that was then to be transferred to their roles outside the group, or so it was hoped. It's worth pausing to consider just how similar the T-group process was to encounter groups, a similarity that was to bedevil NTL.

When NTL started in 1947, the participants were mainly teachers and middle-level industry or government managers; within fifteen years enthusiasm for the training had spread to top executives of major companies like Exxon, General Mills, American Airlines, and TRW. By the end of the 1960s an estimated twenty thousand employees of various companies had experienced T-groups, laying the foundations of the field that has come to be known as Organization Development or OD. NTL became big business, so lucrative that several trainers even copyrighted a version of the training into what they called a Managerial Grid. In 1964, at the height of NTL's success, Kurt Lewin's biographer and benefactor, Alfred Marrow, expressed the popular notion that the biggest problem facing industrial management was human relations. "To some extent we are all strangers. We are strangers in ourselves to the extent that we do not really understand our inner motives and feelings. We are strangers to each other because the image we project to the world is different from the way we see ourselves. We don't really know what we are like until we take off the masks we wear. . . . This is perhaps the greatest discovery a man makes in sensitivity training: in learning through feedback his impact on other people, he begins to understand himself." Breaking down barriers between "strangers," including one's coworkers, inevitably brought up emotional material. And after all, the larger point of T-groups was that, in the course of making its participants better leaders and colleagues, it also made them better people. The British sociologist and historian Nikolas Rose writes that "one could fulfill oneself as a person as one made oneself a more efficient manager and a more democratic leader." In this way the T-group philosophy tracked the humanistic psychology of "self-actualizing persons" that was to become a core value of the human potential movement and encounter groups.

Marrow's remark exposed the tensions at the core of T-groups that would finally bring down NTL as the Lewinites originally understood it. From the beginning there were tensions between trainers who were psychoanalytically oriented and those with a more sociological approach, with the former outnumbering the latter, who were in short supply. The Lewin students worried that the result would be an emphasis on therapy rather than training for the business environment. They were right. Over the years there was a drift to a more therapeutic experience, despite various efforts by NTL's more conservative leaders to change the balance. As Marrow's philosophy suggests, the fact that T-groups often morphed into the realm of group therapy was a natural outcome of the unavoidable intimacy that followed from the pressure to drop external masks and engage in confrontations; human emotions can't always be confined to discrete social roles. These situations became especially awkward when employees from the same company were in a single group, as they naturally worried about the ramifications of the honesty and expressiveness they were supposed to establish. As in encounter groups, tears and anger were not uncommon. A 1968 *Look* magazine article about the groups was called "It's OK to Cry in the Office." But the self-disclosures often went uncomfortably far. In one case a TRW manager confessed to a T-group that he abused his wife. A least one suicide appears to have resulted from T-groups.

NTL's biggest problem was that the same social forces that created T-groups in the postwar period led to other manifestations of the same fascination with group experiences for all sorts of reasons. As historian Scott Highhouse puts it, "[a]ttempts to avoid the trendy, feel-good, unbusinesslike image that was beginning to become associated with T-groups were hampered by the explosive growth of the encounter movement in the general population. The T-group had inspired countless spin-offs, including Esalen groups, Gestalt therapy, Synanon groups, nude workshops, and so forth."

Business school professors and psychologists railed against T-groups. In 1963 University of Michigan management professor George Odiorne said "I can only suggest to businessmen that they avoid the entire cult." The boundary problems that helped sink T-groups were similar to the ones J.L. faced in the relationship between theater and therapy. Regardless of the justified criticism, many individuals and their companies valued their T-group experiences, but ultimately the connection between personal growth and advancing a company's mission was hard to prove. On the other hand, the countercultural younger generation couldn't perceive the idealism at the heart of NTL. They saw these as a part of the "system," as "company men" disguised as reformers: Could capitalists really create a more humane world? Thus, NTL was caught in a kind of pincer movement between nervous corporate leaders and the anti-establishment attitudes of the late 1960s and early 1970s. As enrollments in its groups plummeted, NTL declared bankruptcy in 1975 and is today a very different organization. Though T-groups are gone they left important traces. Writes historian Todd Gitlin, "[m]anagement continues to love sensitivity training as once it loved to paint company lunchrooms green, on the theory that the serene hue would boost worker productivity."

Highhouse notes that the vestiges of T-groups include some of the core concepts of modern organization development, including team building exercises and diversity training.

## LEADERSHIP

A theme that tied J.L.'s first public sociodrama in 1921 to his 1930s sociometric studies, the OSS situations tests, the armed forces compatibility studies, and postwar T-groups was the problem of leadership. What makes leaders? What are their characteristics? How does leadership affect a group's success? For J.L.'s Vienna the immediate crisis was the collapse of the Habsburg Empire. In the 1930s, the democracies faced a crisis of confidence while tyrants flourished. The Allies wanted to know how to improve the chances of strong and mentally healthy clandestine operatives and military officers. T-groups aimed to help corporate culture cultivate visionary executives who were self-critical and sensitive to the needs of their employees. Many also believed that creativity must have something to do with leadership and with other crucial life skills. But what is creativity and how can it be nurtured?

In postwar America no one was more identified with innovative education to enhance creativity than the psychologist E. Paul Torrance, who created the Torrance Tests of Creative Thinking and pioneered educational programs for the gifted and talented. And no one's life work summarized the ideas advocated by J.L. and Lewin better than Torrance. As a young man Torrance worked with teenage boys at a private boarding school. It seemed to him that their parents and teachers had given up on these "problem children" whose offbeat ideas unsettled them, but that their creativity simply needed to be understood and channeled. During World War II at the University of Minnesota he counseled returning veterans who were adjusting to life as college students. When he was drafted in 1945 Torrance became one of the Army's group therapists. Through all these experiences he came to think that many human problems could be solved and people could achieve more if we understood how to identify and develop creativity, especially in children. After the war Torrance became a dean of Kansas State College (now the University of Kansas), and looked around for advisors who could help him pursue his fascination with the connection between creativity and leadership and his interest in group therapy. Among his mentors was J.L., whom he credited with persuading him to complete his PhD.

Torrance took psychodrama and sociodrama to his new job at the University of Minnesota and maintained a close relationship both with J.L. and with the Lewin-oriented social psychologists. In 1954 he and two colleagues published a study in J.L.'s journal about their work: the Air Force Survival Training School. Torrance wondered if combat aircrews continue to respect their aircraft commander in extreme situations, like ditchings, crash landings, or bailouts in tough terrain. It was in important question because the men's "survival expectancy" was known to be affected by the confidence they had in their leader, and not only their technical abilities. Because it was impossible to do careful studies in actual emergency situations, he studied the aircrews when they were being taught survival skills, especially a physically and psychologically challenging "trek" in Colorado, in severe cold at high altitude. It turned out that the most successful crews on the trek were the ones in which the officially designated leaders and the leaders chosen by the men were one and the same. Torrance also found that the men changed their views of their comrades during the trek depending on certain specific behaviors, like continually "griping" about the conditions. The lessons for the aircraft commander of a new unit were clear: "He must help his crew members to accept one another, smooth our differences of opinion and personality, and insure his own acceptance by his men." In other words, the commander needed to have superior interpersonal skills, what might be called emotional intelligence today. J.L. and Lewin, of course, believed that those skills could be fostered in groups that taught people how to be more sensitive to the needs of others and the way others saw them.

A much beloved teacher and colleague, Paul Torrance died in 2003. His legacies include the University of Georgia's Torrance Center for Creativity and Talent Development and his tests of creative thinking, which continue to be refined. Torrance was among those whom J.L. cultivated in the late 1940s and early 1950s when he was at the height of his reputation and powers. But J.L. was not the only teacher Torrance sought out. Another of Torrance's mentors also had a background working with troubled children and was a University of Chicago college counselor who, like Torrance, adopted a sympathetic and humane attitude toward the young people who came to him for help. When Paul Torrance sought him out, he had just published the book that would make him famous, *Client-Centered Therapy*, in which he explained that the attitudes the counselor brought with him into the session—what J.L. would have called the "encounter"—were critical to his interaction with his client. His name was Carl Rogers, and he was the harbinger of a new movement in psychology.

CHAPTER EIGHT

# THE HUMANISTS

J.L. on his stage in Manhattan, around 1960.

*"Meeting" means more than a vague inter-personal relation. It means
that two or more persons meet, not only to face one another, but to live
and experience each other, as actors each in his own right, not like a
"professional" meeting (a case-worker or a physician or a participant
observer and their subjects), but a meeting of two people.*

J.L. Moreno, 1946

THE ENCOUNTER TAKES PLACE in many forms, not all of them placid.
On September 24, 1935, former heavyweight world champion Max
Baer stepped into a boxing ring in Yankee Stadium with Joe Louis. Baer
had lost his title to James J. Braddock in an upset a few months before, and

197

he was eager to get back on track for another challenge to Braddock. These were the days when a championship boxing match was a major cultural event. Vying with baseball as America's most popular sport, boxing provided a welcome respite from the Great Depression for millions huddled around their radio sets or poring over the sports page. They couldn't see the blood and guts spewing around the arena, obvious only to the very few with ringside seats, that would relegate boxing to a corner of American life when the color television era took hold. One of those who had both a close-up and behind-the-scenes view was J.L. His friend at the Associated Press, Howard Blakeslee, suggested that J.L. visit each boxer's training camp and predict the winner based on their spontaneity and their relationships with managers, trainers, family, and assorted hangers-on. Arrangements were made and the wire service carried this story under J.L.'s byline on September 23: "Baer Volcano, Louis Iceberg, By Contrast; Max Covers Uncertainty with Forced Hilarity—Joe is Emotionless." Baer's "uneven jerky fighting, the ups and downs, are due to his emotional makeup."

Baer had just starred in a movie with Myrna Loy, *The Prizefighter and the Lady*. Perhaps his newfound film celebrity had been a distraction. "Every man has a limited supply of emotional energy," J.L. wrote. "If a fighter can concentrate all his emotional energy on the opponent, he gets the greatest effects. But Baer's energy is divided between fighting and acting for spectators. His attention is split. He wants to rule in two kingdoms. He has to betray one or the other. He has both attitudes aroused at the same time, the fighting instinct by his opponent, the acting instinct by the spectators. This divided attitude disintegrated the value of the emotions of fighting, hating and breaking through the defense. It makes him in spots absent-minded while fighting. [Perhaps it occurred to J.L. that he was preoccupied with his own conflicting options at the time between the theater and social science, a conflict he resolved through his work in psychodrama.] Fighting is a job in which you have to forget your ego. You have to fight with your opponent, and not 'solo.' In this conflicting personality makeup lie tremendous powers (most of the things his admirers are banking on) as well as weaknesses." But Joe Louis was calm and collected, totally focused on boxing. He "enters the ring silently like a cat."

The various papers that carried the AP stories applied their own headlines in the days before the fight:

MENTAL EXPERT SIZES UP RIVAL FIGHTERS ON EVE OF
STRUGGLE TO INDICATE PROBABLE WINNER;
DESCRIBES UTTERLY DIFFERENT PERSONALITIES OF FISTIC RIVALS,
COMMENTING ON EMOTIONAL REACTIONS OF BOTH UNDER
STRESS OF EXCITEMENT

VOLCANIC BAER AND LOUIS, THE SMOKELESS BOMBER,
AS A MENTAL EXPERT SEES THEM; DR. MORENO, NOTED
PSYCHIATRIST, GIVES HIS IMPRESSIONS OF 2 FIGHTERS;
CENTRIFUGAL VS. CENTRIPETAL FIGHTERS; ANALYZES TRAINING
THROUGH PSYCHOLOGICAL POINT OF VIEW

MENTAL EXPERT SEES BAER SPLITTING HIS ATTENTION
BETWEEN FOE AND CROWD;
WILD BURSTS OF ENERGY ARE FOLLOWED BY REST PAUSES WHEN MAX IS
OPEN TARGET, DOCTOR SAYS; LOUIS CONSERVES STRENGTH AND GIVES
ENTIRE THOUGHT TO OPPONENT, JOE FORTUNATE IN HANDLERS

PSYCHIATRIST PICKS LOUIS TO BEAT BAER
NEAR END OF BATTLE;
USING SCIENTIFIC ANALYSIS DR. MORENO GIVES BAER AN OUTSIDE CHANCE
ONLY IF HE CAN PUT OVER KNOCKOUT PUNCH IN FIRST THREE ROUNDS
AT STADIUM TONIGHT. REVEALS LOUIS HAS GREATEST PROBABILITY OF
WINNING BY TECHNICAL KNOCKOUT ANY TIME AFTER NINTH ROUND WITH
SECOND CHANCE OF KAYO IN ONE OF MIDDLE ROUNDS.

In the event, the powerful "Brown Bomber" knocked Baer down in the
second round—unprecedented for Baer—and the fight was soon over.
In an AP story the following day J.L. declared that Louis had won "by a
psychological knockout" that "began in the dressing room five minutes
before the fight. Baer, Jack Dempsey, and Billy McCarney were alone in the
shower room. 'Max,' said McCarney, 'go in there fighting at the gong. Don't
box that fellow or he will murder you.' 'Yes.' Cut in Dempsey, 'there will be
no boxing.' 'I'll go in fighting,' Baer promised. Which is exactly opposite to
what he did do. What happened to Baer in the dressing room, the psychological knockout there, was the climax of training camp events." It was the

beginning of the end of Baer's career and the sealing of a love affair between J.L. and the boxing press. (The fact that Baer's right hand was still broken from the Braddock fight, which was only learned weeks after the match with Louis, might have had as much to do with his loss as his psychology.) J.L. covered several more fights, including the title bout between defending world champion Rocky Marciano and Ezzard Charles in 1954. "After making a psychological study of Rocky Marciano and Ezzard Charles, and weighing all the factors involved, I pick Marciano to knock out Charles tonight in one of the middle rounds, probably the seventh or eighth. Charles, a split personality, has to fight himself as well as the champion." Marciano won in the eighth round. J.L. was never wrong in his predictions about the outcomes of the title fights he studied. He was also not a gambler, so presumably others made money on his prophecies.

The notion that a professional athlete's psychological preparedness can be analyzed for its potential contribution to victory or defeat is a familiar one now, but it was a novel idea in the 1930s. J.L. might have been the first "mental expert" to be so popular with sportswriters. Clearly he enjoyed the attention and understood the power of the press. The raw, elemental nature of the pugilistic encounter provided him an opportunity not only to exercise his social diagnostic skills, but also to convey to a broad public the idea that there is a dramatic aspect in all human events, even those that seem so far from the theatrical stage. In fact, the boxing ring is a stage for a primordial physical and psychological struggle. As J.L. appreciated, some of the most successful fighters have been great actors.

In 1962, J.L.'s prediction of the outcome of the Sonny Liston–Floyd Patterson fight was again carried by the AP. "A vicious, savage and confident Sonny Liston will knock out Floyd Patterson within five rounds," and maybe in two, he said. "The image a man has of himself is most important. Patterson has the image of a man who will defend. Liston has the image of a man who will conquer." Liston knocked Patterson out in the first round with a powerful left hook, but this time J.L. based his prediction only on observing the fighters on television. For the rematch in 1963, the producers of CBS's late morning television program *Calendar* invited J.L. to participate on a panel. The show was hosted by the sharp-tongued Harry Reasoner, who asked each guest to predict the winner. This time J.L. had not visited the training camps or studied the boxers from afar. Knowing he was not well prepared J.L. gave a meandering response. "Doctor," Reasoner asked impatiently, "who's going to win?" Not wanting to jeopardize his own undefeated record, J.L. demurred. "I prefer not to commit myself," he said to an obviously annoyed Reasoner.

To American sports writers and their readers in the 1930s J.L. was an appealingly exotic creature. On the leading edge of a wave of accented intellectuals from Europe, as a Jewish emigrant from German-speaking Europe well before the Nazis took power his timing with the American public could not have been more fortuitous. As well, psychology was becoming a matter of widespread curiosity in America. It seemed to be a science that had many practical applications. Early in the century Harvard psychologist and philosopher William James argued that teachers needed to understand and apply psychology. The behaviorist John B. Watson published a popular book on child-rearing in 1928; he had been forced to give up his academic job at Johns Hopkins due to a scandalous affair with his future wife and moved on to a lucrative career at the J. Walter Thompson advertising agency. At the same time Edward Bernays coined the term "public relations" and also went into advertising, applying ideas he had learned from his uncle, Sigmund Freud. But while Freud spurned popular culture, saw one or perhaps two movies in his life, turned down a $100,000 offer from Hollywood to consult on a movie and an offer to be an expert witness in the trial of Leopold and Loeb, "these would have been rather easy choices for Moreno," observes Graham Lazar. The allure of appearing in the sports pages was only one example of what Lazar describes as J.L.'s record of courting America's culture of celebrity. J.L., with his raft of new ideas, his mastery of psychological concepts, his connections to influential New York cultural institutions, the legitimacy bestowed by a medical degree and his colorful personality, was in a good position to become a media star.

## Existentialists

It was J.L.'s good fortune, and that of his immediate family who followed him and his brother to America, that he avoided the catastrophe about to overtake and destroy European Jewry. Even in the midst of a Great Depression, life was far better in America for a talented immigrant with a little luck than it was in Europe. Paradoxically, though, the fact that J.L. was not in the thick of the crisis also effectively isolated him from participating in the development of a welter of ideas that were to shape complementary and powerful movements in Western philosophy and psychology, ideas that in some respects had greater impact in a thriving postwar America than in a shattered Europe struggling to rebuild. During the years that J.L. was struggling for a foothold in New York, being embraced by America's social reformers, gaining public attention, and settling into his haven at Beacon Hill, a German philosopher was developing ideas that profoundly influenced the future of psychology and the way it would be applied to human relations.

Existentialists since the Dane Soren Kierkegaard have argued that human beings are self-creating creatures, that the choices human beings make define what they are, their essence. Martin Heidegger's early writings—and especially his weighty and obscure *Being and Time* (1927)—focused the attention of German-speaking philosophers on what Heidegger called the question of Being: What is it to be? Two thousand years of philosophy had covered over the question with confusions and distractions that needed to be peeled away, like so many layers of paint. What, Heidegger asked, is the nature of the creature for whom Being is a problem, namely the human being (called *Dasein*), whose fundamental nature is that of finding itself thrown in a world? As a result of this quality of "thrownness" human experience is grounded in an "intentional" relationship to the world; that is, human experience is always about something that is prior to the human being, a world about which human beings care deeply, a world of possibilities that include death and therefore the special relationship toward death that is unique to human beings. Heidegger argued that Western philosophy since Plato had obscured the underlying question of the meaning of Being or "ontology."

Because human beings are thrown into an existence in which death is always possible and finally inevitable, we need to be resolute in the face of mortality and push beyond the superficialities of everyday life. In the later 1930s the ideas of resoluteness and authenticity impressed the future leaders of what would be known as humanistic psychology. They sought an approach to human problems that would not subject them to a classical Freudian interpretation based on repression of unconscious desires, but rather as problems that naturally face people as self-aware beings living with others and grappling with mortality. How can I be who I am to myself and others in a way that is honest and authentic? As an intentional being who makes choices what responsibilities do I have for my choices? Given the fact that death is unavoidable, how can I find meaning in life? These were problems that in the late nineteenth century Nietzsche believed to be beyond the abilities of human beings to resolve, but which the humanists thought could be addressed if human potential was realized. Ever since the late 1930s, the humanistic psychology movement has sought ways to expand that potential. Nietzsche laid down a marker for humanistic psychology by anticipating various elements of its practical application in the human potential movement. For example, Nietzsche argued that a higher, post-human being could embrace the cycle of eternal return so common in Eastern philosophy, that an Overman would want to relive every moment of his life an infinite number of times, which is something that no human being would want to do. The human potential movement valued Eastern philosophy, and especially Buddhism, as one of the keys to expanding human capacities and achieving transcendence.

Other sources also influenced the humanists, including personalists like Martin Buber through *I and Thou*, but the personalists' emphasis on individual human uniqueness had its greatest impact on Christian and Jewish theology rather than on secular philosophy. Also, in the 1930s Buber was subjected to restrictions on his teaching and publishing by Nazi authorities before leaving for Jerusalem in 1938, at which point he increasingly focused on the problems of Jewish survival during and after the Holocaust. Buber's encounter philosophy would re-emerge as a point of interest to the humanistic psychologists in the 1950s; meanwhile, the themes that *Being and Time* addressed were among those that stimulated a new generation of social scientists in both Germany and the United States, especially as German Jewish scholars were forced to flee their homeland. Many of them joined a University in Exile at the New School for Social Research in New York City (now The New School), where J.L. sometimes lectured.

Heidegger's writings contributed to an atmosphere in which new ideas about the meaning of human life were being raised, especially that of personal moral responsibility. On the other hand, Heidegger himself embodied the problem of moral choice that was of such great interest to the generation of scientists that were beginning their careers in the 1930s. He was a member of the Nazi Party through the end of the war and in 1933 his inaugural address as rector of the University of Freiburg declared his support of the Nazi social revolution. He resigned the post the following year. Before that he had a number of Jewish students who went on to distinguished careers, including the political philosopher Hannah Arendt, with whom he had a tempestuous extramarital affair while she was his student. After the war, many of his students defended him, including Arendt, but a vigorous battle over the relationship between Heidegger's early Nazi sympathies and his philosophy—or whether one is even relevant to the other—has provoked a highly emotional debate in philosophical circles. J.L.'s energetic promotion of his ideas about the therapeutic theater, group therapy, and institutional reform sharply distinguished him from Heidegger, who dismissed engagement in public matters (though evidently not early Third Reich politics) as "forgetfulness of Being." J.L. was never happier than when he was on stage producing a psychodrama; Heidegger was at his most content reflecting on the meaning of Being in his Black Forest cottage. Nonetheless, there were links between them. Heidegger and J.L. shared a preoccupation with personal authenticity and meaning just enough to be considered part of the trends that led to postwar existentialism and fueled the new humanistic psychology, NTL, and encounter groups.

## THE GROUP

A few months before the flower children gathered at the Woodstock Festival in 1969, some frolicking in the nude to make the best of a wet and wildly disorganized Catskills summer retreat, *Newsweek* magazine published a "special report" on encounter groups called "The Group: Joy on Thursday," illustrated by a discreetly photographed nude encounter. The article explained that "[g]roup leaders draw on a mixed bag of psychological theories and techniques to accomplish this aim, including the experiences of group-psychotherapy and group-dynamics laboratories, the erotic theories of the late Dr. Wilhelm Reich, the psychodrama techniques of J.L. Moreno, and the peak-experience psychologies of Carl Rogers and Abraham Maslow." The article's description of an encounter group prepared readers for a similar scene in *Bob & Carol & Ted & Alice*, which was released just a few months later. "'All right,' bellowed the baldish, bearded leader to some 200 men and women sitting cross-legged and shoeless on the wooden floor. 'Let's everybody begin by screaming as long and as loud as possible.' A wild, raggedy, piercing shriek rose from the crowd. When it subsided, participants dispersed into smaller groups, where they arm wrestled, fell backwards into each other's arms, occasionally hugged each other warmly and kept pouring out to whomever was in earshot the most intimate emotions. By the end of the three-hour session, the participants were euphoric; one matronly woman wept softly, 'Why can't it always be like this?' she asked."

"These groups are the most rapidly spreading social phenomenon in the country," psychologist Carl Rogers told the *Newsweek* reporter. They are helping break through the alienation and dehumanization of our culture." The other most prominent psychological theorist who was often associated with the encounter group movement was Abraham Maslow. Though Maslow was far more ambivalent about the groups than was Rogers, expressing concern about "an awful lot of charlatanism," in the magazine article Maslow, too, endorsed the movement's promise. "If we take the best of it, it's of the utmost importance. It's the great frontier in social psychology now." Cited in opposition was a behaviorist at the University of California at Berkeley, who called encounter groups a new religious cult.

Insistent as usual on his own priority and independence, J.L. refused to identify fully with the human potential movement he helped to inspire and with which he was sometimes identified. To him they were latecomers, however well intentioned. From his point of view, so were the new humanistic psychologists. As his ideas were adopted by government and industry and as he continued to attract favorable public attention, he must have seen little reason to change course. As late as 1963 a favorable three-page spread in *The Saturday Evening Post* described J.L.'s psychodramatic philosophy with no mention of the budding human potential movement. And despite his rebellious style, J.L.'s relationship with the psychiatric establishment remained surprisingly strong. Over the years he collaborated with numerous leading psychiatrists, especially those who were in charge of large mental institutions. Even among Freudian analysts his ideas about group therapy made inroads, especially in postwar Britain and France because they provided tools to use in counseling. But just as J.L. and his contemporaries were formed by *fin de siècle* social disruptions and by World War I, there was a new generation emerging with its own leaders for whom the Great Depression and World War II were formative experiences.

## A NEW GENERATION

Superficially at least, what Maslow called the "great frontier" of social psychology in the late 1960s bore little resemblance to Kurt Lewin's highly mathematized frontier of social psychology twenty years before. As the *Newsweek* article pointed out, though encounter groups were more explicitly oriented to personal growth they were the direct descendent of Lewin's NTL. Esalen founder Mike Murphy's first experience with encounter was at a five-day session for management executives in Carmel, California in 1963. Determined to install group dynamics among Esalen's offerings, in 1966 he recruited Will Schutz from NTL. As historian Jenna Alden reports, Schutz was already shaking things up at NTL, introducing "imagery work from photosynthesis, emotion-releasing techniques from bioenergetics, and action methods from psychodrama." By the mid-1960s the NTL leaders grew more concerned about their reputation melding into the encounter group movement, so it was a good time for Schutz to take his leave. Thus it was that the golden age at Esalen was indelibly marked by Schutz and the sensitivity training formerly most identified with NTL.

Will Schutz held a doctorate from UCLA, taught group dynamics at Harvard, and was a professor at Albert Einstein College of Medicine in New York before accepting the full-time job at Esalen. His career illustrates how much World War II changed American psychology. Like every other institution, the imperatives of the national emergency put science on a war footing. Every possible advantage over the enemy needed to be exploited. The professionals who were supposed to be expert in any field, including the new ideas about group dynamics, were brought into rapidly expanding government institutions, especially the military. A *quid pro quo* that survives to this day was established between colleges and universities and the federal government: You provide the experts and we will provide the dollars. The expansion of knowledge was not optional, it was necessary, perhaps a matter of national survival, certainly as a matter of the survival of Enlightenment ideals of personal freedom and tolerance for differences.

The war also impressed many with the fragility of those ideals. If in the 1930s democrats despaired of the future of institutions "of, by and for the people," in the 1940s philosophers and scientists despaired of the future of humanistic impulses. Especially in light of tens of millions dead, neither psychoanalysis nor behaviorism seemed to have answers to questions of human longing and despair: Was cruelty simply a matter of neurotic impulses or reinforcement histories? For many, of course, traditional religious beliefs continued to be a rock of stability. Some who were newly aware of the "Orient" because it had been a major theater of war became curious about non-Western forms of spirituality. But others took their cues from the tradition of Voltaire that rejected prevailing religious dogma. Like Kierkegaard and Nietszche they refused to turn away from the evidence that there is no inherent meaning in human existence.

J.L. had a foot in both these movements. His social reform methods, a combination of drama-based group therapy and the measurement of group structures, had made him a favorite of progressive administrators of the large institutions of the day—hospitals, prisons, schools, and even the armed forces. His insistence on the priority of the "here and now" and the "encounter," for which he had advocated since the 1910s, made him a natural ally of the new wave of interest in immediate, open dialogue between people of good will, including especially between psychological counselors and their patients or clients. Yet he was neither fish nor fowl. He was not the head of a large organization like an asylum or a full-time member of a research university (though he was a frequent lecturer at several), where more and more scientists and intellectuals were being housed and where they were producing students with graduate degrees. Nor was he prepared to sign on to the more abstract existential philosophy that lay behind much of the new interpersonal psychology.

## Client-Centered

Psychotherapy was a natural setting for assessing the meaning of life and one's personal authenticity. Among the existential therapies that appeared after World War II, Swiss Medard Boss developed a form of psychotherapy inspired by Heidegger's philosophy that he called *Daseinanalysis*. Viktor Frankl's wife and daughter died in the concentration camps, but he returned to his native Vienna to found *logotherapy*, literally the search for meaning. Both were psychiatrists, were friends of J.L., and used psychodrama techniques in their work. The war gave psychologists higher status than they had before, partly due to the shortage of psychiatrists and the introduction of group therapy. As Irvin Yalom observes, in the 1940s psychologists like Carl Rogers had to fight with psychiatrists, behaviorists, and psychoanalysts over his form of therapy. Rogers' "client-centered" therapeutic style is familiar to anyone who has seen modern film or television portrayals of therapy, like those in the series *In Treatment*, but the emphasis on openness on both sides of the therapist–patient relationship was something new. "Experienced therapists today agree that the crucial part of therapy, as Rogers grasped early in his career, is the therapeutic relationship. *Of course* it is imperative that the therapist relate genuinely to the patient—the more the therapist avoids self-protective or professional masks or roles, the more the patient will reciprocate and change in a constructive direction. *Of course*, the therapist should accept the patient non-judgmentally and unconditionally. And, *of course*, the therapist must enter empathetically into the private world of the client" (emphases in original).

J.L. had warm professional ties to Rogers, who invited him to lecture at the University of Chicago in the early 1950s and who was included in a 1956 anthology on psychotherapy that J.L. coedited with Frieda Fromm-Reichmann, psychoanalyst Erich Fromm's first wife, the first of a series J.L. would publish with Fromm-Reichmann. That same year, Fromm published the book that made him famous, *The Art of Loving*. Fromm's lack of medical training was at first a handicap, but his energy and the power of his popular writings coincided with greater opportunities for nonphysicians in the world of psychotherapy after World War II, when he helped found several institutes. Fromm was a pioneer in combining Marxism with Freudian psychology, though most Americans came to known him through *The Art of Loving*. Many assumed it was a self-help book or even a sex manual, but readers quickly discovered that it was actually a deep philosophical exploration of different kinds of love, including self-love and love of God. Although Fromm wrote from a Freudian perspective that the humanists rejected, the themes he explored—self-acceptance as a precondition for loving others and the decline of the ability to truly love in the modern world—fit well with the growing interest in personal growth that flowered in the early 1960s. Fromm was not only more psychoanalytic, but also more political than the humanistic psychologists, who for the most part believed that change, even revolutionary change, must begin with the self rather than with social movements. Though the humanists preferred to do an end-run around the political upheavals of the 1960s, their commitment to the individual as the locus of change later proved to be problematic.

J.L.'s idea of the encounter as an authentic meeting between two people who were not hiding behind masks or roles written for them by others fit well with Rogers' view of the therapist–client relationship, yet Rogers came to his position independently of J.L. Instead, the person who exercised the crucial influence on Rogers, as well on other humanistic psychologists like Rollo May, was a psychoanalyst whom Freud had once held close as one of his favorites, but who was finally rejected by Freud and the classical analysts. Born Otto Rosenfeld, Otto Rank was for twenty years one of Freud's closest collaborators and very like an adopted son. As was common among Jews at the time, including in J.L.'s family, what funds were available for education in the Rosenfeld home went to the eldest boy, who in that case was Otto's older brother, who studied law. Otto therefore became an autodidact, wrote poetry and literary essays and was brilliant in his comprehension of psychoanalytic theory, drawing out its nonmedical aspects especially as applied to artistic creativity. The politics of Freud's inner circle were intense, however, and Rank's loyalties changed as he matured. For a time, Rank proposed that all anxiety is a result of birth trauma, so that the mother relation is crucial, and must be "acted out" so that the patient could be psychologically reborn, a provocative connection to J.L.'s ideas about psychodrama. Freud saw the goal of psychoanalysis as subjecting the patient's neuroses to reason, but Rank came to emphasize the main problem as weakness of will, the inability of neurotics to release themselves from dependent relationships. Patients needed to exert their creativity by sloughing off old parts of the self, as he believed healthy people do throughout life, freeing themselves from birth trauma. The goal of analysis should therefore be to promote the patient's self-confidence and independence. Key was the relationship with the therapist, who should be an affirming and accepting presence, encouraging patients to be open about their emotions in the process of rediscovering their wills. Finally, the patient can transfer this affirming situation to the rest of life and terminate analysis.

In Freud's circle, disagreements about psychoanalytic theory were wrapped up with ideas about the needs of its members for further psychoanalysis. Scientific controversies became matters of personality. Ultimately, Freud concluded that Rank had rejected him as a father figure and Rank's peers rejected him as a brother. Rank liberated himself from these complexities by coming to America in 1926, where he became a member of what is now the University of Pennsylvania school of social work. His social work colleagues began to apply Rank's ideas about the need for a supportive style of therapy to their work in the Philadelphia Child Guidance Clinic, where they emphasized the patient's present experience rather than the usual psychoanalytic focus on the past. The themes of the "here and now," of the encounter between therapist and patient, and of encouraging the patient's self-confidence were among those that were adopted by Carl Rogers in his client-centered approach to counseling and by Rollo May's existential psychology. These themes also happened to be present in J.L's philosophy and psychology, helping to explain why Rogers found J.L.'s approach compatible with his own. They shared attitudes that became prominent in the new humanistic psychology.

## PEAK EXPERIENCES

Although Carl Rogers personified the earnest, open, and sensitive humanistic therapist, Abraham Maslow was the great theorist of the new psychology. He was well equipped for the job, having worked his way through excellent preparation in psychoanalysis, behaviorism, and experimental psychology. Impressed by Rogers' approach to counseling young people, while he was teaching at New York's Brooklyn College, Maslow also provided therapy to some of the students, which proved instrumental in developing his psychological theories. In those years, Maslow often brought his psychology classes to Manhattan to participate in J.L.'s psychodrama demonstrations. He was brilliant, unfailingly kind, and possessed of the emotional resources that allowed him to survive an unhappy childhood, a background that proved instructive when he set out to develop a psychological theory that aimed to answer the questions: What motivates people to do what they do? Why do they want what they want? Why do they play, write poetry, sing, and dance? Again, neither psychoanalysis nor behaviorism seems to provide the answer. Once basic physiological needs are satisfied—needs for air, food, sex—a person seen as a whole organism has further, "higher" needs. "And when these in turn are satisfied, again new (and still 'higher') needs emerge, and so on."

Maslow's hierarchy of needs may be the most important concept in the history of humanistic psychology. Influenced by mentors like the psychoanalysts Erich Fromm and Alfred Adler and the physiologist Kurt Goldstein, Maslow provided an alternative framework for explanations of human activity. Unlike Freud and Watson, Maslow saw the challenge for a psychology of motivation as that of making sense of all the aspects of a human being as a whole, including acts of love and altruism and work for social improvement, without reducing them to libidinal energy or reinforcement histories or viewing them at their worst rather than at their best. At the apex of Maslow's hierarchy was the need for self-actualization, which was informed by his study of certain people widely recognized as remarkable human beings, including historical figures like Thomas Jefferson and his friend, the anthropologist Ruth Benedict. As Maslow's biographer explains, "[a]mong the specific traits of self-actualizers that [Maslow] listed and briefly discussed were greater self-acceptance and acceptance of others, autonomy, spontaneity, esthetic sensitivity, frequent mysticlike or transcendent experiences, a democratic rather than authoritarian outlook, and involvement in a cause or mission outside oneself. . . . He also found that, regardless of their particular occupation or station in life, self-actualizers tend to be highly creative as an outpouring of their very personality. . . ." The list of self-actualizing traits is revealing for the implicit influences it summarizes: esthetic sensibility from Nietzsche, spontaneity and creativity from J.L., mystical experiences from Buber, a democratic leadership style from Lewin, and many others. Here were the implicit building blocks of the kind of person the later encounter groups idealized as elements of our human potential.

As people who have come to a high level of maturation, health, and self-fulfillment," self-actualizers "have so much to teach us that sometimes they seem almost like a different breed of human beings." They may experience temporary disorientation as to time and space, feelings of awe and wonder, supreme happiness, and a sense of connection with the universe that drains them of fear. Peak experiences as understood by Maslow are reminiscent of accounts given by mystics in virtually any culture. In *Nature* Ralph Waldo Emerson, who might well have qualified as a self-actualized person for Maslow, wrote that "[c]rossing a bare common, in snow puddles, at twilight, under a clouded sky, without having in my thoughts any occurrence of special good fortune, I have enjoyed a perfect exhilaration. I am glad to the brink of fear." J.L.'s role reversal with God that gave him a sense of unity and of personal responsibility for the entire universe might be another case. After these kinds of experiences, "the person is more apt to feel that life. . .is worthwhile, even if it is usually drab, pedestrian, painful, or ungratifying, since beauty, truth, and meaningfulness have been demonstrated . . . to exist."

Maslow denied that self-actualizers who have peak experiences are merely neurotics with infantile wish-fulfillment fantasies. These experiences have value and meaning for all of us, even if not all can attain them. "If self-actualizing people can and do perceive reality more efficiently, fully, and with less motivational contamination than others do, the we may possibly use them as biological assays. Through *their* greater sensitivity and perception, we may get a better report of what reality is like . . ." (emphasis in original). Indeed, that is precisely the function of the wise man or guru. Perhaps even more important, Maslow implicitly denied that a different type of creature than the human being is required to achieve these experiences. Though Nietzsche argued that only a new type of being, an Overman, can reach these heights, Maslow believed that human beings have the potential to do so, though only a few get that far in their emotional and intellectual development. Here, again, Maslow articulated what came to be a core value of the human potential movement. As his biographer observes, "[t]erms like *peak-experience* and *self-actualization* began to penetrate the popular vocabulary and help shape the zeitgeist of 1960s America. Before long, nearly every college student in the country was hearing such phrases, as legions of admirers promoted Maslow's approach" (emphases in original).

Even more than the hierarchy of needs and self-actualization, Maslow's concept of peak experiences was seized upon by popular culture, and often not in ways that he approved. In many ways Maslow was a quite conventional person despite his adventurous intellect. He was dubious about claims of easy routes to peak experiences through psychedelics. Though he was personally fond of LSD guru Timothy Leary and encouraged his unconventional approach, he doubted that drugs could be sufficient for self-actualization. "To have a peak-experience, you have to sweat," he told Leary. Toward the end of his career he expressed reservations about esoteric pursuits without any scientific basis that had become so popular in the 1960s, like astrology, tarot cards, the I-Ching, and Jewish mysticism. Like many old-fashioned liberals he saw America's war in Vietnam as a noble effort and was disheartened by what he regarded as the arrogance and willful ignorance of his Brandeis University students in the late 1960s. He was having medical problems and found the Boston winters increasingly difficult. At a sensitivity training workshop sponsored by NTL he met the cofounder of Saga, a food-services company based near Palo Alto. The wealthy businessman offered him a fellowship with no responsibilities. Somewhat to his surprise Maslow found that he was happier in the company of corporate leaders than in that of most of his academic colleagues. Retracing the path of the postwar American and British social psychologists, Maslow spent his last years working on enlightened, humanistic management with Saga's executives.

## GETTING ORGANIZED

The humanistic psychology and group therapy movements operated in parallel and sometimes intersecting universes. In 1953, J.L. founded an international organization of group therapists (mainly psychoanalysts and psychodramatists), who put their philosophical differences aside to pursue the group work they had in common. Like the humanistic psychologists, J.L. and at least some of his cofounders in the field of group psychotherapy saw themselves as representing a third way apart from psychoanalysis and behaviorism. J.L. in particular saw his approach as a social therapy, with a theory that was simultaneously psychological and sociological. For J.L. and many of the group therapists the human being can only be understood and treated in a social context, whereas the humanists were striving to develop a distinctive movement based on their ideas about individual human potential. Up to the early 1960s, like the group therapists, they were mostly unified by their opposition to Freud and behaviorism. According to one commentator, "Maslow numbered among this band [of humanists] Rankians, Adlerians, neo-Freudians, Gestalt psychologists, and Gestalt therapists, as well as such renegades as Herbert Marcuse, J.L. Moreno, Thomas Szasz, and Norman O. Brown."

To create a positive message of its own the bookshelf of humanistic psychology needed to grow. To this end, Maslow, Rogers, and others articulated core principles like a holistic approach to the human being and the importance of moral choice and responsibility. In 1956 Clark Moustakas published *The Self*, a collection of papers by Maslow, Carl Jung, Gordon Allport, Karen Horney, Jean-Paul Sartre, Erich Fromm, Otto Rank, and others. The same year Rollo May published *Existence*, a collection of papers that explained how European existentialism was being used in psychology and psychotherapy, especially Heidegger-inspired *Dasein-analysis*. In 1961 Alan Watts' *Psychotherapy East and West* argued for the integration of Eastern philosophy and Western psychotherapy. That year a professional Association for Humanistic Psychology was organized.

An invitational conference at Old Saybrook, Connecticut, and at nearby Wesleyan University in 1964 was a milestone for the leaders and supporters of what Maslow called the "third force" in psychology. Leading lights at the Old Saybrook meeting included Rogers, Maslow, Moustakas, existential psychologist Rollo May, and several of J.L.'s close associates, including Gordon Allport, Gardner Murphy, and Henry Murray. Some of the most important public intellectuals of the 1960s were there as well, like Columbia dean Jacques Barzun and biologist–environmentalist Rene Dubos. In his keynote address the first day of the conference, Murray expressed ambivalence about the nature and purpose of humanistic psychology. On one hand, the field would need to appeal to the "straitjacket" of conventional academic psychology in order to be recognized by the establishment; on the other hand, he wasn't at all sure that it could be rigorous enough to "appeal to the kind of all-A students that are nowadays selected for admission to our various graduate schools." Murray's hostility to the psychology establishment had only intensified since his 1952 letter to my mother. After the Old Saybrook conference, Murray effectively removed himself from the humanistic psychology movement, however, concluding that its premises were too vague to effect change in the world of psychology. At the time Murray was in a minority. Humanistic psychology, and especially its personal expression as the human potential movement, was about to enter its golden age. But there was a burr in its saddle, a flamboyant, irritating, charismatic, maddening, crude, colorful, divisive yet magnetic former psychoanalyst named Fritz Perls.

# FRITZ

Born in Berlin, Frederick S. "Fritz" Perls was just four years younger than J.L. He, too, was a German-speaking Jewish medical doctor who grew up amid turn of the century avant-garde culture, was drawn to theater as a youth, and studied under a famous neurologist, Kurt Goldstein, who also influenced Rogers and Maslow. Like Maslow Perls had a miserable childhood. His father physically abused his mother and verbally abused him, calling him "a piece of shit." He grew to hate the hypocrisy of his parents' middle-class Judaism, sought refuge in Zen Buddhism for a while, but finally rejected all religion. Humiliated by a prostitute when he was thirteen, he turned to Wilhelm Reich for psychoanalysis fearing the consequences of his compulsive masturbation. (Reich was a tragic figure who later advocated various radical ideas like a cosmic energy he called the "orgone" and whose writings were burned by the United States government while he languished in a federal penitentiary in the final throes of mental illness.) Although J.L. found his sense of cosmic moral responsibility through spirituality and mysticism, Perls found it through the rejection of all intellectualisms, concluding that there is no alternative to personal choice. Perls left Germany for South Africa where he started a psychoanalytic institute. He received a cold shoulder when he visited an aging Freud, a snub he never forgot, unlike J.L. who remembered his own confrontation with Freud as a personal triumph. If spontaneity and creativity were the themes that propelled J.L, humiliation and disgust seem to have been those that moved Perls. His wife Laura described him as "a mixture of a prophet and a bum."

Fritz and Laura moved to New York in 1947 where they got caught up in the flowering postwar bohemian culture and the excitement about psychological exploration that moved beyond classical Freudian analysis. "He went to Moreno's psychodramas in New York," writes journalist and encounter group leader Walter Truett Anderson, "and developed his own dramatic form of group therapy." Perls called it "Gestalt therapy," "an attempt to focus on a subject's conscious experience and construction of the here-and-now. ... Within this total field of social relations and perceptions, the self co-constructs both its own experienced reality 'out there' and its own running narrative-of-who-I-am 'in here.'" As Fritz had aspired to the theater when he was young, the idea of life as a performance came easily to him. He concluded that many of our problems can be traced to the fact that we are prisoners of the scripts that others write for us. His goal was to make people aware of these imposed scripts to make them write their own, to take responsibility for their own performance. (The similarity to J.L.'s early insights is too great to ignore.) Among the other experiences that shaped his development of Gestalt therapy were Zen meditation, which he practiced in Kyoto, and LSD before it was banned. In his autobiography he recorded peak experiences along the lines described by Maslow.

In his early sixties Perls left Laura and their New York institute and took up residence at Esalen, where he became famous for exercises like the "hot seat." As a consummate performer Fritz conducted his therapy in a group setting while working one-on-one with his Gestalt therapy subjects. "People would sit around and Perls would ask for volunteers to sit in the hot seat. He would then proceed to take the person apart by noticing and commenting on every defense mechanism, every body posture, every quiver of the voice or eyes. . . . A kind of one-person psychodrama would ensue— the more crying and volume, the better." These emotionally intense experiences were supposed to lead to self-discovery and growth, both core values in the human potential movement. Alan Watts, whose seminar on Eastern philosophy marked the de facto opening of the Esalen Institute, approved of Gestalt for breaking down dualism and brought it into his integration of Eastern religion with Western psychotherapy. For his part, Fritz regarded this kind of philosophizing as "mind fucking" and "elephant shit." Excretory references were common in Perls's discourse, including his nickname for his rival at Esalen, the popular young encounter group leader Will Schutz, whom he called "Bull Shits." But at least one can say that he applied the same framework to his approach to therapy. "I teach people to wipe their own ass." What can one say of a man who called his autobiography *In and Out of the Garbage Pail*? There was nonetheless something fascinating about Perls's grim, in-your-face world view. Fritz became a counter-cultural anti-hero. Sometime in the later 1960s posters of his "Gestalt Prayer" appeared in stores selling drug paraphernalia and New Age products:

I do my thing, and you do your thing.

I am not in this world to live up to your expectations

And you are not in this world to live up to mine.

You are you, and I am I,

And if by chance, we find each other, it's beautiful.

If not, it can't be helped.

With his unruly grey beard, nicotine-stained lips, jumpsuit, scatological language, and sexually aggressive behavior, Perls became a self-styled freaky psychiatrist who resembled the underground cartoon character Mr. Natural. "I am who I am, I fuck when I can. I'm Popeye the Sailor Man," was Fritz's other most famous line. His womanizing at Esalen was notorious. Sociologist Lewis Yablonsky recounted one incident in 1968 when he and Fritz were in the nude coed hot tub with an attractive young woman. As Fritz made his move the subject of his interest told him in unmistakable terms that his attentions were unwelcome and suggested a physically impossible alternative. Nonetheless, he was often an insightful therapist who could identify and attack a psychological block and provide relief. According to Jeffrey Kripal, Perls's behavior can partly be explained by his obsession with the blind obedience of so many to Nazism and his fears for its resurgence in late-1960s America. His outrageous behavior was a form of protest against intellectual and physical oppression. But it was also a manifestation of his personal sense of humiliation, his generalized disgust and disdain.

Besides separating himself from intellectual "elephant shit," Perls wanted to distinguish his Gestalt therapy from psychodrama. For example, he said that unlike psychodrama, in Gestalt therapy the subject plays all the roles of people in their lives rather than using others who don't know them, and that unlike psychodrama objects can be put in the empty chair, not only people. (In fact both of these techniques are often used in psychodrama.) The New Age psychiatrist John C. Lilly, famous for his LSD experiments and attempts to communicate with dolphins, described an encounter weekend with Fritz in which he took the hot seat to work on a "problem" in his professional life, that whenever he spoke to a group he expected them to react in certain ways, which he found an enormous waste of time and energy. Perls instructed him to talk to his audience about his feelings. "Why are you always there? Why do you bother me? Why do you sit there watching and listening? Why don't I get any responses from you?" and so on. Then Fritz told him to get in the chair of the audience. "You are a posturing fool," Lilly said in the audience chair. Finally Fritz said, "Okay, shift," at which point Lilly got back in the chair in which he was himself again, berated the audience, and smashed a barrel that represented the audience. "How do you feel?" Fritz asked him. "Great," said Lilly, who had had a cathartic experience. He then delivered a personal message to each member of the group (no word on the way the barrel felt). All these elements—taking the various roles, reversing roles, emotional catharsis, sharing with the group—were core concepts of psychodrama.

J.L. rarely spoke of Perls. My impression is that, at least at first, he didn't consider him a heavyweight worthy of a rivalry, unlike others with whom he had tangled over the years. But he was rankled by all the publicity Perls received in the later 1960s. The journalist and encounter group leader Walter Truett Anderson describes an incident often recounted by old-timers in the human potential movement: "Later, when Fritz and his mode of therapy became famous, Moreno often claimed that Gestalt was only a bastardized form of psychodrama. Once at a psychological convention in [1969], they appeared together on a panel. Moreno said to Fritz, 'I don't mind you stealing my stuff, but you should have stolen all of it.' Fritz replied, 'Ah, Jacob, Jacob, when will you just accept your greatness?'" It was a brilliant repost under the circumstances, sure to annoy J.L. first by calling him Jacob; second by adopting a superior role as J.L.'s "therapist"; and third by insightfully identifying J.L.'s insecurity about public recognition of his stature. To some the incident smacked somewhat embarrassingly of two old bull elephants having it out in the savannah. What J.L. and the overflow audience of a thousand did not know was that Fritz was already suffering the debilitating effects of pancreatic cancer; that and heart disease ended his life a year later.

## THE RIFT

Perls's contempt for intellectualizing and academic authority were on display during a Maslow-led seminar at Esalen in 1966. "This is just like school," Perls shouted during the first meeting while Maslow was answering a question. "Here's the teacher, and there is the pupil, giving the right answer." The next day Perls "dropped to the floor and began to make whining, infantlike sounds before the astonished gathering as he slowly wrapped himself around Maslow's knees." "This begins to look like sickness," Maslow said. After struggling through the seminar, a disturbed Maslow berated the Esalen staff for tolerating this kind of anti-intellectual behavior and for enabling a disdain for science. "We've got brains . . . And that's part of spontaneity," he told them, expressing doubts that he could recommend Esalen to others if their permissive attitude persisted. The incident not only permanently put Maslow off Perls, but also created a breach among those who wanted to apply humanistic psychology to human potential. From the beginning Esalen's leaders Murphy and Price had been at best ambivalent about Perls, "having been more impressed with his rudeness than his skill" according to a later Esalen catalog, but he was allowed to remain.

The core issue about encounter for the human potential movement was bigger than Perls. Although the groups were only a small part of Esalen's offerings, they became both an outsized source of publicity and a problem for the Institute's reputation. Perls had not only alienated Maslow, but the conflict between him and encounter group leader Will Schutz was no secret; worse still were the bizarre and sometimes dangerous practices within the groups. One experiment called "Pandora's Box" involved women exposing their genitals in order to work through their fears about them. Then the group acted out the myth of Pandora, supposedly in order to transcend misogyny. Although participants indeed reported moments of transcendence, Esalen cofounder Dick Price summarized Schutz's method as "beat 'em up, fuck 'em at the first opportunity."

Meanwhile, enthusiasm for Esalen ran high in Hollywood. In an event that proved to be historic and counterproductive, actress Jennifer Jones (who became famous when she starred in the film version of Franz Werfel's *Song of Bernadette*), hosted a party for Esalen regulars with guests that included Rock Hudson, Glenn Ford, Eddie Albert, Shirley MacLaine, Dennis Hopper, and James Coburn. After dinner Carl Rogers ran an encounter group, then Perls held his own Gestalt session near the pool with Natalie Wood in the hot seat. Matters soon got out of hand. "You're nothing but a little spoiled brat who always wants to get her own way," Perls snarled at Wood. As former *Life* magazine editor George Leonard remembered it, Wood "gasped and her mouth fell open. A moment later Fritz had her on his knee, spanking her. It was a brief episode, hard for the senses to register or credit. Natalie flounced away, and her friend Roddy McDowell offered to fight Fritz. Fritz ignored this offer. About two minutes later, Natalie marched out of the party with no goodbyes, her nose angled sharply upward." A few minutes later Tuesday Weld was in the hot seat, "with approximately the same results, minus the spanking. She too stormed out, her long blond hair streaming." Both of the offended stars later satirized the human potential movement in films, Wood in *Bob & Carol & Ted & Alice* and Weld in *Serial*.

Esalen was not the only setting for conflicted feelings about encounter groups within the human potential movement. *Love and Will* author Rollo May was among the leaders who were dismayed by the way that humanistic psychology was being taken as a justification for the human potential movement's anti-intellectual tendencies. I remember standing about ten feet away from an obviously disgruntled May one evening near the elevators in Miami's Fountainbleu Hotel in 1970 during a psychology convention. May looked distracted as his second wife Ingrid, a tall German woman, wrapped her arms around him while she fended off one of his camp followers. "Now," she said, "would you mind if I had some time alone with my husband?" At the time I thought that May was simply tired from all the hugging, laughing, weeping, and nonstop trolling for peak experiences at these meetings. Just as likely he was upset about the hang-loose proceedings, despite his stardom among the attendees. In a 1971 profile, the *New York Times Magazine* said that "May seldom participates in encounter sessions, and at the Miami Beach convention, when he was caught in a group that celebrated its ecstasy by jumping up and down, he simply jumped his way to the door and out of the room. . . . Yet he does not deride all encounter therapy, recognizing that there is a vital area of communication that is below the level of words. 'But I would like to deny the importance of touch when it's isolated at the expense of the brain, or concepts or thinking,' he adds." May had the same reservations as Maslow did about the anti-intellectual tendencies of the human potential movement.

J.L., too, was conflicted. Should he continue to fight for what he believed to be his unsatisfied recognition or was it best to keep his head down amid the decidedly mixed image of encounter, especially as the Sixties went on? In 1969 he again felt compelled to retrace for the record "The Viennese Origins of the Encounter Movement," and complained that too many of the practitioners were poorly trained and incompetent. "There are thousands of little groups today, spread over the American continent, especially in the U.S.A., practicing what is called 'encounter groups,' frequently not conducted by professionally trained leaders, but rather by laymen or 'hippiephrenic' individuals." (Here J.L. was coining a term for a new type of obsession, with the hippie counterculture that he suspected rivals like Perls were only too happy to join in a vain effort to recapture their youth.) The results were too often damaging to group members. Acknowledging that his psychodrama centers have also been criticized "for over-exposing their trainees by action methods and stimulating them to violence," J.L. created a graphic that contrasted the Moreno Institute with the encounter groups; not surprisingly, the encounter groups didn't come off well.

## GAMES PEOPLE PLAY

One problem with humanistic psychology's premises was identified by Henry Murray: the vagueness of its premises. How, for example, could two people with such different temperaments and philosophies as Abe Maslow and Fritz Perls be part of the same movement? Transactional analysis (TA) was an alternative that did develop a tight theory and that roughly straddled group psychotherapy and humanistic psychology. TA was rocketing to fame just at the time of the Old Saybrook conference. The founder of TA, psychiatrist Eric Berne, published a best seller in 1964 called *Games People Play*. French-Canadian by birth, Berne was yet another psychoanalyst with a Jewish background who broke from the Freudian gospel. He became a group therapist after his World War II service, noticing that in dealing with one another people engaged in repeated seemingly scripted behaviors or "transactions" with one another, which he called "games." These behavior patterns correspond to certain states of mind or "ego states." The three ego states are Parent, Adult, and Child. At different times people shift from one state to another, though we all have them in us. As Berne explains, "This is your Parent" means that "You are now in the same state of mind as one of your parents (or a parental substitute) used to be, and you are responding as he would, with the same posture, gestures, vocabulary, feelings, etc." "This is your Adult" means that "You have just made an autonomous, objective appraisal of the situation and are stating these thought-processes, or the problems you perceive, or the conclusions you have come to, in a non-prejudicial manner." "This is your Child" means "The manner and intent of your reaction is the same as it would have been when you were a very little boy or girl." An example of an appropriate Adult–Adult transaction of a very simple kind is when a surgeon holds out her hand during a procedure and the nurse hands the surgeon a scalpel. Another is when a fevered child asks for water and a parent gives it to him. Inappropriate transactions involve people operating in inappropriate ego states with one another, and transactions that begin as appropriate often cross over.

Berne's view of human life and people's relationships with one another is pretty grim. The games we play with each other are often not fun, but in the real world they are all but inevitable. Games involve a series of moves or "gimmicks" aimed at achieving a "payoff" or being "stroked." To Berne there is an economy to human relationships; they are literally transactions. "Because there is so little opportunity for intimacy in daily life. . .the bulk of the time in serious social life is taken up with playing games. Hence games are both necessary and desirable, and the only problem at issue is whether the games played by an individual offer the best yield for him." He calls the most common game between spouses "If It Weren't For You" or IWFY, in which one partner accuses the other of keeping him from being or doing something that in fact he didn't want to be or do (which is why his Child had chosen her), but in the process their IWFY arguments jeopardize their relationship. This is a "two-handed" game between a restricted partner and a domineering one that takes place on at least a couple of levels, but there are also many-handed games that take place on multiple levels and require fairly complicated analysis to make sense of what's going on. Among the other games are "I'm Only Trying to Help You" or ITHY, "Why Don't You—Yes But" or YDYB (which is the inverse of ITHY), "You Got Me Into This" or UGMIT, "Why Does This Always Happen To Me" or WAHM, and (my personal favorite), "You're Uncommonly Perceptive" or YUP.

Transactional analysis gave people the feeling that they could achieve insight into their own and others' behavior by paying attention to Berne's games. *Games People Play* had the distinction of inspiring a chart-topping hit of the same name by country singer Joe South. The song was an angry diatribe about inauthenticity and the refusal to take responsibility for one's actions, games that occupy most of human life as we count off the hours toward death. Transactional analysis also produced another best-selling book. In 1970, psychiatrist Thomas Harris's *I'm OK–You're OK* was written in a less technical style than Berne's and delivered a more positive message about the possibilities for change through therapy based on TA principles, while nearly all of Berne's book was about destructive games. Harris emphasized a four-cell system of general feelings about life that reflects attitudes about oneself and toward others:

- *I'm OK and you're OK.* This is the healthiest position.
- *I'm OK and you're not OK.* I feel good about myself but I am critical of others.
- *I'm not OK and you're OK.* I am self-critical and you are stronger and better off, making me ripe for abuse.
- *I'm not OK and you're not OK.* I'm in a bad way and so is the world; this is the least hopeful position.

From these simple principles Harris developed his view that the point of psychotherapy is the freedom to change. "This freedom grows from knowing the truth about what is in the Parent and what is in the Child and how this data feeds into present-day transactions."

Transactional analysis swims in the same waters as psychoanalysis and humanistic psychology. Berne built his theory on top of his experience with psychoanalysis, but TA's list of paradigmatic games made it much more accessible to the layperson. The Child, Adult, and Parent ego states are similar to Freud's id, ego, and superego. As per Freud, according to TA unconscious motivations drive the impulse to engage in transactions. The immediate appeal of TA owed much to its offering a menu of games that it seemed everyone could apply to their own relationships. Unlike the artful nuances of psychoanalytic theory and the open-ended nature of psycho-analyis, after reading one of these books everyone could analyze at least a simple transaction. Berne refers to "the attainment of autonomy" as getting beyond games, not nearly as grand a goal as Maslow's self-actualized person. but much more within reach. The last page of Berne's *Games People Play* is an apologetic summation of "[t]he somber picture presented" in the main parts of the book, "in which human life is mainly a process of filling in time until the arrival of death, or Santa Claus, with very little choice, if any, of what kind of business one is going to transact during the long wait, is a commonplace but not the final answer." For "certain fortunate people" classifications of behavior can be transcended by awareness; the programming of the past can be overcome by spontaneity; and intimacy can be more rewarding than games.

Though J.L. and psychodrama are not mentioned in either Berne's or Harris's books, the fingerprints of his influence are easy to make out. A core idea of the games themselves is that they are performances, akin to the dramaturgical model in sociology in which people are seen as actors on stage. Each transaction involves underlying scripts with certain key phrases that the players utter without realizing it until they are pointed out in therapy. Was it merely coincidental that Berne, Perls, and so many others adopted J.L.'s ideas about role-playing and spontaneity in the 1950s and 1960s? J.L. had been asserting since at least 1921 that people need to learn how to play roles they create rather than those created by others, but he never reduced an understanding of human relations to formulaic scripts. One explanation is that these theorists were responding to the emotionally stifling "phoniness" of the 1950s, as illustrated by J.D. Salinger's iconic young character in *Catcher in the Rye*. Being phony meant working from a script instead of disclosing oneself and engaging in an authentic relationship.

The ego states Parent, Adult, and Child are said not to be roles. Nonetheless, the diagrams of the ways they interact in particular games are strikingly similar to J.L.'s sociograms. Both seek to chart the externalization of a person's inner life, to make the invisible visible. And in *I'm OK–You're OK* Harris argues that groups are far superior to individual therapy for the use of TA. Berne was a handsome and charming man who was a familiar figure at meetings on group therapy and psychodrama. During the 1940s and 1950s, he saw many of J.L.'s psychodrama demonstrations. In 1970, not long before he died, Berne reviewed a book by Perls in which he said that both of them suffered from "the Moreno problem: the fact that nearly all 'active' techniques were first tried out by Moreno in psychodrama, so that it is difficult to come up with an original idea in this regard."

J.L. often felt insufficiently recognized, feelings of exclusion that became more acute as the human potential movement thrived and his energies waned. But though his visibility was diminished by the glare of the new pop therapies, in the years before J.L.'s death there were a number of tributes from peers like Berne. In 1971, Will Schutz said that "virtually all of the methods that I had proudly compiled or invented [Moreno] had more or less anticipated, in some cases forty years earlier. . . ." In his scholarly study of sensitivity training in 1972, Duke's Kurt Back wrote that "psychodrama, sociometry, the cult of spontaneity, the notion of encounter, the term 'here and now,' and the acceptance of psychotic states as valid states of the individual—all seem to be derived from Moreno's work." Following a 1968 *Life* magazine article about Esalen by Jane Howard, Abraham Maslow wrote a carefully worded letter to the editor. "Jane Howard's article on Esalen and the developments in education was excellent. I would like to add one 'credit-where-credit is due' footnote. Many of the techniques [described in the article] were originally invented by Dr. Jacob Moreno, who is still functioning vigorously and probably still inventing new techniques and ideas." J.L. expressed his gratitude in a letter to Maslow. "I take it as a testimonial of our old friendship and mutual respect," he wrote, and expressed the hope that they would see each other at a meeting the following month. Weakened by illness, Maslow responded by returning J.L.'s letter, having circled the words friendship and respect and written "Yes." Then, in a scrawl next to J.L.'s mention of the meeting, he added, "Sorry won't be there. Cardiologist forbids. Heart attack some months ago. Convalescing nicely. Abe."

Maslow never fully recovered. He died suddenly two years later at the age of sixty-two.

## EUPSYCHIA

By the late 1960s, encounter groups had become closely identified with the opportunity for personal growth despite the growing doubts among some of the leading humanistic psychologists—and the directors of the centers where the groups were conducted, about how encounter was playing out in practice. Once the emotional power of group dynamics was let loose in the human potential movement's encounter groups, the humanistic psychologists found themselves in an awkward position. The humanistic theorists like Maslow, Rogers, and May were focused on individual growth, as was the human potential movement. Maslow called his utopian vision "eupsychia," a desert island community consisting of "one thousand self-actualizing people and their families." But how would these self-actualizing people and their families get along? As J.L. pointed out years before, and as Lewin understood, the whole of human groups is greater than their parts. Even the psychologically healthiest people have disagreements and in various ways are not ideally suited for one another. Within the framework of the human potential movement, the quest for personal growth was both facilitated by group encounter and threatened by it. Although they strove to be practical, emphasizing individual striving for fulfillment rather than perfection, in the end the early humanistic psychologists were sociologically naïve. The "Third Force" theorists lacked an orientation to what J.L. called sociometrics and what Lewin called group dynamics. Encounter groups forced this problem home, as they presented all the complexities that groups can produce.

## CHAPTER NINE

# THE GREAT CROSSOVER

The Moreno Institute in Manhattan, 1960s.

*Theatre and therapy are closely interwoven. But also here there are many steps. There will be a theatre which is purely therapeutic, there will be a theatre which is free from therapeutic objectives and then there will be also many intermediary forms.*

J.L. Moreno, 1973

T HE YEARS 1960 TO 1975 were the era of the "Great Crossover." Just as the foundations for the human potential movement and "therapy for normal people"—people J.L. called "normotics"—were being laid by NTL and the humanistic psychologists in the 1950s, the number of patients in huge mental hospitals was reaching its peak. Yet smaller institutions were cropping up: personal growth centers for adventurous elites, treatment centers for desperate drug addicts, and self-organized small groups for political liberation. As mental patients were being released into the community, experimental theatre companies portrayed what they considered the madness of American society, some inviting audiences to break down emotional and physical barriers with the actors. And there were still other efforts to use theatre to energize oppressed groups and resolve racial conflicts. From many directions theatre as therapy was brought out of closed institutions and into public life.

## ASYLUMS

Like countless Baby Boomer college students, I read University of Pennsylvania sociology professor Erving Goffman's *Asylums* in an introductory sociology class. The beginning of the end of vast mental hospitals, a process known as deinstitutionalization, can be linked to Goffman's book. From 1954 to 1957 he observed one of the world's most famous psychiatric institutions, St. Elizabeths in Washington, DC, which claimed among its famous patients the poet Ezra Pound. Today, St. E's (thinly disguised as "Central Hospital" in Goffman's book), is a shadow of its former self, far smaller in size and population from its heyday in the 1950s and 1960s, its huge historic campus on the banks of the Potomac River threatened by neglect. Now property of the District of Columbia rather than the federal government, it remains the home of John Hinckley, Jr., the attempted assassin of President Ronald Reagan. Goffman's was not only one of the most influential books in the history of sociology, but one of the few books in any academic field to embody and fuel a turnabout in the treatment of millions of people. He claimed that being in "total institutions" inevitably undermines selfhood and adapts people to an artificial world, after which they can barely function anywhere else, no matter how progressive or humane the asylum. Patients feel abandoned by society and mistrustful of everyone in charge of their incarceration. The cycle of dependence, frustration, and depersonalization cannot be broken.

The description of St. E's had personal significance for me, as I'd been a visitor there several times, first when I was twelve years old. That was 1964 during the annual meetings of the American Sociological Association in Washington, DC, when J.L. brought a large group of his colleagues to the hospital for a demonstration of psychodrama. J.L.'s methods had been adopted by many mental hospitals, especially in the

Veterans Affairs system and at the famous Menninger Clinic in Kansas (relocated to Houston, Texas in 2003). But J.L. had especially deep connections to the hospital that Goffman portrayed. The powerful psychiatrist who befriended J.L. in the early 1930s, William Alanson White, spent most of his career as superintendent of St. Elizabeths. His successor, Winifred Overholser, was also well disposed toward J.L. and built the country's second psychodrama theater on the grounds in 1941. For forty years, thousands of patients had therapy and dozens of therapists were trained in role-playing and group therapy at St. E.'s. A 1956 *Harper's* magazine article, published while Goffman was doing his research, said that St. Elizabeths was experiencing "great success with psychodrama." Goffman witnessed a number of psychodrama sessions, which he called an example of the "modern treatment" available at large mental hospitals of the day. In a later book, *The Presentation of Self in Everyday Life* (1959), Goffman became famous for arguing that human beings are role players, that there is no such thing as the self, only the roles we play in the drama of life. In that sense, everyone in total institutions learned to play certain roles. The mental patients learned how to be mental patients, the staff learned how to be staff. One sociologist argues that Goffman got this idea from his experience at St. Elizabeths. The last time I was at the hospital, in the mid-1970s, it was already well on the way to being emptied of its patients and the campus on the bluffs overlooking the Potomac River was showing signs of deferred maintenance.

Until the closing of the asylums tens of thousands of people thought to have intractable mental problems spent many years apart from the outside world, some from adolescence to death. But new developments challenged this huge system of incarceration. There were novel drugs that could control the more obvious symptoms of psychotic delusions, especially those associated with schizophrenia. Professionals began to think that it would be better for everyone if most mentally ill people could be taken care of outside of massive, impersonal institutions, in smaller community-based mental health centers. There were also legal challenges to long-term incarceration as a violation of human rights. And brilliant, innovative, and controversial psychiatrists like Thomas Szasz and R.D. Laing helped establish an "anti-psychiatry" movement, which argued that psychiatric treatment can often do more harm than good and even questioned the very idea of mental illness. Others argued that everyone needed to be in treatment, not just people who said they heard voices. Ironically, the end of the asylum was accompanied by the Great Crossover, an explosion of a culture of therapy.

Popular culture also primed the American public to welcome a new policy for the mentally ill. In fact, the movies tracked—and surely influenced—changing attitudes about insane asylums. In 1948, *The Snake Pit*, starring Olivia de Havilland, depicted horrific conditions in a fictional mental hospital. In 1968, the French film *King of Hearts* portrayed mental patients as sweet, simple people who show no evidence of needing to be in an asylum once they are given the opportunity to take over an abandoned town during the chaos of World War I. In 1975 the far more hard-edged *One Flew Over the Cuckoo's Nest*, with Jack Nicholson as the lead, coincided almost perfectly with the emptying out of mental hospitals on a vast scale, not only in the United States, but also in Europe. Its political subtext, embodied in the Nurse Ratched's puritanical, fascist dictatorship, fit well with the anti-establishment temper of the times in post-Vietnam, post-Watergate America.

No doubt the back wards of vast institutions like St. Elizabeths had qualities of the snake pits of popular imagination. The efforts of reformers, including J.L., could not overcome the sheer volume of illness or the lack of medical options to treat it. Goffman's book provided a comprehensive, sophisticated rationale for integrating all but the most seriously mentally ill persons into the community. It seemed that no amount of psychodrama, group therapies, creative arts therapies, or any other innovation within the asylum could compensate for the dehumanization the institutions caused, in sharp contrast to the self-actualization advocated at the time by Maslow and other humanistic psychologists. There is no doubt that many patients needlessly languished in asylums. But the new medications had serious side effects. Federal funding for community mental health centers to aid in the transition and continuing care of the patients has been spotty at best, leading to a nationwide problem of homeless mentally ill people who in some cases might have been better off in the old hospitals. Although the failures of deinstitutionalization have been widely acknowledged in the psychiatric community, recently scholars have revisited Goffman's description of conditions at St. Elizabeths as well. Michael E. Staub points out that Goffman's view was out of step with other visitors to the hospital in the

1950s, which *Harper's* magazine called a "pacesetter." Historian and psychiatrist Matthew Gambino also questions Goffman's diagnosis; though conditions were certainly harsh in some wards, the sociologist failed to fully appreciate the progressive features of St. E's, like its patients' self-governance program that emerged from group therapy. "Psychodrama, art therapy, and dance therapy created an environment that valued individual self-expression."

## THERAPEUTIC COMMUNITIES

Therapeutic communities, fondly known as "TCs", emerged as another model for greater autonomy for people with emotional problems, especially if they involved substance abuse. Rather than large institutions they are residential or day programs with a relatively small number of participants. Therapeutic communities got their start in England after World War II, but by emphasizing group therapy in a setting where patients and therapists lived together, they resembled J.L.'s Beacon Hill Sanitarium. In a democratic spirit, at Beacon Hill and in the TCs the usual hierarchy of authority between patient and therapist was broken down. Therapeutic communities were promoted by innovative British psychiatrists like Maxwell Jones, R.D. Laing, and J.L.'s friend Johsua Bierer. In the far more free-wheeling United States, the pioneering TC was founded in 1958 by a former alcoholic named Chuck Dederich for drug addicts. Its name was Synanon (supposedly a recovering alcoholic's mash up of "seminar" and "symposium"), and it became the most colorful and controversial—and for a time the wealthiest—therapeutic community in history.

Partly inspired by Alcoholics Anonymous, but with his own vision of a rehabilitation program for ex-drug addicts, Dederich founded Synanon with $33 from an unemployment check. Within a few years he had turned the organization into a multimillion dollar business that operated out of the Casa del Mar, an historic building on the beach in Santa Monica that is now a posh hotel. The principal method at Synanon was called "the game," a combination of group therapy and encounter group. According to an older ex-addict at Synanon named Charlie Hamer, interviewed by sociologist Lewis Yablonsky, "People here go to these sessions three evenings a week. In the game, people can dump their emotional garbage, have their self-deceptions exposed, and learn about themselves. It's kind of [a] pressure-cooker group for working out your problems." Yablonsky frequently visited Synanon and wrote the first book about the program, *The Tunnel Back*, in 1965. Years later Yablonsky remembered his introduction to the game by Hamer, who "showed me one of the rooms set up for the groups," Yablonsky wrote. "Chairs were placed in a circle, so that everyone faced everyone else. The room began to fill up with the assigned people. Soon loud curses and shouts were coming from the various rooms. I was somewhat disturbed by the violent voice pitch. I knew, from past institutional experience, that the type of shouting I was hearing was often a prelude to, or accompanied by, physical violence." Synanon claimed that physical assault and using drugs or alcohol were forbidden. "One thing we encourage in our groups is that people speak out their true feelings," Yablonsky was told. "What you are hearing is a lot of angry people speaking their truth."

The extreme emotional displays that were common at Synanon, especially in the early years, were not typical of the therapeutic community movement, especially in England. The atmosphere Yablonsky described in Santa Monica was more a reflection of the hothouse environment of the early 1960s in certain southern California precincts and of Dederich's personality than of the TC idea. But intense group sessions have always been a key part of TCs, including methods from psychodrama. Yablonsky, who helped to incorporate psychodrama into many TCs in America and Europe, wrote that "many TC directors have told me how the psychodrama method often emerges spontaneously in an encounter-group session. One typical example involved a young woman on a marathon [an innovation that did not come from psychodrama]. When her ego defenses were low on the third day of the group meetings, she began talking about her unresolved hostility toward her father, who had sexually abused her. At a certain point in her monologue to the group on her painful and hostile feelings toward her father, she said, 'It's weird but Dominic here (another addict) really reminds me of my father.'" Dominic then played the role of her father in a drama that culminated with the woman "without too much encouragement, viciously raining down blows on the pillow. . . ." The session ended with the other women sharing their experiences of sexual abuse.

Yablonsky told me that Synanon's controversial founder was one of J.L.'s admirers. At a conference in Los Angeles in the late 1960s J.L. walked into a hotel coffee shop looking every bit his eccentric self—dark suit, bow tie, and significant girth of waist in his later seventies. Yablonsky and Dederich were sitting in a booth with a notorious ex-addict biker. "Look at that crazy old guy," the fellow said. Dederich cut him off. "If it weren't for that 'crazy old guy' you wouldn't be here." But Synanon was in for a bad end. Dederich ran into just about every imaginable ethical and legal problem, involving allegations of illegal prescriptions, zoning violations, violence, forced vasectomies and abortions, and child abuse. In 1974, he declared the organization a tax-exempt church, sealing its reputation as a cult. Nonetheless, the Synanon model of group encounter has influenced the hundreds of TCs all over the world that do a great deal of good for people with a history of substance abuse, including a German offshoot of Synanon that bears its name.

## Open Sessions

Many of the large state mental hospitals tried to adopt J.L.'s ideas in watered-down form, but he had little confidence in the care they provided. For several years he had just one patient, Joe, the man with schizophrenia. Fearing Joe would be abused if transferred to a public mental hospital, J.L. held onto his sanitarium license until 1968, when the fees and insurance cost became unmanageable. Yet ever since his work at the girls' reform school in the 1930s, his professional prestige and his stature among the hospitals' powerful leaders in the psychiatric community were tied up with his reputation as an institutional reformer. As those institutions seemed less amenable to reform, he turned his attention more and more toward the mental health problems of society as a whole. J.L. was well-disposed toward the TC model, but he still wanted to find ways to integrate role-playing-based therapy into the lives of people who didn't require such intensive experiences. He never wavered in his conviction that individual therapy alone could not resolve emotional problems because society is composed of groups. And group experiences were key parts of the Great Crossover.

Until the 1960s, there were only a few places other than mental hospitals or other residential settings where people could experience something like group therapy, and even then human relations groups were generally not open to the general public. But J.L. continued to believe that the therapeutic theater should be open to all, just as it was in Vienna and in his Impromptu Theatre. From the late 1940s through the early 1970s, six nights a week, anyone could go Manhattan's Moreno Institute (first near Grand Central Station and then on the Upper West Side), and participate in a psychodrama session for about the price of a movie ticket. The public sessions followed the usual structure of a psychodrama as he conceived it, beginning with a "warm-up" (often a short lecture by J.L. or some group exercise like the empty chair). A volunteer from the audience would agree to enact his or her psychodrama, such as a conflict with a boss or a parent. Someone else would be chosen to play the role of that person and various scenes were enacted, with the aim of exploring ways to resolve the conflict. If the protagonist had trouble seeing options, members of the audience might take her role and model ways to approach the problem. If very emotional content got stirred up and the protagonist had a hard time expressing herself, another person might "double" for her and try out various lines to see if the protagonist thought they were helpful or revealing, such as "Mr. Smith, I'm very angry that you treat everyone in the office like an idiot and it makes me so anxious that I keep making mistakes." Or "Dad, I can't be the child you've always wanted me to be. I've got to be my own person." Though free to reject the double's statement, often the protagonist would nod and say, that's how I feel, I just couldn't say it. After about two hours the session would end with members of the audience sharing their own experience with a difficult boss or parent, but always being warned not to analyze the protagonist's behavior. It was not uncommon for the person whom the protagonist had chosen to play an important role in the psychodrama to report that he had had a very similar experience. J.L. cited these as cases of tele, where we seem to sense an emotional connection to another even though we often can't explain why.

These public psychodrama sessions were a fixture of Manhattan life from the late 1940s to the early 1970s. Groups ranged from ten or twelve to over a hundred, even two hundred, people. Not once was there any problem finding a volunteer to enact her or his psychodrama. Often, several volunteers briefly described their issue and the audience was asked to vote for the psychodrama they wanted to see, leaving the runners-up disappointed, but determined to try again another night. For some, this was an opportunity for cheap therapy or for exhibitionism, cases that had to be sensitively but firmly handled. Weeping was common, especially when the psychodrama involved an adult's "unfinished business" with a deceased parent or the loss of a child. But there was also a lot of laughter. With little urging, people were willing to disclose and share their conflicts and troubles. A group that began as dozens of strangers felt an emotional closeness after witnessing a powerful enactment, even though only a couple of hours had passed. Many new friendships ensued, sometimes love affairs. By the early 1960s, J.L.'s public psychodramas were a hip, offbeat way for city people and sub-urbanites to spend the evening, including even first dates. Professors like Abe Maslow brought their classes from local colleges, suburban couples showed up by the dozens, and actors and other performers observed as discreetly as they could, among them Alan Alda, Woody Allen, and Dustin Hoffman. A journeyman named Walter Klavun, who was in the original cast of the musical comedy *How to Succeed in Business without Really Trying* and frequently played the judge on the courtroom drama *Perry Mason*, became a regular director of the public psychodramas.

As popular as these open psychodrama sessions were with their select and experientially adventurous audience, they were doomed by changing times. Even if my mother hadn't decided to sell the small building that housed the Moreno Institute in 1973 due to J.L.'s failing health and the burdens of running the business, an increasingly litigious society might have all but forced the outcome. J.L. was well aware that the group setting created special challenges for the traditional medical ethics of confidentiality. In 1955 he proposed a "group oath" to supplement the Hippocratic Oath, a remarkably far-seeing concept at a time well before modern widespread concerns about medical ethics. But at some point, a vindictive participant whose emotional life had been the subject of a psychodrama in front of dozens of strangers or colleagues would have found an enterprising attorney. Even a case without merit would have been a magnet for publicity. Paradoxically, in the 1980s exploitive displays of private lives and violent outbursts became daytime television fodder, and hardly for therapeutic purposes. But unlike J.L., the powerful broadcasters and producers could protect themselves by "lawyering up." His determination to bring a healing catharsis to the world originated in a different time and could not account for the changed distribution of money, power, and access to the media of late twentieth-century America. Much later a new communications medium would change the playing field. It is called the Internet, and though it equalizes access to worldwide communications it also jeopardizes privacy in a way that dwarfs the open psychodrama sessions that were a staple of J.L.'s efforts to broadcast his therapy for all.

## SOCIODRAMA REDUX

Back in 1921, in Vienna's Theater of Comedies, J.L. wanted to embody and alleviate social crises through enactment. At that time his first sociodrama was motivated by the crisis in Austria stemming from the disintegration of Habsburg rule. Though the effort was widely judged a failure, especially by theater critics, J.L. was as usual undeterred. Exactly forty years later he invited those involved in the trial in Jerusalem of Nazi war criminal Adolph Eichmann to join him in at his institute in New York. Arguing that a legal resolution of the case was not enough, that a sociodrama was required to address the collective trauma of the Holocaust, he suggested that

> Eichmann be taken out of his cage [the defendant was caged in the courtroom] and given the full range of the courtroom to act out crucial episodes of his life, carefully selected and known to be true . . . his early childhood, his meetings with Hitler, Heidrich, Himmler his superiors and subordinates . . . his dreams, his delusions, his hallucinations, his delusions of grandeur, his fears and panics, and his complete abandonment of any feeling, episodes after the Nazi war was lost and he tried to escape. . . . He should be instructed by the director to reverse roles with every Jew he has put into the gas chamber and should be made to relive the anxiety and panic of such a victim, he should be made to reverse roles with every Jew hiding from his men and being caught . . . he should be made to play the parts of children and young people whom he starved and sent to the deathcamps, he should be put in coffins, playing the part of corpses, he should be buried. . . .

Moreover, J.L. wrote, "all mass media should be used to make a mass coexperience possible." The point was to bring to light the universal moral catastrophe of the Holocaust, for all of humanity to begin to heal and to learn from it using psychodramatic techniques. Predictably, Israel's attorney general saw the whole idea as a circus. "I wish to dissociate myself unequivocally from your suggestions," he wrote J.L. "What we are conducting in Jerusalem is not a psychodrama nor a sociodrama. It is a case against an accused under due process of law and will not be turned into anything else." Undaunted, J.L. followed up by sending the Israeli a copy of his group therapy journal and his monograph on his recent trip to the Soviet Union, as well as a citation to one of his famous cases: psychodrama therapy with a delusional New York City butcher who believed he was Adolf Hitler. "I am referring to these publications so as to acquaint you with my point of view," J.L. wrote.

Several years later, after the assassination of President Kennedy and the murder of his assassin Lee Harvey Oswald in front of a national television audience, J.L. again proposed that psychodrama be employed to provide an opportunity for a society-wide catharsis. He argued that the death of Oswald at the hands of Jack Ruby required more than a legal resolution but a mass experience of group psychotherapy. Forty years after his triumph at the American Psychiatric Association (A.P.A.) meetings where he defended Lincoln and introduced sociometry, J.L. opened the 1964 psychiatric conference in Los Angeles with a sociodramatic trial of Ruby. As in the proposed psychodrama of Eichmann, legal authorities refused J.L.'s request to release Ruby to participate in the event. Ruby's lawyer accepted the invitation, but didn't show. Nonetheless, the session attracted hundreds and drew the attention of national media. *Time* magazine described it as "a Kafka-style reconstruction of the personalities and possible motives. . . ." Though the sociodrama was not the collective healing that J.L. desired, "at the play's end, the entire audience of 400 seemed to feel better—as if the doctors of the mind had need to get something off their minds." The next day "they turned to the main business of the A.P.A." It was the only major press notice of the psychiatry meetings that year.

## GUERILLAS

J.L.'s attempts to stage these mass psychodramas could be seen as the lifelong obsession of a naïf, the self-promotions of a megalomaniac, or the insights of a visionary. Whatever the verdict, his lifelong efforts to use theater as a public social therapy was a the predecessor of 1960s "happenings," a vaguely defined form of performance art conceived and named by artist Allan Karprow in 1958. Happenings both participated in and became a vehicle for the Great Crossover. They were the art world's contribution to efforts at social change and personal growth. Though J.L. resisted the association, like psychodramas happenings eschew the standard narrative arc of formal drama and aim to break down the barrier between the performers and the audience. Often partially scripted happenings may include readings and exhibits of plastic art. They are meant to provoke audience reaction and improvisation. Modern prank fads, like flash mobs organized through social media, are eventful and entertaining, but they lack the intentionally disruptive artistry of happenings and the goal of a therapeutic effect that happenings sometimes share with sociodrama. But to J.L. these amorphous events lacked the organizational form that psychodrama gives to human relations.

Augusto Boal's Theatre of the Oppressed (TO) is sometimes seen as a version of the happening. When I met the great Brazilian director at a psychodrama conference in the 1980s, he struck me as someone who rivaled J.L. in sheer magisterial presence. Like J.L.'s sociodrama, the mission of the TO is to use theater as a medium for bringing citizens into dialogue about social issues, especially concerning political oppression. Boal started to work in experimental theater in Sao Paulo in the late 1950s after becoming acquainted with the Actor's Studio as a student in New York. He founded his famous Theatre of the Oppressed after returning to Brazil from exile in 1986 when the military dictatorship fell. Though Boal and J.L. never met, Boal recalled participating in psychodrama "as a patient, not a technician," and he was a student of J.L.'s writings, even once describing his work as "psycho-theatre." One of his techniques, called "the cop in the head," addresses internalized oppression by embodying its sources on the theater stage, a maneuver J.L. would have appreciated. But Boal rightly insisted on his own originality, pointing out that his concept of the theater as a setting for social protest is decidedly more political than J.L.'s emphasis on theater as therapy.

American experimental theater was also often political. President Roosevelt's New Deal theater project was shut down partly because it raised concerns about its left-wing orientation, even as it provided jobs to its participants and some emotional relief to its Depression-era audiences. As a war raged in Southeast Asia, guerilla theater performances by antiwar groups were staged in places like the US Capitol, acting out violent episodes between American soldiers and Vietnamese civilians. Like J.L.'s religion of the encounter in Vienna, some theater groups also implemented direct social action. The Diggers were an improv group based in San Francisco that combined social services like free food and medical care with performances critical of capitalism; their most famous member was actor and director Peter Coyote. Closely resembling happenings but with a bitter political edge, guerilla theater was designed to elicit media coverage, and it did. Despite his misgivings, during the last decade of his life J.L. was intrigued by the new, radical experimental theaters of the 1960s; to him they were direct descendants of his revolutionary theater. "In the last twenty years," he wrote in 1973, "the American tendency to overcome the old, dogmatic theatre has become visible. Theatre producers attempt to incorporate the spectators in the action. It frees theatre partially from written plays but it uses theatre for social and political aims in the sense of Brecht and other playwrights. They hold conferences in which the actors are involved in a psychological change in order to deliver slowly a theatrical piece." Thus J.L. framed the new experimental groups in the terms of his spontaneity theater. The "psychological drama" that attracted so many young actors in the crisis years of the 1920s and 1930s was revived in response to a new period of social uncertainty. Unlike much of the new theater, J.L.'s sociodrama was never ideological, nor did it try to upend the status quo. Perhaps naively, he believed that his philosophy transcended politics.

The oldest continuously operating experimental theatre in America is the Living Theatre, and it was perhaps the most visible of the theater groups with a political message in the 1960s. Though founded in the late 1940s, the Living Theatre intensified its radical, anti-establishment approach through plays that included reciting lists of prohibited sex acts as the actors disrobed. The Living Theatre's philosophical inspiration was playwright Antonin Artaud, whose influential essays published as *The Theatre and Its Double* (1937) expressed the same contempt for theater conventions as J.L. had two decades before. One of Artaud's spiritual heirs was the Polish playwright Jerzy Grotowski, who created the Poor Theatre in the 1960s. He described it as an "encounter with the spectator" that would enable "discarding of masks. . . . Here we can see the theatre's therapeutic function for people in our present-day civilization." Drama therapist Robert Landy writes that "in these voices are also echoes of the spiritual Moreno searching for ways to take on the role of God and become the holy actor."

Some of the most colorful theater performances were hard to distinguish from encounter groups. The Liquid Theatre performed at the Guggenheim Museum in New York. Attendees put their shoes and ties into colored bags, were assigned to small groups and led in various games by cast members, and then were paired off. Instructed to gaze into the eyes of his partner, one male reviewer reported that his partner was "an attractive young lady" named Marcia. "It was at once embarrassing, pleasant, troubling and exciting, with the result that Marcia and I parted friends." After an intermission "hands stroke your face and brush your hair, you are hugged and find yourself hugging back, you feel cool, warm, alone and loved." The same words could have been used by any of the pop writers about encounter groups. As J.L. perceived in his youth, the boundaries between theater, therapy, political expression, and social change are always frail. In 2013, not far from the Guggenheim, the Whitney Museum mounted a retrospective exhibit on performance art in 1970s Manhattan called "Rituals of Rented Island: Object Theater, Loft Performance, and the New Psychodrama."

A limitation of overtly political theater is its dependence on prevailing issues and attitudes; its hard edge risks alienating rather than liberating audiences. One post-1960s experimental drama group, Playback Theatre, has instead modeled itself on ancient traditions of storytelling, citing as its inspirations psychodramatic method (founder Jonathan Fox was a student of my mother's), and the Brazilian philosopher Paolo Freire, who was linked to the Theatre of the Oppressed. Like J.L., Playback's leaders are interested in recapturing the original experience of the theater. For the ancient Greek dramatists, the production was intended as a reflection and interpretation of the inner life of the audience through stories that might have originally been told by goat herders. In Playback audience members are asked to relate an experience or event, which is then "played back" by the performers. Like all theater, a Playback performance might stimulate a therapeutic result or catharsis for audience members, but the goal is to aid in self-expression and the creation of social networks. Reminiscent of the work of J.L. and Lewin in organization development and reform, Playback works with refugees and victims of natural disasters and has been applied to improving workplace communication and management. Though prepared to work in politicized contexts, like performances with Palestinian villagers, Playback represents a "softer" approach to social change. The success of the Playback model can be measured in its global reach. With dozens of training schools, companies and festivals Playback might be the most influential improvisational theater in the world.

## SCANDAL

As 1960s experimental theater sharpened its edge, one of its favorite tools was nudity, becoming the most-remarked feature of the hit musical *Hair!* Human beings' confused and conflicted attitudes toward nakedness are bound to help any nude practice to attract attention. In 1969 *Newsweek* covered—or rather uncovered—nude encounter groups. Though he wasn't the only group leader to conduct them, they were a specialty of Los Angeles-based psychologist Paul Bindrim. "If a participant disrobed physically," Bindrim said, "he might, by this gesture, gain the freedom to also disrobe emotionally." At the time of the article Bindrim had conducted thirty such nude groups. Bindrim attributed his inspiration to Abe Maslow, who had wondered what T-groups would be like with nudity. "People would go away from there an awful lot freer," Maslow said, "a lot more spontaneous, less guarded, less defensive; not only about the shape of their behinds, or whether their bellies are hanging or not, but freer and more innocent about their minds, as well." Though Bindrim stressed that his groups' nudity was carefully desexualized, fairly or not his experiments—and the encounter movement itself—got caught up in the public mind with highly publicized scandals about psychiatrists having sexual affairs with patients. Esalen leaders Murphy and Price wisely declined Bindrim's offer to run nude encounter groups at Big Sur; they had enough on their hands with Fritz Perls' priapic pursuits.

Though one can't be sure about the dangers that encounter groups' experiments in nudity presented, at least ostensibly they took place among consenting adults. But sex with patients involves a self-identified vulnerable person who is, nearly by definition, dependent on the therapist and emotionally disturbed. One lawsuit that obsessed the New York City tabloids in 1971 was filed against Dr. Renatus Hartogs, who happened to have been the ex-husband of one of my maternal cousins. Hartogs was a distinguished and very visible psychiatrist. He published a regular column in

*Cosmopolitan* called "The Analyst's Couch" and had treated the troubled thirteen-year-old Lee Harvey Oswald at a New York City facility called Youth House. The Hartogs case was so highly publicized (*Time* magazine gave it a full page) that when his ex-wife met him for lunch in a Manhattan restaurant he wore a disguise. The patient ultimately won the lawsuit. About fifteen years later Dr. Jules Masserman, a former president of the American Psychiatric Association (with whom J.L. had edited a book about psychotherapy), was sued by four former patients who claimed that he had drugged and sexually abused them. The cases were settled out of court. Just before his death in 1994 Masserman wrote a book with his wife in which he denied the charges, a story that became the basis of a made-for-TV movie.

In 1971, the same year as the Hartogs case, the psychiatrist Martin Shephard became famous for his book *The Love Treatment: Sexual Intimacy Between Patients and Psychotherapists*, writing that "[a] sexual involvement can indeed be a useful part of the psychotherapeutic process." In 1972, the feminist writer Phyllis Chesler published an article in *New York* magazine excerpted from her landmark work, *Women and Madness*. Chesler described her interviews with eleven women who had been sexually exploited by their therapists. In some cases, the therapists were psychiatrists who also prescribed medication. Some were in group therapy, some in individual. Chesler's report included the following precise account of the sex. "Nine of the 10 therapists assumed a 'missionary' position during sexual intercourse for the first time and in general throughout the sexual treatment. Seven of the women did not experience orgasm the first time; four women never did throughout the treatment; seven of the women eventually experienced orgasm after from one to nine months. Four of the therapists had difficulty maintaining an erection." The least one can say of the behavior of these therapists is that it was a disgusting violation of medical ethics, and at worst that it inflicted long-term pain and sorrow on the patients. That such behavior is deeply immoral is not a new idea. The Hippocratic Oath prohibits not only sex with patients, but sex with anyone in the household, "free or slave." Of course, the fact that the Oath's authors saw fit to include this prohibition suggests that the practice was far from unknown, even in the ancient world.

Sexual exploitation of patients was no more routine in psychotherapy than nude groups were representative of the encounter movement. But it is undeniable that the trends that emerged at the same time as humanistic psychology too often devolved into bizarre, exploitive, and sometimes dangerous practices. The Great Crossover meant that more people than ever could be involved in therapeutic experiences, but also that they could be exploited by their leaders. Ambivalence about encounter groups among the leadership of growth centers like Esalen was partly due to the disrespect for boundaries on the part of group leaders like Fritz Perls. Even for those of us who lived through this period, it can be hard to recapture the mood of the times. In 1973 at an international group therapy congress in Zurich, I attended a session called "Going Out with the Group." As I recall the principal speaker was a Scandinavian psychiatrist who claimed that there were therapeutic benefits to socializing with group members, for example, taking a therapy group out for pizza after the session. During the discussion an agitated, slightly older male American psychiatrist asked, "How far do you go with your patients? Do you sleep with them?" Pausing, the presenter answered somewhat sheepishly, "only very rarely."

## LIBERATION

The scandalous behavior of a few psychotherapists and encounter gurus met resurgent feminism head on. Despite its progressive self-image, at first the human potential movement did little to address male domination or traditional sex roles. Phyllis Chesler's *New York* magazine exposé of exploitive male therapists appeared the same year as the founding of the Ms. Foundation and a year after the first issue of *Ms.* Magazine, edited by the journalist and feminist leader Gloria Steinem. In the late 1960s, some feminists founded "consciousness raising," or CR, groups to galvanize women in response to male hierarchies while also providing support for one another. It was pointless to draw a clear line between the political and the personal; indeed, "the personal is the political" is a touchstone of the modern feminist movement. When I posed the question about the relationship between CR and encounter groups to Gloria Steinem, she observed that the goal of CR was (and is, as the groups persist in various forms) to give members an opportunity to be heard, to give voice to the voiceless. Unlike encounter groups, which were largely indifferent to social reform, CR engaged both individual and social change.

Nonetheless, according to one observer, "[u]ltimately, consciousness raising moved into the orbit of the group therapy movement." The same problem confronted feminist therapy itself. In her history of American psychology Ellen Herman writes that "'[f]eminist therapy' surfaced early in the movement as a possible alternative to the sexist practice of traditional therapies. . . . What it was exactly and how it differed from CR were notoriously difficult to determine, but the persistence of discussion about it, and the strong demand for it by potential consumers, illustrated yet again the abiding place of the psychotherapeutic sensibility within feminism. . . . [T]he general feeling seemed to be that virtually any school or style of psychotherapy could qualify as feminist—from cognitive reprogramming to psychodrama and Gestalt—as long as a feminist practiced it." A vigorous debate ensued; CR leaders denied that their groups were a form of therapy, while others worried that they were drawing the energy away from political organizing and denounced them as "little more than a 'T' group."

Consciousness raising was part of the Great Crossover. By the late 1970s articles on CR in psychology journals were indexed under encounter groups, sensitivity groups, and human relations training. The CR moniker has been adopted by some self-help groups, such as a cancer prevention program that emphasizes behavior change, including "dramatic relief" through psychodrama and role-playing. A marriage counselor advises that "[r]ole reversal is another effective technique. It is especially useful for helping people get a feel for what the other sex experiences. The experience of one couple in counseling may serve as an example. Alice and Mike were disagreeing about whether to have another child or not. Mike wanted one and Alice didn't. The counselor, after listening to them argue from their own points of view suggested that they reverse roles and argue for the other side. She asked them first to switch chairs and to close their eyes and imagine themselves in the body and role of the other one. Then after a few moments of silence, she suggested that they open their eyes and talk to each other from their new positions."

Resurgent feminism was not the only self-organizing liberation movement to rediscover the value of role-playing and group dynamics in the 1960s. One source of feminists' inspiration for CR was the small group analysis and "rap sessions" of the African American civil rights movement. Role-playing was used to train civil rights workers in nonviolent methods of protest to withstand verbal and physical assaults, much like the situation tests of World War II-era clandestine operatives. The small fraternity of psychodramatists attempted their own interventions during the civil rights struggle. A 1969 *Newsweek* magazine–sponsored documentary called *In the Company of Men* by the distinguished black filmmaker William Greaves featured a series of psychodramas involving unemployed blacks and ambitious white foremen, illustrating their mutual misunderstandings. (Greaves's film received a little renewed attention when it was featured at the Melbourne Film Festival in 2013.) Esalen, too, tried to insert itself into these waters with an interracial encounter group that collapsed after the assassination of Reverend Martin Luther King, Jr., a sad irony considering that the original T-groups were inspired partly from Lewin's work on race relations just after World War II.

## THE TRAINING

Erhard Seminars Training, known as est, epitomized the Great Crosssover. In the 1970s, as hundreds of troubled hospitalized patients were daily being released from their involuntary commitment in vast institutions, hundreds of "normal people" were voluntarily entering hotel ballrooms in the hope of transforming themselves. The attraction was a handsome and charismatic young man named Werner Erhard, who had undergone his own "transformation." The word has a nearly technical significance for Erhard, who uses it to refer to his realization that what stood between him and his completeness as a human being was within his control. A critical part of "the training," as practitioners refer to it, is freeing oneself from the past, accomplished by "experiencing" recurrent patterns and problems rather than repeating them, where "experience" again has a technical significance. To fully experience the pointless repetition of old, burdensome behaviors is to "experience them out." An early biography of Erhard explains that

> [t]he training provides a format in which siege is mounted on the Mind. It is intended to identify and bring under examination presuppositions and entrenched positionality. It aims to press one beyond one's point of view, at least momentarily, into a perspective from which one observes one's own positionality. . . . The setting for the training is arduous and intrusive, . . . In the training ordinary ways to escape confronting one's experience are—with the agreement of the participants—sealed off in advance. On the concrete level this means

limited access to food, water, toilets, bed. Alcohol and drugs are forbidden. There is limited movement, there are no clocks or watches by which to tell the time; one may not talk with others; nor may one sit beside friends. Internal crutches and barriers to experience—such as one's own belief systems—are also challenged by means of philosophical lectures and exercises in imagination.

Participants might have been surprised how both physically and emotionally challenging and how philosophical the training was. Erhard had his own story to tell about coming upon his personal transformation, one in which he was relentlessly self-critical about his previous life, modeling the process for others. Thousands of people attended est training, and Erhard became the object of both popular fascination and an avalanche of criticism. Esalen leaders at first embraced and then tried to distance themselves from him, Rollo May called his methods "anti-humanistic," while others accused him of engaging in brainwashing and of leading a cult, even of fascism. Reasons for skepticism about him seemed legion. He had changed his name from the pedestrian John Rosenberg to one that appeared to be designed to call to mind some German philosopher. Erhard had gone through a variety of experiences and acknowledged a wide range of influences on the way to his transformation, including many self-enrichment texts, hypnosis, Zen Buddhism, physics, the psychology of Maslow and Rogers, Dianetics, Mind Dynamics, and more. The variety of sources of inspiration to which Erhard admitted very nearly invited suspicion: Everyone has reservations about at least one item on this list. It was also true that some people didn't feel they gained much from the training, but many felt they did.

By the time the est phenomenon exploded on the public scene, I was immersed in graduate school and wasn't paying much attention to these kinds of experiences. But I was struck by the controversy over Erhard; having grown up with a controversial man I am inclined to reserve judgment. As I saw coverage about Erhard in various major media I mentally filed it away. Over the next couple of decades the vilification of Erhard only intensified. Allegations of all sorts of personal and financial wrongdoing were hurled at him, none of which were borne out and some were even publicly retracted by major media organizations. As to the training itself, so far as I could tell not only were est participants consenting adults, none had credibly experienced harm and many asserted they had learned useful lessons for their personal or professional lives. From what I had heard and read about it, the training didn't appeal to me, especially the more controlling elements, but neither did I find it repulsive. That there should be such a level of hostility just didn't add up, certainly not as compared to other popular and more likely harmful offerings that grew out of the 1960s and 1970s. I couldn't help but think that there were other factors at work: Erhard was cursed with good looks, a history as a salesman, seemingly instant success, and an obvious enjoyment of his sudden wealth. (Befuddling the critics, he also created a foundation that sponsored physics lectures and with singer and songwriter John Denver founded an earnest effort to defeat world hunger.) He was also doing something that to many resembled some kind of group therapy, though he had no credentials, not even a college degree, a combination that was sure to irritate the establishment: How could this be anything but snake oil?

Whatever its merits, Erhard struck a chord among many, partly because it was simultaneously original and familiar. Erhard brought a uniquely American voice to the themes of the fading human potential movement, and est training was in the American tradition of Great Awakenings and motivational programs. He had a way with pithy, often spontaneous observations about life and living. Even as the spirit of the 1960s lost steam, there was a powerful lingering desire among many for personal exploration and for more authentic connections to others. In many ways the training was the most important cultural event after the human potential movement itself seemed exhausted, with elements of theater, therapy, and social networking.

Somewhere along the line the clunky term "large group awareness training" had been coined in reference to experiences like est that were on a bigger scale than Lewin's T-groups, but still aiming at Maslow's peak experiences. Crucially, est workshops took place on a stage before dozens or even hundreds of people. That was a departure from the usual encounter group size of a dozen or so participants, and further still from the analyst's couch. Erhard also confronted participants one-on-one, challenging them to be themselves rather than playing some role that had been imposed on them, a form of Socratic interrogation reminiscent of J.L.'s story about mounting the stage to confront the actor in the "legitimate" Vienna theater. Erhard was sensitive to the aspect of theater in the training; his biographer even calls it "a new form of participatory theatre, . . . Like most drama, it has catharsis as one of its aims. Unlike most drama, it also aims to bring the participant to an experience of him or herself which is tantamount of transformation." In the early years of est Erhard cited psychodrama as one way of "rehabilitating the imagination in the attempt to bring people to their potential." And he plainly had enormous charisma and self-confidence, qualities that J.L. also didn't lack. Erhard sold his company in 1991; it survives as Landmark Worldwide and its basic program is called the Landmark Forum. Erhard now travels and lectures on leadership education and integrity. Referring to a book he is completing with a friend, Erhard says that "I'd like to live long enough to get the ideas down."

Despite my curiosity about him, a talk with Erhard was not on my to-do list until Claremont Graduate School professor Paul Zak offered an introduction. To my surprise, Erhard immediately agreed (I have the impression he rarely gives interviews), and set no preconditions. I wasn't sure what to expect; one acquaintance who had been in est in the 1970s told me to be prepared for a "big spirit." I thought that being J.L.'s son was about the best preparation I could get. When we met in a Manhattan hotel suite, Erhard immediately struck me as warm, gregarious, and open. Well into his seventies, Erhard is still a tall, well-built man who stands stock straight and whose voice easily projects. When he got warmed up to a topic, his volume rose in the small living room, for which he offered an embarrassed apology. The years don't seem to have lessened his enthusiasm about his ideas or those that influenced him. Erhard is an intense listener who absorbed my summaries of many of the tales told in this book. What ensued was a sometimes breathless conversation about people and events that are important to both of us.

Erhard told me that he doesn't consider himself to have been part of the human potential movement, but he agrees that his concept of the training was part of the confluence of ideas that emerged during that period. I had sent him a couple of early chapter drafts of this book and he had clearly done his homework, as he recalled being intrigued by an improvisational theater group in San Francisco, perhaps around 1967 or 1968. Though he says that particular performance "fell flat," it alerted him to the new experiences that were bursting forth. At Esalen he got to know Fritz Perls and heard him lecture, and also Will Schutz, but not as part of their encounter groups. He was fascinated by the philosopher of Eastern religions Alan Watts with whom he studied and practiced Zen, as well as movement exercises with music educator Charlotte Selver and somatic educator Moshe Feldenkrais. Erhard estimates that he visited Esalen between five and ten times, adding that he was impressed by every visit and every discipline he experienced there. They all helped him to break out of the conventions with which he grew up in suburban Philadelphia. "I was always trying ideas," beginning when he was training people in sales at *Parents* magazine. "Everything I got involved in I learned something from, but none of it was the breakthrough [that led to his transformation and est], but it all added up. It wasn't just one thing, just keep battering at the limits" of the ideas.

## A SCREAM AWAY

In another example of the Great Crossover, while the cries of the severely mentally ill in the snake pits of asylums were being silenced by medication and deinstitutionalization, the cries of others were migrating to individual therapy, clinics, groups, and therapeutic communities. Erhard had a gift for challenging, often cathartic encounters with his participants without the aggressive tone of Perls's hot seat. As he said to me in our conversation, "I don't want to leave people raw." But "raw" was critically important to another catharsis-oriented experience that emerged from the 1960s. Los Angeles psychologist Arthur Janov's primal therapy came to public attention through his 1970 bestseller *The Primal Scream*, joining a long bookshelf of volumes about novel therapies and personal growth training. Primal therapy's purpose is to create the most emotionally raw experience possible by inducing its subjects to relive repressed trauma through a series of psychotherapy sessions that include screaming. This process is supposed to bring emotional pain to the surface where it can be treated. In the face of criticism of primal therapy, Janov and others continue to practice it and to insist on its benefits and scientific basis. In online answers to ten frequently asked questions, Dr. Arthur Janov's Primal Center pays J.L. a backhanded compliment by insisting that primal therapy is an advance over just talking about emotional pain, but it is not psychodrama; any distinction that distanced psychodrama from primal therapy is one that J.L. would have been happy to endorse.

Not to be outdone by Janov, over on the East Coast, New York psychiatrist Daniel Casriel combined his experience as a group therapist and founder of the therapeutic community Daytop Village (inspired partly by Synanon) with screaming as part of his psychotherapy. In 1972, Casriel published yet another innovative therapy manual with an especially catchy title, *A Scream Away From Happiness*. A year later I watched Casriel demonstrate his group primal therapy during a psychotherapy conference in Switzerland. After he offered some words of explanation about a dozen volunteers agreed to sit in a circle in the middle of a classroom at the University of Zurich. Casriel told them to start to scream "I hurt, too!" At first the screams were obviously forced and shallow, but gradually they became and more intense, evolving into shrieks of anger, then wails of pain. "I HURT, TOO! I HURT, TOO! I HURT, TOO!" After a few minutes the words became unintelligible as most of the participants melted into balls of tears, some doubled over. The sounds of a dozen people screaming in primal sorrow from the depths of their being escape my powers of description.

Casriel then spent most of the session comforting the screamers, as they also hugged, stroked and massaged each other. Some of those who had not participated in the circle also came forward to help. When the time for the session was over, we all filed out. In the courtyard outside the building I came upon several people in their mid-twenties who had been in the session, one woman and two men. They were all psychology graduate students from Germany. Although she was not part of the volunteer group of demonstrators, the young woman was distraught and her two colleagues were trying to console her. No effort had been made to check on the reactions of the "observers." Here was unfortunate confirmation of Aristotle's remark about the emotional power of the tragedy, that the stage play evoked emotions of pity and fear in the spectator. The Great Crossover made catharsis possible in all sorts of settings, but with no guarantee of asylum.

## IMPROMPTU MAN

In 1972, two years before his death, J.L. asked one of his students in residence at his psychodrama training institute in Beacon to drive him to the

Hudson River State Hospital in nearby Poughkeepsie. The old-fashioned asylum sprawled over three hundred acres and housed nearly two thousand patients. It required considerable determination for J.L. to mobilize himself for even that modest journey. He rarely left the house and lived mostly in a housecoat and pajamas. Besides suffering from the usual aches and pains associated with advanced age, he was by then carrying around a large belly on the thin legs owing to his childhood case of rickets. As it turned out, this episode was a sort of last hurrah for J.L. in the familiar setting of a psychiatric hospital. Joe Powers, now in charge of group therapy at Harvard's McLean Hospital, recalled the incident.

A patient that he had treated previously had called him to let him know that she was at the state psychiatric hospital and that she would like to see him. J.L. arranged with the hospital officials for a visit and so he asked me to drive him to the hospital and accompany him to the psychiatric unit. We headed off together in the famous white station wagon; he dressed in a dark suit and bowtie. It was a lovely spring day. We arrived at the facility, taking our time walking along from the parking lot to the entrance and found the elevator to the third floor where his former patient was staying. A staff member ushered us into a large common room where patients on the unit were sitting around the room's periphery. He greeted his former patient warmly and sat with her on a large comfortable couch in the center of the room. I stood back, standing directly opposite them across the room.

J.L. was completely comfortable and was warmly inquiring how his former patient was and how her treatment was progressing. That particular tableau in itself was enjoyable to watch but what followed was very mind-blowing. As he talked with her, slowly other patients drew near to him and began to sit on the couch, sit on the floor at his feet, or to draw chairs near to him. He introduced himself to this growing group, shaking their hands, listening to each, patting their hands, smiling, and reassuring. His charisma and therapeutic engagement were remarkable—I, a witness from ten paces away. As a young man and a student who was learning about group work, I was amazed at how he related so comfortably with all the patients, how he addressed them, how he engaged them, and how attuned he was to the whole group. He was completely comfortable and living in the "moment." He was completely comfortable with a group of acutely ill patients. He showed no discomfort with psychopathology; on the contrary, he exemplified compassion, empathy, and encouragement to all who joined him in this group "encounter."

That tableau imprinted in my mind and remained a powerful force throughout my personal and professional life. J.L. Moreno sitting in the midst of a group of inpatients in a state psychiatric hospital, conducting a group therapy in which he welcomed all into the circle. I was tremendously moved by the experience, promising to myself that I too would grow to become a group leader who would also work with acutely ill patients, internalize his methods and personal style and create group therapy experiences that would radiate similar values and virtues of compassion, empathy, and the capacity to listen and role reverse. My many years working at McLean Hospital on inpatient units working with children, adolescents, adults, and families with dissociative disorders, severe depression, psychosis, bipolar illness, personality disorders, and eating disorders has been guided by that one particular moment and led me to begin my groups with the invitation: "How can we help each other?" J.L. was simply extraordinary in creating relationships and a healing environment that fostered safety and recovery. In that amazing experience he demonstrated to me how group work happens in the shortest of time and is guided by the gifts of a group leader who not only "understands" human frailty and psychopathology but also promotes the vision of recovery, humanity, and hope.

J.L. conducted his last psychodrama session among those with whom he was in many ways most comfortable, the mentally ill, and in the kind of enormous asylum he had once tried earnestly to reform. If he couldn't change the system, perhaps he could at least make a difference in the here and now. He was, to the end, the impromptu man.

## CHAPTER TEN

# SIX DEGREES FROM J.L.

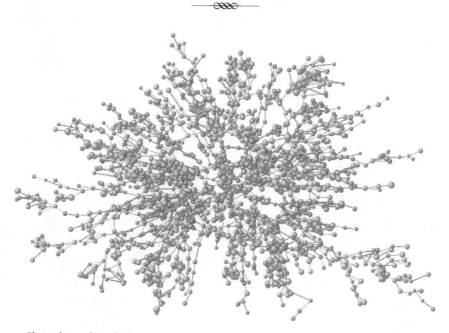

Christakis and Fowler's 2007 representation of a network of twenty-two hundred individuals, with the size of each circle proportional to the person's body-mass index. The lines indicate the relationship between them. In this black and white image, friendships and marital ties are darker and familial ties like siblings are lighter.

*A truly therapeutic procedure cannot have less an objective than the whole of mankind.*

J.L. Moreno, 1934

J.L.'S INSIGHTS ABOUT THE POWER OF SOCIAL NETWORKS are now so familiar we hardly notice them anymore. Who hasn't experienced the amusement of discovering, upon striking up a conversation with a stranger, that your cousin works with his sister-in-law, or that your father and his father worked at the same company in the same town, or that your old friend grew up two blocks from his wife? The phrase "six degrees of separation" is a social network cliché that has become as common as "Freudian slip" in psychology. In the late 1960s psychologist Stanley Milgram wondered what the average length of a social network in the United States would be. The answer was surprising, in that the lengths of connections from one person to another were not nearly as great as might be thought. Milgram gave about three hundred people in Boston, Massachusetts and Omaha, Nebraska packets of information about a friend of his in Boston, including his name and address. Rather than sending their packet to him directly, the participants were instructed to send it to someone they thought might know him on a first-name basis. It turned out that sixty-four of the packets reached Milgram's friend through only six steps in a chain of contacts.

Milgram published his paper about the "six degrees" research in the most successful of the many journals J.L. founded, *Sociometry*, which he donated to the American Sociological Association in 1954. Thus Milgram joined the list of important mid-century sociologists who carried on J.L.'s vision of social networks as indispensable for understanding human relations and group dynamics. What neither of them could have anticipated is the ability of modern social media like Facebook to both capture vastly more complex social networks and create new ones that minimize degrees of separation. The profound questions that the combination of social networks and cyberspace pose for our understanding of ourselves and our relationships remained for a later generation to address. It is no coincidence that Milgram's graphic resembles one of J.L.'s sociograms, which had by the 1960s become enmeshed in modern sociology and in information theory, which is increasingly faced with the problem of representing data in a visually meaning way.

At least one commentator on the new media has noted the J.L. connection. Writing on the popular website *Buzzfeed* in 2012, Russell Brandom points out that "The Future of Facebook Was Born in 1932," when J.L. sketched the world's first sociogram. "He was examining an epidemic of runaways at the Hudson School for Girls," Brandom explains. ". . . [F]ourteen girls had run away in two weeks. Instead of examining each case individually, he mapped all fourteen girls on a graph, showing how each case socially influenced the others, eventually leading to a social kind of epidemic. As you may have noticed, it looks an awful lot like Facebook's social graph. . . . And for anyone skeptical about the social graph, it's a powerful reminder: people have been at this for quite a while, and modern social networks are barely scratching the surface."

Nor could the generations of J.L., Lewin, and Milgram have known that the very knowledge of an individual's place in a network could be transformed into a market commodity. As I was finishing this book the latest star in the corporate social media firmament went public. On November 6, 2013 the microblogging company Twitter raised more than $1.8 billion. Not bad for a company that has never made a profit and whose communications concept of 140 characters of content would have seemed ridiculously constrained to Johannes Gutenberg, whose bibles are said to have required as many as one hundred thousand pieces of type. Starting with its first tweet in 2006 to four hundred million per day seven years later, by 2013 Twitter was the second most popular social networking site, exceeded only by Facebook. Perhaps the simplest explanation for Twitter's success is the most obvious: that it satisfies what is ultimately a very simple human impulse for self-expression and the sense of belonging to a group, however abstract, hypothetical, and distant. For Twitter users to have a message retweeted is some kind of blissful reassurance, a confirmation that their tweet is valued by someone. And so, in some way, are they.

## THERAPEUTIC FILM

Unlike the instantaneous virtual "groups" of social media, the T-group and encounter group leaders generally worked in actual small groups of about a dozen, certainly no more than twenty. In his public psychodrama sessions, J.L. sometimes worked in groups of hundreds, as did Werner Erhard in est, relying on the power of the shared cathartic experience that Aristotle observed. But J.L. was not satisfied with these numerical limitations. If "[a] truly therapeutic procedure cannot have less an objective than the whole of mankind," how could psychodrama reach everyone? This was important not only to assist all who are troubled and to "democratize" the development of individuals' spontaneity and creativity, but also to capture the inherently social and networked nature of human life. Building on his experience with his radio-film invention and the booming film industry in the 1920s, it occurred to him that perhaps the new communications technologies could help him realize his enormously ambitious goal.

J.L. first struggled with these questions in the 1920s, when he was led to reconsider his "nasty thoughts about machines" after his dream that inspired radio-film and ultimately his successful career in America. Yet the idea that ultimately brought him to America, rescuing him from impending difficulties in his personal and professional affairs, was a technology that appeared out of J.L.'s fantasy life, his wellspring of creativity. For the rest of his life J.L. was ambivalent about technology. Spontaneity and creativity are not necessarily at odds with technology, he thought, but they may be inhibited by its seductive distractions and efficiencies. For J.L. the technology symbolized by robots created an interesting philosophical challenge. The Czech playwright's Karel Čapek's 1920 play *R.U.R.* influenced all the intellectuals in the Prague–Vienna axis. In *R.U.R.*, creatures called robots are manufactured from biological parts (shades of Mary Shelley's Frankenstein.) The robots are benign slaves of human beings until they revolt and destroy their masters, a theme that had a profound impact on the last generation in which horses were prevalent in warfare and, within twenty-five years, saw news reports about the atomic bomb. "Why should man want to build robots?" J.L. asked in 1946. "It is perhaps the same reason, in reverse, as the one that in an earlier period made us want a God to whom we were robots. Therefore, if we could understand what we mean to God, we could understand what robots mean to us."

The same question can be asked of all human creations, including communications media like movies or television. After all, robots are only one example of the many kinds of static creations or "conserves" into which human beings pour their creativity, just as from the standpoint of divinity we are God's conserves, the products of diving creativity. Although pretechnological societies could certainly be oppressive, J.L. believed that modern technological advances intensified the risks of oppressive social systems, which he understood as interfering with spontaneity-creativity, a malady he called "robopathology." Robots themselves are not the sources of oppression, but the obstacles to spontaneity are rooted in the social systems that produce and support robots. "The solution of this conflict [with the machine] lies in an heroic measure, not to surrender to the machine, not to halt its development, but to meet it on even terms and to resort in this battle to resources which are inherent within his organism."

J.L.'s critique of technology focuses on social systems rather than the devices that are merely the physical manifestation of the system. He thought that communications technology could help push out his ideas about spontaneity and creativity. "Moreno believed that the technologies of mass communication could dramatically expand the scale and reach of the practice of psychodrama," writes Graham Lazar. When he suggested audio recording of spontaneity tests in the Sing Sing report, for example, it was among only the first of his efforts to put technology to work in the service of therapeutic social reform. Around that time he founded a company called Therapeutic Motion Pictures that produced a silent film depicting the way that he was training girls at the reform school for jobs as waitresses. Perhaps these films could be shown in schools and even movie houses so that other young women with few skills could learn by watching these simulations, and other institutions would adopt these methods.

In 1943, J.L.'s company produced a movie in which he rather frenetically demonstrated psychodrama. (The performance was typical; until he was much older J.L.'s spontaneity was such that he seemed to be about to burst his skin with excitement, especially on the psychodrama stage.) Television created still more provocative opportunities to bring psychodrama to everyone. "The day will come," he wrote in an unpublished manuscript in the 1940s, "when the engineer will provide us with a 'two-way' television system . . . [in which] every tele spectator will be able to televise himself back and so establish a communication between the therapist and himself multiplying the potentialities of the visual telephone by millions." In his 1970 bestseller *Future Shock*, Alvin Toffler predicted "interactive" films that would enable people in their homes to participate in soap operas, "a kind of televised psycho-drama." In his novel *2001: A Space Odyssey*, Arthur C. Clarke describes an astronaut surfing the television networks on Earth: "In the next five minutes, he got a symphony orchestra playing Walton's Concerto, a discussion on the sad state of the legitimate theatre, a panel game in some Oriental language, a psychodrama. . . ."

## FACE TO FACE?

J.L. believed that communications technologies present the opportunity to associate and organize human beings in their original creative capacity. "If a fraction of one-thousandth of the energy which mankind has exerted in the conception and development of mechanical devices were to be used for the improvement of our cultural capacity during the moment of creation itself, mankind would enter into a new stage of culture, a type of culture which would not have to dread any possible increase of machinery nor robot races of the future." If human beings refocus on that which makes them truly human, on their creative potential, rather than on the dead products of creation, they have nothing to fear from robots. J.L. believed that without his sociometric and psychodramatic interventions social systems that undermine human flourishing could even become oppressive. "The weakest point in our present day universe is the incapacity of man to meet the machine, the cultural conserve, or the robot, other than through submission, actual destruction, and social revolution." The problem of conserves is so common we are inured to it. This was the problem he had with scripted plays at the beginning of his spontaneous theater days in Vienna and during his studies at the Hudson reform school. Whenever human beings form groups, or indeed any social institution, at a certain point they may inhibit spontaneity.

Finally, though, for all the cathartic power that is supposed to inhere in the drama, J.L. was never able to make his psychodrama come across on the screen. He was still fighting the battle with those accustomed to the aesthetics of the traditional drama, a battle he began in Vienna and brought to New York, but then the battlefield became film rather than the stage. Even though audiences may find it hard to accept "imperfections, inconsistencies, fragmentariness and imbalances . . . [t]o make a picture perfect and smooth. . .is most undesirable, in fact destructive to therapeutic filming." Others have tried to find an aesthetic for using film or TV with role-playing. In the 1990s the Discovery Channel went pretty far with developing an audience participation psychodrama program. But lacking the secret sauce of having the audience in the room instead of watching on television, along with the importance of a real-time rather than prerecorded experience, the effort fell flat. Instead, so-called reality shows and encounters limited to the studio audience, as in Oprah Winfrey's daytime show, have filled that space as vicarious experiences for the viewers.

Can web-based technologies succeed in bringing healing encounters to all where film and television seem to have failed? Technically it is now realistic to "meet" virtually everyone through social media. But is it an "authentic" encounter or do social media just reinforce the ways that spontaneity can be repressed? Has Facebook redefined the meaning of "liking" someone or something, or has it emptied it of emotional content? There are plenty of skeptics who believe that the easy availability of web-based relationships is destructive of something deeply human. The sociologist and psychodramatist Lewis Yablonsky commented acidly when we were talking about titles for this book, "You should call it, 'From Love to Face-book.'" But is it really necessary to be "face to face, eye to eye" as J.L. put it in his 1914 verse, or can device-to-device contact not only preserve, but even enhance spontaneity? It seems undeniable that there are limits to technologically mediated relationships. As communications theorist Clay Shirky told me, "[p]urely mediated connection turns out to be not merely a terrible substrate for changing people's attitudes and behaviors, it can, in some circumstances, confirm or harden existing biases. The basic intuition of T-groups was that repeated face-to-face contact was the most powerful tool for altering outlook, and the work done on behavior change in games or networked groups seems to back up that insight."

To make matters worse, MIT's Sherry Turkle has argued, it is possible that the more technologically mediated our interactions become the less we expect from actual encounters. "Human relationships are rich; they're messy and demanding," Turkle writes. "We have learned the habit of clean-ing them up with technology. . . . We are tempted to think that our little 'sips' of online connection add up to a big gulp of real conversation. But they don't. E-mail, Twitter, Facebook, all of these have their places—in pol-itics, commerce, romance and friendship. But no matter how valuable, they do not substitute for conversation." Describing her research for her book about digital relationships, *Alone Together*, Turkle found one experience especially disconcerting. She brought a robot in the shape of a baby seal to a facility for the elderly. "[A]n older woman began to talk to it about the loss of her child. The robot seemed to be looking into her eyes. It seemed to be following the conversation. The woman was comforted." But, Turkle continues, "why would we want to talk about love and loss with a machine that has no experience of the arc of human life? Have we so lost confidence that we will be there for one another?" Turkle's worries about machines and human life had precedents in the reaction of the Industrial Revolution. Marx wrote of the way capitalism alienates the worker from his human nature; for the sociologist Emile Durkheim the key term was anomie, the breakdown of social bonds because of regimentation. In J.L.'s case, the underlying problem was a lack of spontaneity and creativity. Their absence results in automatic, machine-like behavior.

In any case, J.L. didn't think that modernity left us any choice. "In a technological era like ours," he wrote in 1946, "the fate and future of the spontaneity principle as a major pattern of culture and living may depend on good fortune in tying it up with technological devices." Considering that this was sixty years before the current worries about the social implications of social media, the remark is prescient. We need to reconcile ourselves to living in a technologically dominated world yet find ways to manage it for human purposes. If sociologist Keith Hampton is right, the challenge is far from hopeless. Disputing Turkle's findings, Hampton's studies of his neighborhood suggest that his more "wired" neighbors recognized one another more than those who were not technologically linked. Comparing decades-old films of public places in major cities with his new films of the same sites, Hampton concluded that people on mobile phones weren't avoiding others, but passing the time while waiting to meet friends or business associates. He argues that one reason we are aware that people are on their cell phones is that people are spending more of their time in public places than was the case thirty years ago, especially women, an increase in "hanging out" for which he has gathered evidence in his films.

Generalizations about technology and social isolation are dangerous. As Facebook's research team leader Cameron Marlow told me, social media are not one thing; people use them for different reasons. Facebook helps us stay in touch with those we know, Twitter is for shooting out pithy observations and factoids, LinkedIn is for making professional connections, and so on. So now consider meetup.com, a way to organize face-to-face meetings for just about any purpose you can imagine: to talk philosophy, to hike, to go to a ballgame, and on and on. One such group in New York, the Humanistic Interpersonal Meetup, is utterly self-aware. Except for the fact that J.L.'s name doesn't appear in their mission statement, he could have written it:

> This Meetup is designed to help people enrich their social relationships, increase creativity, enhance spontaneity, and meet new friends. This is not a superficial singles discussion; it's an exclusive social experience based on the concepts of Fromm, Maslow, Reich, Ellis,

and other greats in humanistic philosophy and psychology. The philosopher Martin Buber said that life is an encounter with oneself, others and nature, but we need to have these encounters enhance warmth, mutual understanding and health.

The Meetup uses social media as instruments that facilitate direct encounters. As digital political strategist Alan Rosenblatt said to me, whether social media can preserve what J.L. called the "spontaneity principle" might depend on whether they can be used in new and surprising ways that their designers did not intend. For example, the social media site Tumblr is famous for arranging meetups. Tumblr's director of outreach for social and political causes is Liba Wenig Rubenstein. Rubenstein told me that her parents were opera buffs who didn't own a TV set. She only discovered popular culture in college and now sees herself as an anthropologist who translates the concerns of a new generation into new modes of communication. "Social media are becoming as much of a utility as water and electricity. For every example of technological alienation there's an example of a kid growing up gay in a small town who had no one to talk to about it before." Or as J.L. would have put it, social media can facilitate sociometric choice.

Perhaps there are latent possibilities for spontaneity in computer platforms. It turns out that some of the people who pioneered the robots we call personal computers had a thing for psychodrama. The somewhat surprising link runs through *Cuckoo's Nest* author Ken Kesey, who volunteered for an experiment at the Menlo Park Veterans Hospital in 1959 while he was a Stanford graduate student in creative writing. The attraction was the easy money: Volunteers were paid $75 a day to be part of a study of "psychotomimetic drugs." A few weeks later Kesey took a job as a night attendant in the psychiatric ward where he had access to all sorts of hallucinogens. Kesey shared his chemical fortune with his network of friends in and around La Honda, south of San Francisco, where their trips bound them together as a clan of spiritual adventurers they called the "Merry Pranksters." They fashioned a 1939 International Harvester bus into a multicolored rolling party palace labeled "FURTHUR," with a sound system that could blast inside and outside the vehicle, and a hole in the roof to provide an upper deck. The Merry Pranksters established the outlandish style of the 1960s American hippie movement: the colors, the music, the clothes (or no clothes), the rock and roll. They drew inspiration from the wacky cartoons, kids' TV shows, and circuses of their childhood. To the degree that early hippiedom was a protest against America's dominant cultural values—it was impish, not angry. They sought not to raise hell, but aided by a drug-induced sense of cosmic purpose, to realize heaven.

The Merry Pranksters were fun and outrageous, but it turns out that perhaps in spite of themselves they had a work ethic. While he was founding the Pranksters Kesey was also busy writing a book inspired by his experience at Menlo Park. Kesey dedicated his brilliant antipsychiatry novel *Cuckoo's Nest* to the man who had initiated him in psychedelics as a human guinea pig at the Veterans Hospital, psychologist Vic Lovell. Lovell was a central cultural figure at the Mid-peninsula Free University (MFU), a radical response to established higher education, where his psychodrama workshops attracted a small group of young engineering wizards who were trying to expand human potential through computers that could make information free to all, not just to university and military scientists operating whirring mechanical behemoths that took up whole rooms. These pioneers of what was later known as personal computing were finding their place in the counterculture, and psychodrama became a popular form of exploration. In his book about these early personal computing pioneers, John Markoff reports that, "While encounter groups quickly became part of mainstream psychology in the sixties, psychodrama remained stronger, more emotionally challenging stuff, more confrontational and intense. Psychodrama became a significant activity in the Free U. . . ."

## THE WHOLE EARTH

The fact that psychodrama and other personal growth experiences appealed not only to counterculture activists and New Age seekers, but even to engineers seems strange in light of the way we usually think of the 1960s. Popular social criticism like Charles A. Reich's *The Greening of America* advocated a new consciousness of human liberation with help from hallucinogens. Reich tapped into widespread disillusion with corporate domination, the military–industrial complex, and poverty and violence at home and abroad. Underlying these philosophical misgivings about modern Western society were a common longing for a more authentic and wider network of human relations that could leverage the knowledge and insights of many different people so that all could live in a more egalitarian way. If the nineteenth-century consciousness was shaped by agriculture and the twentieth-century consciousness by industrial bureaucracy, the new consciousness would level bureaucracy and create harmonious collaborations. Reich called the new phase of socioeconomic history "Consciousness III."

Consciousness III did not abandon the technological accomplishments of the previous era; on the contrary, according to Reich in 1970, "today's emerging consciousness seeks a new knowledge of what it means to be human, in order that the machine, having been built, may now be turned to human ends." Frederick Turner has chronicled what he calls the "New Communalists" who were in the process of creating the consciousness that Reich articulated. They might have sported a hippie appearance and lived in communes but the New Communalists were not stereotypical new leftists. "[E]ven as they set out for the rural frontier, the communards of the back-to-the-land movement often embraced the collaborative social practices, the celebration of technology, and the cybernetic rhetoric of mainstream military–industrial–academic research. . . . For the New Communalists, the key to social change was not politics, but mind." One person who came to see technology as a key rather than an obstacle to realizing Consciousness III was Stewart Brand. Brand had befriended Ken Kesey and become part of the Merry Pranksters scene. Psychedelics, and especially LSD, were viewed as a technology of the new consciousness. They were combined with electronic technologies like strobe lights, stereo equipment, and slide projectors to make performance art. The Pranksters' "acid test" happenings were celebrations of consciousness expansion aided and abetted by both pharmaceutical and electronic technology. In that spirit, the first edition of Brand's *Whole Earth Catalog* in 1968 provided a guide to useful tools, from garden equipment to the first personal computers that could support the making of a new counterculture. Brand and his likeminded associates never indulged in wholesale rejection of the world left to them by the World War II generation. They had too much they wanted to do with the tools at hand.

By the mid-1980s those tools included a computer-based teleconferencing system called the WELL, the Whole Earth 'Lectronic Link, through which Brand extended his communal ideals into cyberspace.

Counterculturalists, journalists, hackers, and Whole Earth Catalog follow-ers joined discussion groups and exchanged information about a vast range of topics from parenting to electronics to the Grateful Dead, in a largely self-governed online community. To its participants the cooperative spirit of the WELL embodied the virtues of the virtual community and in the early 1990s attracted the attention of commercial ventures like America Online that sought to capture its high mindedness. Most of all, though, for its true believers the WELL represented the expansion of consciousness in a disembodied form, much as LSD seemed to do just a few years before. Indeed, in the Bay area that was spawning the most important new indus-try of the late twentieth century, the two technologies were complemen-tary. Frederick Turner writes that "even as technologists worked to build a sort of placeless space, that space quickly became linked to local, Bay area stories of LSD and countercultural transformation. [The software firm] Autodesk, for example, hired famed acid guru Timothy Leary to appear in its promotional video for its cyberspace initiative." The experience helped inspire Leary to spend his last years propounding the possibilities of cyber-space. Declaring "The PC is the LSD of the 1990s," he urged countercultur-alists to "turn on, boot up, jack in." Shortly before he died in 1996, Leary enjoyed a final reunion with Kesey over the World Wide Web by means of Apple's then-primitive version of a Skype system.

## HCE

In 2008, the communications theorist Clay Shirky published a book enti-tled *Here Comes Everybody* about the ways that the Internet has changed interpersonal relations and group dynamics. Taking social media sites like MySpace, blogging software like WordPress and Twitter, and col-laborating platforms like Wikipedia as examples, Shirky observed that these adaptations of the technical possibilities inherent in the Internet could surmount the inefficiencies and costs of traditional institutions for human interaction. They enabled conversation and experimental forms of organization that would previously have been too expensive to justify. Implicitly new forms of social networks could be realized and older ones could be made obvious. To Shirky, the advent of social media represents as monumental a change in the potential for group dynamics as did the printing press and the telephone.

In 1971, Will Schutz, the Harvard-trained Esalen encounter group leader and alumnus of National Training Labs, published his second popular book on encounter groups. In his book, Schutz wrote that "virtually all of the methods that I had proudly compiled or invented [Moreno] had more or less anticipated, in some cases forty years earlier. . . ." Schutz's title *Here Comes Everybody* called to mind the seemingly inexhaustible appeal of the human potential movement. It was also a shrewd reference to the initials of the main character of James Joyce's experimental, comic novel *Finnegans Wake*, Harold Chimpden Earwicker. The novel had acquired a special fascination for followers of New Age philosophies as Joyce was a favorite of mythologist Joseph Campbell. Adding to the popular appeal of the word, in 1964 the physicist Murray Gell-Mann took the name of his hypothesized subatomic particle from a nonsense word in the novel ("Three quarks for Muster Mark!"). Since then, Gell-Mann's curious quarks have been experimentally confirmed, in six "flavors" no less.

I was astonished when I noticed that Schutz's book on encounter groups and Shirky's on social media had the same name. I could have dismissed it as a coincidence attributable to every author's search for a catchy title had it not been for Shirky's response when I called his attention to Schutz's book. "There's certainly an indirect relationship," Shirky told me in an email, "since the kind of work done in T-groups (and, on the other side of the pond, in some of [Wilfred] Bion's work, which I cite in HCE), were inputs to social network analysis." Indeed, as Shirky noted, the link from T-groups and encounter groups to social network analysis is a matter of record. And T-groups themselves are rooted in J.L.'s studies at the girls' reform school and Sing Sing prison in the 1930s and Lewin's adaptations.

What about the historical connection between social network analysis and social media? That turns out to be more complicated. Shirky told me that early social network analysis "did not much inform social networks services such as LiveJournal, Friendster, MySpace, and Facebook, which were built on simpler (or simplistic, if you prefer) models of human connection. SNA has become a great tool for *extracting* information from such systems, but was not used much in their original design." Sociologist Dave Knoke and computer scientist Joseph A. Konstan, both at the

University of Minnesota, agreed that the social network theorists and the social media developers were largely separate groups, with the social media developers "rediscovering" social networks as their technology matured. As Konstan observed, "they [social media developers] were mostly not researchers, but inventors and entrepreneurs looking to create something of interest."

## A TRAIL OF BREADCRUMBS

Apart from his justifiable wish for recognition as his ideas were absorbed by the culture, J.L.'s principle objection to the ways his ideas were used was the separation between network analysis and social interventions that could help a community satisfy the emotional needs of its members. All sorts of social interventions are based on social network analysis, some of them in very lucrative industries. Canadian sociologist Sergio Sismondo studies the way that the pharmaceutical industry finds "key opinion leaders" (KOLs), who are physicians paid to give talks to other physicians about the company's products; the industry often uses social network analysis in its efforts. Sismondo traces the systematic use of KOLs as a form of commercial promotion to Paul Lazarsfeld, the sociologist who helped J.L. to interpret the data from his early sociometric studies and from whom, I believe, he learned about the use of sociograms. Their collaboration continued through the early 1950s, including Lazarsfeld's paper about the role of personality in job-hunting by young people, which was published in J.L.'s journal in 1941.

Considered by many to be the founder of modern empirical sociology, Lazarsfeld played a key role in rendering into mathematically sophisticated forms the information about social networks that J.L. and Helen Jennings accumulated. The need for mathematics to analyze data about social networks has only grown with the advent of social media. As social network theorist Michael Kearns said to me, today Facebook, Twitter and other social media face a challenge that J.L. and Lazarsfeld would have appreciated: What to do with the deluge of data that they are producing? The open source advocate Tim O'Reilly (who attended courses at Esalen in the early 1970s), used the apt phrase "continuous trail of breadcrumbs" when I spoke with him, describing the data stream left by Internet communications. J.L., Lewin, and their social science heirs perceived the trail before the technology helped it to be rediscovered by the new generation of social media explorers. One of them is Duncan Watts, a sociologist who uses social media to study the ways that networks shape the behavior of social systems. Watts' work on "small-world" networks ingeniously replicated Stanley Milgram's six degrees experiment, but with the vastly richer tools provided by modern communications technology.

As the physician and social scientist Nicholas Christakis puts it, social media sites "created the terrain for being able to use social network analysis." And as just about everyone knows, those uses have been prodigious. Christakis, who keeps a framed print from J.L.'s 1934 book on the wall of his lab, and his colleague James H. Fowler have taken social network analysis into public health. They've shown that people who suffer from obesity are more likely to be closely connected to others with the same problem. If they are right that "obesity is spread through social ties" because people who are socially connected to one another influence one another's behavior, then, as they also point out, there is hope for the obesity epidemic. "[M]edical and public health interventions might be more cost-effective than initially supposed, since health improvements in one person might spread to others." The graphics they use are close relatives of J.L.'s sociograms. In fact he would have called the exercise involved "near sociometry," because the relationships are not intentional choices or rejections. Nevertheless, he would have loved the evidence that his idea of interpersonal rapport or tele could be the key to both explaining and tackling a serious health problem.

Another lesson of the breadcrumbs left by social networks is the opportunity to contrast different levels of engagement between people. Using data from Facebook, several researchers have shown that there are systemic differences between the networks of all one's friends, those who had clicked on a Facebook newsfeed or their profile more than once ("maintained relationships"), one-way communications, and mutual communication. Graphic representations of these data in sociograms give an idea of the way that information can travel through an online medium.

The uses of data from networked data systems have been made famous in another way by Edward Snowden, a former CIA employee and National Security Agency contractor with a security clearance, who in 2013 leaked information to *The Guardian* newspaper about secret United States government surveillance programs. One of them, called PRISM, collects and analyzes virtually all the electronic data that passes through the United States, including cell phone calls, e-mails, and chats. This information can be graphically represented in a sociogram and reproduced in MIT's Immersion program much the way it must appear in the NSA graphics. As summarized by *International Business Times* writer Ryan Neal, the Immersion program "asks users for their G-mail address and password; it then scans every e-mail in their accounts and scrapes the metadata to create a portrait of their personal network. With the circles and lines of a network diagram, it highlights the hundred people with whom you've communicated most, and shows how closely they're connected to you and how thickly interconnected with one another in your mailbox." Neal reproduced his own Immersion results in a graphic that, like the obesity and Facebook relationships images, owes much to J.L.'s sociograms.

Snowden leaked the information about the United States programs to the press almost exactly one hundred years after J.L. first proposed that Austro-Hungarian authorities assign new refugees to shelters based on an analysis of their interpersonal choices rather than by random assignment. Would J.L. have thought that the combination of digital information and national security needs could result in the use of sociograms to track possible terrorist planning? I think J.L. appreciated the vast potential of his insight into social networks and group dynamics, including in national defense and counter-intelligence. And there is evidence that his work directly influenced the American intelligence community during the Cold War. Though it is impossible to trace the NSA's modern use of social network analysis directly back to their experience with J.L.'s sociometry and psychodrama, in 1955 staff members of the NSA visited J.L.'s psychodrama institute at our home in Beacon, New York at least once, and the psychodramatist at St. Elizabeths Hospital in Washington lectured NSA employees. The deputy chief of the NSA Office of Training wrote the hospital director that the agency's trainees were interested in "human relations, group dynamics, and group behavior," and that those who had participated in psychodrama training at J.L.'s institute spoke enthusiastically about that experience. Ironically, around that time radical conservatives were accusing J.L. of being a Communist tool, or worse. At least one can say that J.L.'s methods resisted ideological classification.

## COPS, CORPORATIONS, AND COURTS

Not only sociometry, but also psychodrama lives on in the national security world. Federal contracting guidelines for the training of federal law enforcement officers in hostage negotiations specify that the trainers must be certified psychodramatists. Since the late 1970s they were drawn from the psychodrama training program at St. Elizabeths, including skilled psychotherapists like Barry Spodak, who is also an expert on campus violence. Spodak told me that in the late 1970s there was a growing awareness among law enforcement officials of the need for an understanding of people with psychiatric problems. The big hospitals like St. E's were being emptied and there were far more of these people on the streets than before. Simulated domestic conflicts, which can so often turn violent, were the basis of the training provided by the psychodramatists for the FBI hostage-rescue teams. After the attempted assassination of President Reagan in 1981, Spodak and his colleague Dale Buchanan ran psychodrama sessions on the ward that housed the would-be assassin, John Hinckley. That experience, Spodak said, gave them credibility with the Secret Service, which then engaged them in psychodrama training for their agents. Ultimately, he also worked in psychodrama with the US Marshall's Service and the US Capitol Police. When Spodak was asked why the role-playing he did in psychodrama was so much more effective than the role-playing done by others for law enforcement organizations he would respond, "Well, it's because it all comes out of psychodrama theory which is so complex and sophisticated, and we take the theory seriously."

Corporate consultant David Swink started as a colleague of Barry Spodak in federal law enforcement training. Like Spodak, he has built on his background as a psychodrama therapist. Swink's company, Strategic Interactions, got its start in 1990 when it did a course on diversity training for MCI. Of course Swink wasn't the only one offering diversity training to industry, but he believed he could approach difficult topics that face employers using psychodrama-based role-playing that others could not, topics that made people walk on eggshells and often sparked legal action, from racial issues to demeaning workplace interactions. Instead of putting people on the spot, Swink and his staff use J.L.'s idea of the sociodrama to present various models for handling difficult conversations with employees, and invite the audience to comment on the models. Gradually, audience members become active participants in the scenarios. For a particularly antagonistic situation involving, say, an allegation of sexual harassment, Swink helps the group recreate the likely experience of a woman in a largely male company. "We've found we can't explain what we do," Swink says, "we can't convey the power of the method. It's like describing a sunset or a great Rolling Stones concert. You have to experience it."

Whether it's called psychodrama or not, improv is common in professional education. Northwestern University medical humanities scholar Katie Watson is a Second City trainer and uses "medical improv" to improve doctor–patient communication. Perhaps the most unlikely constituency for psychodrama training is trial lawyers. Many litigators are intuitive actors who appreciate that the coutroom is a stage. J.L.'s fascination with the proceedings at Vienna's law courts was rooted in his apprecation for the inherently dramatic quality of a trial, but few have taken the insight as far as Gerry Spence, who lays fair claim to being the most successful trial lawyer in America. The charismatic Spence has represented some of the most famous defendants in history, including Karen Silkwood, Imelda Marcos, and Geoffrey Fieger, and won a lawsuit against McDonald's. In a bit of theater that J.L. would have appreciated, he defended Lee Harvey Oswald in a televised British mock trial. Spence is especially interested in public interest law. He began using psychodrama to train lawyers when he first saw it demonstrated at a meeting of criminal defense attorneys in 1978. When he founded his Trials Lawyers College at his thirty-four thousand acre Montana ranch, Spence made psychodrama a key part of the curriculum and brought in another former St. Elizabeths Hospital therapist, Don Clarkson.

Psychodrama fits well with Spence's basic premise that unless a lawyer cares about what happens to her client, she can't expect the jury or anyone else to care. Akron University law professor Dana Cole explains the rationale this way: "Through psychodrama, the lawyer is able to 'experience' the event. The lawyer can reverse roles with the witness and experience the event from the vantage point of the witness. The lawyer will have access to the emotional content involved in the story that is not otherwise fully available. The lawyer will have a deeper understanding of the 'truth' involved—an understanding grounded in empathy, not sympathy." Through psychodrama techniques the incident is reenacted, witnesses are prepared to testify, cross-examinations are developed, and opening and closing statements are prepared so as to capture the emotional detail of the case.

## SIX DEGREES

It's hard to exaggerate the extent to which J.L.'s pioneering ideas have penetrated the culture. As the Harvard sociologist Samuel Stouffer said to a student who was feeling overwhelmed by J.L.'s prolific and often unruly production of ideas, "Whatever else, how many of us can look forward to leaving two such important contributions as role-playing and the Sociometric Test?" Role-playing has impressed itself in just about every imaginable domain of human activity, including sexual practices and computer games. It also has a special place among the most ethically controversial experiments in social science. In 1961 Yale psychologist Stanley Milgram, who had also done the "six degrees" study, wondered how far a person would go if ordered to hurt another person by someone in an authority role, like a scientist. His famous "obedience to authority" experiments suggested that ordinary persons would often go very far indeed, even giving what they thought was a potentially dangerous shock on command. Coming on the heels of the Eichmann trial and Hannah Arendt's famous conclusion that the Nazis were not pathological, but ordinary people for whom evil became a banal part of everyday work, the Milgram experiment sent shockwaves through the country. Milgram was accused of damaging the self-image of the research subjects, who might have been traumatized to realize they could hurt an innocent person when told to do so by someone in a high-status role. Another famous social psychology experiment was undertaken at Stanford University about ten years after Milgram's. In 1971, psychologist Philip Zimbardo recruited a number of young men for a prison study. He arbitrarily assigned them the roles of prisoner or guard and set them up in a prison-like facility on campus. The planned two-week study had to be aborted after only six days because of the sadistic behavior of the "guards" and the depression that overtook the "prisoners." Again, role-playing turns out to be a powerful instrument.

Fortunately, there are far happier examples of the close connections between J.L.'s ideas and popular culture. The television institution

*Saturday Night Live* has drawn many of its brightest starts from the Second City theater company, which has roots in Viola Spolin's theater games. Although quick to distinguish between theater and therapy, at least some Second City alumni continue to feel a kinship with psychodrama. In his memoir *An Improvised Life*, actor Alan Arkin, one of the early Second City cast members, says that when he's conducting his acting workshops "[o]nce in a while someone yells, 'This is turning into a lot of psychodrama!' . . . The second time someone yelled 'This is psychodrama!' another voice yelled back, '*Everything* is psychodrama!'" (emphasis in original). Arkin writes that in his theater workshops "working on one's psychological issues happens almost by accident," precisely the experience that led J.L. to psychodrama a century ago.

Tina Fey is one of the most successful Second City alumnae. She told an interviewer for *The New Yorker* magazine in 2011 that she had been in psychodrama. "Fey told me that she has been systematically imagining—and rehearsing—a knock-down fight with terrorists. She entered a course of psychodrama, a form of therapy that uses acting techniques to banish sadness, anger, and fear. In sessions, she said, she faces down imaginary terrorists, sometimes represented by chairs. She also punches a pillow that stands in for President Bush." On her hit TV show *30 Rock* Fey used role-playing as a setup for a number of hilarious scenes in which her characters reverse roles in the manner of a psychodrama session. Fey even closed the circle with J.L. in Vienna, as she writes (facetiously but more accurately than she might realize) in her book *Bossypants* that "I made [my husband] fly once before we married because he was offered a free trip to Vienna, Austria, to direct a sketch comedy show for an English-language theatre. If you know anything about Vienna, you know that they love Chicago-style sketch comedy!"

Whether they are known for improv or not, comedians seem to have a special affinity for psychodrama. Joy Behar, the comedian and former co-host of the daytime talk show *The View* told me that she has been directing psychodramas in a small group with a therapist present since the mid-1970s. During a debate on her TV show about the kids' game tag with other *View* personalities, Behar suggested that children who play the game too aggressively should be required to undergo a "psychodrama technique where you reverse roles with the other child." (Whoopi Goldberg was not impressed with this suggestion.) In a moving 2011 interview with Jane Fonda, Behar observed that Fonda's role opposite her dad Henry Fonda in the film *On Golden Pond* was "almost a psychodrama" in which Fonda was able to say things to her dad that she couldn't say in their difficult real-life relationship.

Even politicians find it convenient to use opaque references to J.L.'s psychological drama. In *The Audacity of Hope* President Obama wrote that "in the back and forth between [Bill] Clinton and [Newt] Gingrich, and in the elections of 2000 and 2004, I sometimes felt as if I were watching the psychodrama of the baby boom generation—a tale rooted in old grudges and revenge plots hatched on a handful of college campuses long ago—played out on the national stage." Not to be outdone, in 2011 the conservative magazine *Commentary* referred to "The Psychodrama of the Obama Presidency."

Somewhere J.L. is smiling.

# JOHN WILCOCK: NEW YORK YEARS

**WOODY ALLEN –AND– DR. MORENO'S THEATER OF THE PSYCHODRAMA**

In the early 60s, I became fond of a local comic nicknamed Walter Allen, or "Woody", as he's now *much* better known. I'd first met him at one of my weekly parties. He had a good act:

> See ... I got her a turtle for a GIFT! .... Who knew she'd be a-**ALLERGIC**!

HAW HAW HAW

LATER, bumping into each other at an Automat, I suggested an interview:

> Sh-Sure thing, b-but let's do it somewhere ...entertaining.

A FEW DAYS PASSED, and I called Woody on the phone. He asked if I knew about **DR. MORENO'S PSYCHODRAMA** — and would I care to accompany him to a session?

> ...Not to *participate* ...It'll just be fun to watch!

First developed by Doctor Jacob L. Moreno in 1910,

## PSYCHODRAMA

is a form of **GROUP THERAPY THEATER**, where participants **ACT OUT** roles to deal with issues of anxiety, confusion and grief. A blend of **PSYCHOLOGICAL ANALYSIS** and **COMMUNITY PERFORMANCE**, a night of "Psychodrama" in the Sixties was similar to an evening of improv, with participants being selected from the audience. However: The master of ceremonies was a **SHRINK!**

Proponents of Psychodrama have called it a **REAL CURE** (the talking cure is the only cure, they say) ... while others have derided its public performance aspect to reflect more a medical quack sideshow, or scam. Or worse, a cult.

Woody and I arrived to the theater JUST IN TIME for the night's session

It was there, where Woody surprised me...

> Any volunteers? Oh yes, you *lovely* young lady — Yes! come right up!

wow.

> I need **JUST one more** volunteer!

ZOING!

Sorry, I know what I said about not participating ... but check out the CANS on the girl he picked!
— *Ripe!!*

> Right this way, young man!

Woody Allen and Village Voice columnist John Wilcock
attend a night of Psychodrama in the early 1960s.

From the comic biography "John Wilcock, New York Years"
© Ethan Persoff and Scott Marshall, used with permission.
More information at http://www.ep.tc/john-wilcock

# A ROLE REVERSAL

J.D.M.: Well, that's the book. What do you think?

J.L.: I think you did a pretty good job, though your mother deserves a lot of credit for bringing my ideas to the world.

J.D.M.: There's no doubt about that. You know, I finished this book almost exactly forty years after you died. So we are in surplus reality here. Do you have any advice for me about how to do this role reversal?

J.L.: It's a lot of responsibility, speaking for someone who can't speak for himself, especially from the eternity of the cosmos, a great challenge for spontaneity and creativity. The key thing is you have to preserve my unique identity, my voice as it would have been.

J.D.M.: Some might say it's odd that you reversed roles with God and now I'm reversing roles with you, a Godplayer.

J.L.: And why shouldn't you? Anyway, many people called me crazy, but I knew I was crazy like a fox. I knew my ideas would prevail even though they were criticized and picked apart.

J.D.M.: Toward the end of your life you decided that your self-confidence wasn't always a big advantage.

J.L.: I had an *idee fixe,* but I was often too hard on other people. Finally, I realized how much I owed to others for following through on my ideas and carrying them forward.

J.D.M.: Yet when you were young and started the Religion of the Encounter you understood the importance of disciples, and in psychodrama you called people who play the roles of important people in the protagonist's life auxiliary egos. Isn't it surprising that it was hard for you to accept that you needed others to fulfill your work?

J.L.:  It was a contradiction, I admit. But I had to fight hard in the early years. It's easy to look back and second guess.

J.D.M.:  Fair enough. Anyway you did succeed in getting your ideas accepted though they were adapted in ways you didn't approve.

J.L.:  I still think that ultimately they will have to be brought together. Group psychotherapy, psychodrama, and sociometry work best as a unity. For now, the important thing is that they are accepted even if they are not intact.

J.D.M.:  So what's it like being a Godplayer where you are now? You have some company in that department.

J.L.:  Let's just say that we see eye to eye.

J.D.M.:  And for us who are still in this world? Any parting advice?

J.L.:  Remember that spontaneity and creativity are what the world needs now.

J.D.M.:  I was hoping you'd say that.

# Acknowledgments

AUTHORS ARE OFTEN ASKED, "When did you start writing this book?" I'm tempted to respond, somewhat impolitely: "Define writing." Although it would have looked odd for a little kid to wander around social science conferences in the late 1950s and early 1960s taking notes and doing interviews, it has occurred to me more than once that that would have been a great help in the writing of this book. It also would have made it easier to acknowledge the contributions of so many psychologists, psychiatrists, sociologists, theologians, psychiatric patients, actors, dramaturges, and spiritual seekers—heralded and unheralded, living and dead. As a child, teenager, and young adult I ran across many of the big thinkers and large personalities mentioned in these pages, but until I was in my late teens I mostly took no notice of them nor certainly they of me, save perhaps to wonder what I was doing there.

Growing up the way I did was a total immersion experience in some of the great ideas of the day. I have come to think of those years as an extended continuous interview with my father. My mother who carried on and advanced my father's work, not to mention gestating me, must be gratefully acknowledged. My sister Regina showed up a dozen years before I did; her unique perspective on what our household was like has enriched my own.

At my urging my father undertook an autobiography a couple of years before he died, but like many older people the memories of his youth are both more detailed and more predominant than those of his mature years. His recall was also characteristically laced with imaginative renderings that are far more interesting than what he would have considered mere facts. Fortunately, his biographer Rene Marineau opened up many avenues for deeper insight both into my dad's career and the way it intersected with the times. Since Rene's work in the 1980s many new sources have arisen, especially concerning the humanistic psychology and human potential movements. In 2012 my mother wrote her own beautifully crafted memoir that has helped me round out the story and led me to some very valuable interviews with her. Even after more than ninety-six years on the planet, her intellectual curiosity is undiminished.

Besides scaling a mountain of reading, anyone writing about unfolding ideas and events still in living memory needs to talk to lots of people. I've been lucky to be surrounded with friends and colleagues who both in some way experienced the movements I have sought to understand, but are also thoughtful about them and were willing to share their thoughts. Some I have quoted or cited in the book or have led me to another valuable source—or both. Nearly every extended conversation I have had in the last couple of years (and in some cases long before) has come around to some question or other that preoccupied me at the time; so the risk that I have failed to acknowledge someone is especially great. At the very least I want to thank Robert Abzug, Jenna Feltey Alden, Walter Truett Anderson, Roderick Bailey, David Baker, David Barker, Nancy Barskey, Joy Behar, Bill Behrman, Dan Berger, Adam Blatner, Dale Buchanan, John Casson, Nicholas Christakis, Peter Sachs Collopy, Don Clarkson, Lisa Corrigan, Abdallah Daar, Robert DeRubeis, Rick Doblin, James DuBois, Ken Dychtwald, Robert Epstein, Werner Erhard, Linton Freeman, Paul Gaffney, Tom Gage, David Gibson, Barry Glassner, James Giordano, Sergio Guimaraes, Keith Hampton, Andy Harmon, Scott Highhouse, Kathryn Hinsch, Charles Kadushin, Samy Kamkar, Marcia Karp, Michael Kearns, Scott H. Kellogg, Alan Kirschenbaum, Frances Kissling, David Knoke, Joseph Konstan, Marc Lenzenwger, Jeanne Loring, Katia Mai, John Markoff, Cameron Marlow, John Markoff, Roddy Maude-Roxby, Frank Miller, Donna Murch, Mike Murphy, John Nolte, James Ogilvy, Tim O'Reilly, Sam Osherson, Randy Papadopoulos, Sheldon Patinkin, Ed Paisley, Malcolm Pines, Joe Powers, Judith Roberts, Ann Rondeau, Nikolas Rose, Alan Rosenblatt, Sandy Rosenzweig, Liba Rubenstein, Cary Sparks, Pamela Sankar, Keith Sawyer, Beryl Satter, Ulf Schmidt, Jay Schulkin, Dennis L. Serrette, Clay Shirky, Barbara Silverstein, Maj. General Jack Singlaub (US Army, Ret.), Robert Siroka, Wendy Smith, Stuart Sotsky, Gonneke Spits, Barry Spodak, Mark Stahlman, Gloria Steinem, David Swink, Tom Treadwell, Marlene Vasilic, Barbara Wallace, Kathleen Wallace, Katie Watson, Mark Wentworth, Lewis Yablonsky, Paul Zak, and Daniel Zemel.

Special thanks to Betsy Amster who helped me through multiple revisions of the proposal, a process that proved critical to settling on the story I wanted to tell.

In 1978 the Francis A. Countway Library of Medicine at Harvard accepted the stewardship of my father's papers. I want to thank the library and Jack Eckert in particular for their cooperation in making those documents available for my use.

Lara Maggs attended my seminar in the history of technology at the University of Pennsylvania, did her senior honors thesis under my supervision, and stuck around for a master's in bioethics. Fortunately, her patience didn't run out before I asked her to be my research assistant. Although this project was some distance from Lara's undergraduate work in the life sciences, she took it up with alacrity. Her combination of intelligence and persistence was invaluable. Probably Lara never thought that having her home only a few minutes from Harvard's Countway Library would come in so handy.

I was delighted to learn that a recent Harvard graduate named Graham Lazar had also been immersed in the Countway collection for his honors thesis in the history of science. Taking on primary source material with little context is a challenge for a writer of any age, yet Graham dove in and produced a fascinating paper. It was wonderful to have Graham's fresh insights into my father's work.

There is no more collegial or supportive institution than the University of Pennsylvania. Among the unexpected pleasures of writing this book were my conversations with colleagues at the university whose work involves one or more aspects of the ideas I examine, and the discovery that several of the important figures that are part of the story were distinguished members of the faculty decades ago. Thanks as well to the Center for American Progress, where I have learned a great deal about the policy process and the role of social media.

This is the fourth project I've undertaken with my editor and friend Erika Goldman. It has been so important for me to enjoy her confidence, patience, and sound judgment all these years. Every time I've had a moment of doubt—and there have been plenty of them—I've told myself that if Erika thinks I'm on the right track all will be well.

Thanks to Jarrett for deepening my appreciation of the way communications networks have helped to shape the consciousness of a generation and to Jillian for her critical and sensitive reading of drafts at a moment's notice. J.L. would have been exceedingly proud of them both.

More than 40 years ago J.L. looked into Leslye's beautiful blue eyes with his own. I have no doubt that he approved of my taste. Fortunately for me she did as well.

## ILLUSTRATION CREDITS

Psychodrama theater image used with permission of John Nolte.

Cartoon panels of Woody Allen's encounter with psychodrama in the early 1960s are from the comic biography *John Wilcock, New York Years*, http://www.ep.tc/john-wilcock
© Ethan Persoff and Scott Marshall, used with permission.

Obesity network sociogram used with permission of Nicholas Christakis.

# Notes

Introduction

p. 21   "... among Iranians on Facebook and other sites."
http://knowyourmeme.com/memes/events/
clint-eastwoods-empty-chair-speech-eastwooding-invisible-obama.

p. 25   "... and the revolution of encounterculture was joined." Robert Karoly
Sarlos, *Jig Cook and the Provincetown Players: Theatre in Ferment*
(Amherst, MA: University of California Press, 1982), p. 40.

p. 25   "... for a book dealing with the history of ideas." Ibid., fn. 16, p. 214.

Chapter One

p. 27   ... from a *Time* magazine article. Patrick Goldstein, "The Year that
Movies Got in Touch with the Cultural Revolution," *Los Angeles Times*,
July 7, 2009.

p. 27   "... for educational and institutional change." Robert L. Schwartz, "New
Hope for the Dull," *Life Magazine*, June 12, 1970, p. 16.

p. 28   "... by other means." Todd Gitlin, *The Sixties: Years of Hope, Days of
Rage* (New York: Bantam Books, 1987), p. 426.

p. 29   "... to tell the truth in our personal relationships." Roger Ebert, "Bob
and Carol and Ted and Alice," *Chicago Sun-Times*, December 22, 1969.

p. 31   "... distinctions between sensitivity training, group encounter, and
group psychotherapy are blurred. ..." "Foreword," Robert W. Siroka,
Ellen K. Siroka, and Gilbert A. Schloss, eds., *Sensitivity Training and
Group Encounter* (New York: Grosset & Dunlap, 1971), p. vii.

p. 31   "... considered the forerunner of the Group Encounter movement."
Gilbert A. Schloss, Robert W. Siroka, and Ellen K. Siroka, "Some
Contemporary Origins of the Personal Growth Group," Robert W.
Siroka, Ellen K. Siroka, and Gilbert A. Schloss, eds., op, cit., p. 3.

p. 32   "... anything you fancy for the hell of it." Alex Comfort, *The New Joy of
Sex* (New York: Simon & Schuster, 1991), p. 152.

p. 32   "... frequently producing negative results." "Introduction," Robert W.
Siroka, Ellen K. Siroka, and Gilbert A. Schloss, op, cit., p. 103.

p. 34   "... to some quiet activity like that of an artist." "Psychodrama Institute
to be Established Here," *Los Angeles Times*, June 29, 1945.

p. 35    ". . . I am the controversy." J.L. Moreno, *Who Shall Survive?* (Beacon, NY: Beacon House, 1953), p. cviii.

p. 35    ". . . in the field of group psychotherapy." George Gazda, *Basic Approaches to Group Psychotherapy and Group Counseling* (Springfield, IL: Charles C. Thomas, 1982), p. 10.

p. 35    ". . . has receded into the shadows." Karl E. Scheibe, *The Drama of Everyday Life* (Cambridge, MA: Harvard University Press, 2000), p. 5.

p. 36    ". . . a psychiatry and sociatry for all mankind." Jane Howard, *Please Touch: A Guided Tour of the Human Potential Movement* (New York: Dell, 1970), p. 255.

p. 37    "strong group experiences." Kurt W. Back, *Beyond Words* (New York: Russell Sage Foundation, 1972), pp. 3–4.

p. 38    ". . . an excitable young Austrian psychiatrist named Jacob Levy Moreno." Walter Truett Anderson, *The Upstart Spring* (Reading, MA: Addison-Wesley, 1983), p. 80.

p. 39    . . . nearly 80 percent were in private practice. Ellen Herman, *The Romance of American Psychology* (Berkeley: University of California Press, 1995), pp. 258–259.

p. 39    ". . . in the realization of certain ethical values." Nevitt Sanford, quoted in Ellen Herman, Ibid., p. 261.

p. 40    ". . . but which usually leads to ecstasy." William C. Schutz, *Joy: Expanding Human Awareness* (New York: Grove Press, 1967), p. 19.

p. 41    ". . . Only physical assault was prohibited." Tom Wolfe, "The 'Me' Decade and the Third Great Awakening," *New York Magazine*, August 23, 1976.

p. 41    ". . . and carried him into the group circle." Schutz, op. cit., p. 80.

p. 44    ". . . I sensed a gallantry in their efforts to change the world." Howard, op. cit., p. 5.

p. 44    ". . . draping and became a drapee myself." Howard, op. cit., p. 14.

p. 45    ". . . and who founded that much-used technique of psychodrama." Howard, op. cit., p. 45.

p. 45    ". . . a one-armed lady who often conducts group psychodrama sessions." Howard, op. cit., p. 45.

p. 45    ". . . backward from 2000." Correspondence with Jane Howard, June 1, 1970. Moreno Papers, 44:699.

p. 45    "LIFE has never done a proper review. . . ." Correspondence with Jane Howard, December 8, 1971. Moreno Papers, 44:699.

p. 45    ". . . the sort of article you suggest." Letter from Jane Howard, January 5, 1972, Moreno Papers, 44:699.

p. 46    ". . . and think it's a cop-out when they don't get one." Pauline Kael, "Waiting for Orgy," *The New Yorker*, October 4, 1969.

p. 46   ". . . would have buried the movie's small, but poignant, message." Roger Ebert, op., cit., 1969.

CHAPTER TWO

p. 51   ". . . its creativity and spirituality." Malcolm Pines, "Moreno in Context: A Sketch of the Shapes of Two Elephants," unpublished paper.

p. 51   ". . . a psychology of possibility, of openness to the future, of indeterminacy. . . ." Malcolm Pines, "Psychoanalysis, Psychodrama and Group Psychotherapy: Step-Children of Vienna," *Group Analysis* 19(101): 1986.

p. 51   ". . . through Jewish mystical traditions." David Bakan, *Sigmund Freud and the Jewish Mystical Tradition* (Princeton: D. Van Nostrand, 1958).

p. 51   . . . chaos on all sides. Gershom Scholem, *Sabbatai Sevi: The Mystical Messiah*: 1626–1676 (London: Routledge Kegan Paul, 1973).

p. 54   ". . . co-existing with an urge to destroy." Ackerl, op. cit., p. 6.

p. 54   ". . . secure, righteous, and repressive. . ." Carl E. Schorske, *Fin-de-Siecle Vienna: Politics and Culture* (New York: Vintage, 1981), p. 6.

p. 54   ". . . opening her creative side." Rene Marineau, *Jacob Levy Moreno, 54–1974* (London, Routledge 1987), p. 36–38.

p. 55   ". . . but died with a considerable estate." Josephine Mary Nelmes Simpson, *Peter Altenberg: A Neglected Writer of the Viennese Jahrhundertwende* (Berlin: Peter Lang GmbH, 1987).

p. 55   ". . . accomplish a regeneration of culture as a whole." Allan Janik and Stephen Toulmin, *Wittgenstein's Vienna* (New York: Simon & Schuster, 1973), p. 70.

p. 56   ". . . for the movie adaptation of his novel." Jonathan D. Moreno, ed., "J.L. Moreno, The Autobiography of J.L. Moreno," M.D. *Journal of Group Psychotherapy, Psychodrama & Sociometry* (42:1–2), 1989, p. 71. Unless otherwise noted all further references to J.L.'s personal recollections are attributed to this autobiography.

p. 56   ". . . both a scientist and a theologian." Marineau, op. cit., p. 26.

p. 56   ". . . he entered the University of Vienna in 1909." Marineau, op. cit., p. 26. (J.L. reports that he entered the university in 1908, but Marineau inspected the registration records and reports the date as 1909.)

p. 59   ". . . that responsibility to colleagues." Britta MeEwen, *Sexual Knowledge: Feeling, Fact and Social Reform in Vienna, 1900–1934* (New York: Bergahn Books, 2012), pp. 29–31.

p. 60   ". . . the general condition or 'race hygiene' of the social body." Ibid., p. 29.

p. 61  "... the Jewish hospital." Wolfgang Neugebauer, *Racial Hygiene in Vienna 1938* (wird publiziert in: wiener klinische wochenschrift, Sonderheft, März 1998. http://www.doew.at/information/mitarbeiter/ beitraege/rachyg.html.

p. 63  "... nor even that the draft letter was sent." Rene Marineau, op. cit., p. 43–44.

p. 64  "... and at another with an 'i.'" Marineau, op. cit., p. 172, n. 8.

p. 65  "... and began applying it to psychotherapy." Robert Karoly Sarlos, *Jig Cook and the Provincetown Players* (Amherst, MA: The University of Massachusetts Press, 1982), p. 56.

p. 66  "... philosopher of humanistic psychology." Robert Waldl, Doctoral thesis: "The Influence of Martin Buber's I and Thou by J.L. Moreno," University of Vienna, 2006.

p. 67  "... Austria at that time." Marineau, op. cit., p. 55.

CHAPTER THREE

p. 73  "... nothing but the text and its interpreter." Janik and Toulmin, op. cit., p. 82.

p. 74  "... someone else's play again." Marineau, op. cit., p. 46.

p. 75  "... of someone who is dead." J.L. Moreno, *The Theater of Spontaneity* (North-West Psychodrama Association U.K., 2010).

p. 76  "... as they looked at the speaker as a fool." Quoted in Eberhard Scheiffele, "The Theatre of Truth," doctoral dissertation, University of California, Berkeley, 1995, pp. 20–21.

p. 76  "... with much temperament, energy and brilliance...." Ibid., pp. 84–85.

p. 76  "... they repeated a given plot." J.L. Moreno, *The Theater of Spontaneity, Third Edition* (Ambler, PA: Beacon House, 1983), p. 55.

p. 77  "... died a slow death." J.L. Moreno, *Psychodrama, Volume One* (Beacon, New York: Beacon House, 1946), p. 12.

p. 78  "... engaging than the well-respected classics, including Strindberg." Quoted in Eberhard Schiweffele, "The Theatre of Truth," doctoral dissertation, University of California, Berkeley, 1995, pp. 22–23.

p. 78  "... in recognition of his talent for mimicry." Youngkin, op. cit., p. 19.

p. 78  "... of psychic complexes at the same time." Youngkin, Ibid., p. 16.

p. 79  "... to 'de-conserve' his 'mimic behavior.'" Youngkin, Ibid., p. 18.

p. 80  ... to bring news to illiterate peasants. J.W. Casson, "Living Newspaper: Theatre and Therapy," *The Drama Review* 44(2):107–122, 2000.

p. 80  ... which his friend Robert Muller had written about. Jonathan Fox, *Acts of Service, Spontaneity, Commitment, Tradition in the Nonscripted Theatre* (New Paltz, NY: Tusitala Publishing, 1986).

p. 80   ". . . similar to J.L.'s view of the theater as a divine instrument." For an extended argument on the similarity of Evreinoff's ideas J.L.'s see John Casson, "Monodrama and Psychodrama." http://www.psychodramansp.co.uk/index.php/resources.

p. 81   . . . an article about psychotherapy and drama in 1916. S.E. Jelliffe, "The Physician and Psychotherapy," Medical Record, August 26, 1916. Reprinted as "The Drama and Psychotherapy" in S.E. Jelliffe and Louise Brink, *Psychoanalysis and the Drama* (New York: Nervous and Mental Disease Publishing Company, 1922.

p. 81   ". . . were actually on stage and in performance." Richard and Richards, cited in Ebert Schieffele, op. cit., p. 83.

p. 81   ". . . in front of a paying audience." Keith Sawyer, *Improvised Dialogues* (Westport, CT: Ablex, 2003), p. 17.

p. 83   ". . . saw themselves in a 'psychological mirror.'" J.L. Moreno, op. cit., 1946, p. 3–5.

p. 84   ". . . into a freer and broader world." J.L. Moreno, *Psychodrama, Volume I* (Beacon, NY: Beacon House, 1959), p. 315.

p. 85   ". . . Muller seems to have been besieged by creditors." Thomas Schwarz, "Robert Muller: A Barbarian of the Twentieth Century." http://robertmueller1887.wordpress.com.

p. 85   "She should be remembered." Robert Muller, "The Impromptu Theater in Vienna," Prager Presse, 1924; reprinted in J.L. Moreno, ed., *Impromptu* 1(1):24–26, 1931.

p. 86   ". . . but not in connection with the stage." Peter Weibel, *Beyond Art: A Third Culture: A Comparative Study in Cultures, Art and Science in 20th Century Austria and Hungary* (Berlin: Springer, 2005), p. 66.

p. 86   . . . for the United States Navy. Richard Rhodes, *Hedy's Folly: The Life and Breakthrough Inventions of Hedy Lamarr* (New York: Doubleday, 2012).

p. 87   . . . complete with caricatures. Reprinted from Barbara Lesak, *Die Kulisse Explodiert: Friedrich Kieslers Theaterexperimente und Architecturprojekte, 1923–25* (Vienna: Locker Verlag, 1988).

p. 88   ". . . examples in Vienna, Munich and New York." Hiram Motherwell, *The Theater of To-day* (New York: John Lane Company, 1914), p. 38–39.

CHAPTER FOUR

p. 97   ". . . Adler referred some of his patients to J.L." A. Paul Hare and June Rabson Hare, *J.L. Moreno* (London: Sage, 1996), p. 21.

p. 98   ". . . impromptu theatre for the intellectuals of Vienna." Robert Muller, "The Impromptu Theater in Vienna," Prager Presse, 1924; reprinted in J.L. Moreno, ed., *Impromptu* 1(1):24–26, 1931.

p. 98     ". . . a 1923 article called 'Impromptu Express.'" Hans Kafka, "Impromptu Express," Die Buhne, 1923; reprinted in *Impromptu* 1(1):17–18, 1931.

p. 98     ". . . where her illustrious grandfather preached in his Plymouth Congregational Church." Marineau reports that Beatrice was born in 1892 (Marineau, op. cit., p. 180, n. 4), but a genealogical website for the descendants of John Beecher lists her birthdate as 1894 and her death in 1972. Interestingly, in his autobiography J.L. states that she died in the mid-1930s, but this was almost certainly an error—or perhaps a way to "resolve" his friendship with her that somehow ended in those years. Apparently she never remarried. http://wc.rootsweb.ancestry.com/cgi-bin/igm.cgi?op=GET&db=billjim&id=I2137.

p. 99     ". . . in schools, churches and universities." Marineau, op. cit., p. 97.

p. 99     ". . . J.L.s book on the Theater of Spontaneity." Marineau, op. cit., p. 96.

p. 100    ". . . herself an instructor at Hunter." "Girl's Parents Make Charges and Hunter Professor Quits," *Brooklyn Daily Eagle*, November 30, 1929. http://fultonhistory.com/Newspaper%205/Brooklyn%20NY%20Daily%20Eagle/Brooklyn%20NY%20Daily%20Eagle%201929%20Grayscale/Brooklyn%20NY%20Daily%20Eagle%201929%20a%20Grayscale%20-%200421.pdf.

p. 102    ". . . his influence cannot be entirely ruled out." John Casson, "Living Newspaper: Theatre and Therapy," *TDR: The Drama Review* 44(2):107–22, 2000.

p. 104    ". . . the financial stability of the theatre." J.L. Moreno, *The Theatre of Spontaneity, Third Edition* (Ambler, PA: Beacon House, 1983), p. a.

p. 104    ". . . entirely absent in the legitimate theatre." A.B.W. Smith, "The Impromptu Theatre in New York," *Impromptu* 1(1):11–13, 1931.

p. 105    ". . . personable members of the opposite sex." Robert Mitchell, "Impromptu for us Lowbrows," *Impromptu* 1(1):46, 1931.

p. 106    ". . . their own memories to recreate emotion." Gilbert Laurence, interview, March 2005, Psybernet: Moreno Page. http://www.psybernet.co.nz/gilbert_laurence_moreno.html.

p. 106    ". . . a living embodiment of communal values and aspirations." Wendy Smith, *Real Life Drama: The Group Theatre and America, 1931–1940* (New York: Knopf, 1990), p. 199.

p. 107    ". . . is said to have used psychodrama in his rehearsals." Paul Portner, "Psychodrama: Theater der Spontaneitat," *Theater Heute*, 8(9):10–14, 1966.

p. 107    ". . . on twentieth century theater. . . ." Keith Sawyer, op.cit., 2003, p. 20.

p. 107    ". . . a therapeutic party-game for a small, close-knit group," Robert Karily Sarlos, *Jig Cook and the Provincetown Players* (Amherst, MA: University of Massachusetts Press, 1982), p. 14.

p. 107    ". . . in an increasingly mechanized and impersonal world." Ibid., p. 40.

p. 108    ". . . whose theatre he shared." Ibid., p. 40.

p. 108    ". . . a hallmark of Chicago improv." Keith Sawyer, op. cit., 2003, p. 22.

p. 108    ". . . However, the actor and director Andrew Harmon. . . ." Andrew Harmon, telephone interview, February 7, 2013.

p. 109    ". . . and perform naturally and spontaneously." Jeffrey Sweet, *Something Wonderful Right Away* (New York: Proscenium Publishers, 2003), p. xvii.

p. 109    ". . . it started with The Compass back on 55th Street." Ibid., p. 13.

p. 109    ". . . a backstage observer of The Compass. . . ." Janet Coleman, *The Compass: The Improvisational Theatre that Revolutionized American Comedy* (Chicago: University of Chicago Press, 1990), p. 152.

p. 110    ". . . in the style of Second City." Marcia Karp to JDM, e-mail, January 6, 2014.

p. 110    "As the director Andrew Harmon pointed out to me. . . ." Andrew Harmon, telephone interview, February 7, 2013.

p. 110    ". . . in a theater setting is impossible." "Bernie Sahlins, co-founder of Second City, dies at 90," *Chicago Tribune*, June 17, 2013.

p. 112    "an asylum for the creator. . . ." J.L. Moreno, "Ave Creatore," *Impromptu* 1(1):9–10, 1931.

p. 113    ". . . incident 'most psychoanalysts turned against Moreno.'" Marineau, op. cit., p. 129.

p. 114    ". . . he was unable to disburden himself of his depressive moods." "Lincoln Analyzed by a Psychiatrist," *Lawrence (Kansas) Journal-World*, June 5, 1931. http://news.google.com/newspapers?nid=2199&dat=193106 05&id=Wz9XAAAAIBAJ&sjid=7EMNAAAAIBAJ&pg=1231,6001564.

p. 114    ". . . through the lens of childhood traumas and sexual conflicts." Joshua Wolf Shenk, *Lincoln's Melancholy* (New York: Houghton-Mifflin, 2005), p. 6.

p. 115    ". . . versus the President of the United States." J.L. Moreno, *Who Shall Survive?* (Beacon, NY.: Beacon House, 1953), pp. xlvii–l.

p. 115    ". . . based on unproven and unsubstantiated conclusions." Lucy Ozarin, "J.L. Moreno, M.D., Founder of Psychodrama," *Psychiatric News* 38(10):60, 2003. http://psychnews.psychiatryonline.org/newsarticle. aspx?articleid=106261.

p. 116    ". . . he called Fortinbras to take over." J.L. Moreno, op. cit., 1953, pp. xlvii–l.

p. 116    ". . . what they say as facts." A.A. Brill, quote in *Toronto Evening Star*, June 5, 1931, as reported in J.L. Moreno, *Who Shall Survive?* (1953), p. xlvi.

p. 116    ". . . J.L.'s real target was not Brill but Freud and psychoanalysis itself." Marineau, op. cit., p. 129.

p. 117    ". . . one of the two greatest presidents of this republic." "Lincoln
Analyzed by a Psychiatrist," op. cit..

p. 117    ". . . I see nothing of which we can complain." "The American
Psychiatric Association Proceedings Eighty-Seventh Annual
Meeting," *American Journal of Psychiatry*, 88:333–383, 1931. http://ajp.
psychiatryonline.org/article.aspx?articleID=140424.

p. 117    "akin to hypnotism." Lawrence R. Samuel, *Shrink: A Cultural History of
Psychoanalysis in America* (Lincoln, NB: University of Nebraska, 2013),
p. 42.

## Chapter Five

p. ??    ". . . under Moreno's direction." E. Stagg Whitten, "The Application
of the Group Method to the Classification of Prisoners, " *Sociometry*
8(3–4), Group Psychotherapy: A Symposium (Aug.–Nov., 1945), p. 33.
Whitin's name appears to be misspelled in this document.

p. 119    ". . . defined experimentally the interpersonal situation and developed
interpersonal measurement." J.L. Moreno, *Who Shall Survive?* (Beacon,
NY: Beacon House, 1953), p. lx.

p. 119    "Network research is 'hot' today. . . ." Stephen P. Borgatti, Ajay Mehre,
Daniel J. Brass, Giuseppe LaBianca, "Network Analysis in the Social
Sciences," *Science* 323:892, 2009.

p. 120    ". . . with another lonely mortal." Charles Mercer, Associated Press,
October 31, 1958. http://news.google.com/newspapers?nid=2202&dat=19
581031&id=TCkmAAAAIBAJ&sjid=U_4FAAAAIBAJ&pg=1096,19966.

p. 121    ". . . metaphor into an analytic diagram." John G. Scott, *Social Network
Analysis: A Handbook* (London: Sage, 1991), p. 10.

p. 123    ". . . modern social network analysis." Massimo Franceschetti, "The
Power and Beauty of Networks," http://users.dimi.uniud.it/~massimo.
franceschet/netart/talk/netart.html

p. 125    ". . . by group attraction, repulsion, and indifference." "Emotions
Mapped by New Geography," *New York Times*, April 3, 1933.

p. 128    ". . . is in effect a sociometric test." Kurt W. Back, *Beyond Words* (New
York: Russell Sage Foundation, 1972), p. 96.

p. 130    ". . . of an equal number of adolescents." J.L. Moreno, op. cit., 1953, p. 527.

p. 131    ". . . had decreased to about one half of the former frequency." Ibid., p.
523.

p. 131    "in education and social activities white and colored mix freely." J.L.
Moreno, op. cit., 1953, p. 220.

p. 132    ". . . destroyed by the State of New York." "Ward of the State: The Gap
in Ella Fitzgerald's Life," *New York Times*, June 23, 1996. http://www.
nytimes.com/1996/06/23/weekinreview/ward-of-the-state-the-gap-in-
ella-fitzgerald-s-life.html.

p. 134    "... a measure of economic security for its families." Shepard Wolman. "Sociometric Planning of a New Community," *Sociometry*, 1(12):220–221, 1937.

p. 134    "Neighbors for New Communities May Be Lined Up By 'Sociometry.'" Howard Blakeslee, Associated Press, August 25, 1935.

p. 135    "... they did this in groups." Charles P. Loomis, oral history interview, SfAA News, Society for the Study of Applied Anthropology (n.d.). http://sfaanews.sfaa.net/2013/02/01/sfaa-oral-history-project-conversation-with-one-of-sfaas-founders-an-interview-of-charles-p-loomis.

p. 136    "... the far-right bullies of that era." Jo Hindman, "Social Engineering for 1984," *Human Events*, December 15, 1958, pp. 5–8.

p. 136    "... and hounded for much of the rest of his career." Cooke, Bill. (2007). "The Kurt Lewin—Goodwin Watson FBI/CIA Files: A Sixtieth Anniversary of There-and-Then of the Here-and-Now," *Human Relations*, 60(3):435–462.

p. 136    "... may be harmful to the liberal cause." J.L. Moreno to Doris Twitchell Allen, January 21, 1959.

p. 136    "... that the time and money weren't worth the trouble." Doris Twitchell Allen to J.L. Moreno, February 27, 1959.

p. 136    "... since the beginning of time." Gordon Allport to J.L. Moreno, February 13, 1959.

p. 136    "... believing J.L. would win." Howard Becker to J.L. Moreno, February 24, 1959.

p. 136    "... urged him to ignore the matter." Paul Tillich to J.L. Moreno, February 26, 1959.

p. 136    "... and have since discarded is libel action." David Riesman to J.L. Moreno, February 20, 1959.

p. 136    ... as that would play into the critics hands. Margaret Mead to J.L. Moreno, April 3, 1959.

p. 140    "... and his inter-relations with other people." William Alanson White, op. cit., 1945, p. 21.

p. 140    "... in the successive stages of their development." Ibid., p. 19.

p. 141    "... from 13,000 to over 24,000." Federal Bureau of Prisons, "A Brief History of the Bureau of Prisons," http://www.bop.gov/about/history.jsp (accessed March 22, 2013).

p. 141    "... which threatens our civilization." Whitten, op. cit., p. 33.

p. 143    "... American sociology and psychology at the time." Linton C. Freeman, *The Development of Social Network Analysis* (Vancouver: Empirical Press, 2004), p. 31.

p. 144    "... to cast any light on sociological questions." Ibid, p. 42.

CHAPTER SIX

p. 147    ". . . such as William Alanson White, Winifred Overholser, Pierre Renouvier, S.H. Foulkes. . . ." J.L. Moreno, Concerning the Origins of the Terms Group Therapy and Group Psychotherapy (Correspondence), *American Journal of Psychiatry* 116, August 1959, p. 176.

p. 149    ". . . within the fold of the American Psychiatric Association." J.L. Moreno, op. cit., p. 176.

p. 152    ". . . and his work with psychodrama and sociometry." Howard Blakeslee, "Psychiatrist: God Speaks Constantly to Each and Every Man," Associated Press, November 30, 1941.

p. 152    ". . . not in his new psychodrama theater." Associated Press, "Public Quarreling On Stage Seen To Be Cure for Marital Rifts," September 20, 1937.

p. 152    "The Odds Against True Love Are . . . ?" Lillian C. Genn, *The Edwardsville Intelligencer* (syndicated column), June 26, 1937.

p. 155    ". . . partly because of his embrace of psychoanalytic theory." Samuel Slavson, *An Introduction to Group Therapy* (New York: The Commonwealth Fund, 1944).

p. 155    "When Slavson's group therapy association published a brief history . . ." American Group Psychotherapy Association, "A Brief History of the American Group Psychotherapy Association, 1943–1968," *International Journal of Group Psychotherapy* 21(4), October 1971.

p. 155    ". . . with the claim of a still earlier priority." Robert K. Merton, *The Sociology of Science* (Chicago: University of Chicago Press, 1973), p. 396.

p. 155    ". . . that divided the American group therapy world ever since." Zerka T. Moreno, personal interview, May 30, 2013. . . .Trist quoted J.L. during the wartime work. Pearl King, ed., *No Ordinary Psychoanalyst* (London: H. Karnac Ltd., 2003), p. 53.

p. 157    ". . . can be traced back to him. . . ." Art Kleiner, *The Age of Heretics* (New York: Jossey-Bass, 2008), p. 21.

p. 158    ". . . for use in his own research." Susan T. Fiske, Daniel T. Gilbert, Gardner Lindzey, eds. *Handbook of Social Psychology*, 5th Edition, Volume 2, (Hoboken, NJ: John Wiley, 2010), p. 1220.

p. 158    ". . . research for her work on Lewin." Jenna Feltey Alden, personal interview, July 24, 2013.

p. 159    ". . . at Columbia University's psychology department." Marineau, op. cit., p. 182, n. 7.

p. 161    ". . . in adequate structures of communication." Peter Miller and Nikolas Rose, "*Production, Identity, and Democracy,*" *Governing the Present: Administering Economic, Social and Personal Life* (Cambridge, England: Polity Press, 2008), p. 182.

p. 161    ". . . every Wednesday night, Nancy?' " Kleiner, p. 25.

p. 162    "I would like to pass this feeling on to you." Kurt Lewin, "Action Research and Minority Problems," *Journal of Social Issues* 2(4):42, 1946.

p. 164    ". . . to maturity of individual and group functioning." Ronald Lippitt, Kurt Lewin, 1890-1947: Adventures in the Exploration of Interdependence," *Sociometry Monographs* (17), (Beacon NY: Beacon House Inc., 1947), p. 27.

p. 167    ". . . advice that J.L. took." Personal interview, Lewis Yablonsky, May 21, 2013.

p. 167    ". . . the work of Moreno and his numerous associates. . . ." Kenneth D. Benne and Bozidar Muntyan, "Preface," *Human Relations in Curriculum Change* (New York: The Drydren Press, 1951), p. x.

p. 167    ". . . influenced the development of group dynamics. . . ." Alfred J. Marrow, *The Practical Theorist* (New York: Basic Books, 1969), p. 167.

p. 168    ". . . only by considering both facets of his personality." Linton C. Freeman, *The Development of Social Network Analysis* (Vancouver, B.C.: Empirical Press, 2004), p. 31.

p. 168    ". . . to be associated with him." Ibid., p. 41.

p. 169    "'Of course you know,' J.L. muttered in passing, 'I said that first.'" Lewis Yablonsky, personal interview, May 21, 2013.

## Chapter Seven

p. 171    ". . . including having all her teeth pulled out." Lewis Banks III, MAJ, USA, "The Office of Strategic Services Psychological Selection Program," Master's Thesis, US Army Command and General Staff College, 1995, p. 10.

p. 171    ". . . would play 'Boo, Boo, I'm a Spy' whenever he walked in." Banks, Ibid., p. 11.

p. 172    ". . . 'electronic brains' could become 'cybernetic organisms' or 'cyborgs.'" Matthew Farish, *The Contours of America's Cold War* (Minneapolis, MN: University of Minnesota Press, 2010), pp. 147–148.

p. 172    ". . . (earning the OSS the sobriquet 'Oh So Social')" Charles Pinck, "General Donovan's Glorious Amateurs," *The OSS Society Journal*, Fall 2012, p. 14.

p. 172    ". . . tests to assess variables like emotional stability and leadership skills." Ibid., p. 151.

p. 173    ". . . the connection between information theory and psychology." See Norbert Wiener, "Introduction," *Cybernetics* (Cambridge, MA: MIT Press, 1948), p. 18. I am grateful to Mark Stahlman for this point.

p. 173    ". . . connected around the mind and heart." Kathleen Dannemiller, interview in Bill Cooke. The Kurt Lewin—Goodwin Watson FBI/CIA Files: A Sixtieth Anniversary of There-and-Then of the Here-and-Now. *Human Relations* 60(3):435–462, 2007.

p. 174     ". . . for the Office of Strategic Services (OSS) during World War II." Kimball Young, Linton Freeman, "Chapter 19: Social Psychology and Sociology," Howard Paul Becker and Alvin Boskoff, eds. *Modern Sociological Theory* (New York: McGraw Hill, 1957), pp. 550–557.

p. 174     ". . . better than blind guesses, but not by much." Daniel Kahneman, "Don't Blink: The Hazards of Overconfidence," *The New York Times Magazine*, October 19, 2011.

p. 174     ". . . similar to that in the English War Office Selection Boards (WOSBs) be set up in the OSS." Donald W. MacKinnon, *How Assessment Centers were Started in the United States*, Development Dimensions International, Inc., 2005, p. 3.

p. 175     ". . . but was resisted by many in the organization." MacKinnon, Ibid., pp. 2–3.

p. 177     ". . . including undergoing simulated interrogations under stressful conditions." Banks, p. 68.

p. 177     ". . . if confronted with such a situation. . . ." MacKinnon, op. cit., p. 10.

p. 177     ". . . a variety of objective and projective psychological tests." Ellen Herman, *The Romance of American Psychology* (Berkeley: University of California Press, 1995), p. 45.

p. 180     ". . . bubble like a spontaneous fountain all his life." Henry Murray to Zerka T. Moreno, June 24, 1952.

p. 180     ". . . much of which is Grain, the rest Chaff." Henry Murray to Lewis Mumford, quoted in Forrest Robinson, *Love's Story Told: A Life of Henry A. Murray* (Cambridge, MA: Harvard University Press, 1993), fn. p. 438.

p. 180     ". . . being a mysterious man with secret knowledge." Henry A. Murray, quoted in Richard Harris Smith, *OSS: The Secret History of America's First Central Intelligence Agency* (Berkeley: University of California Press, 1972), p. 5.

p. 180     ". . . the making and remaking of selves. . . ." Lewis Mumford, *The City in History: Its Origins, Its Transformations and Its Prospects* (New York: Harcourt, Brace and World, 1961), p. 116.

p. 181     ". . . the real identities of the people they were assessing." Banks, p. 54.

p. 181     ". . . the 'OSS entrance exam.'" Review Leonard W. Doob, *The Saturday Review*, May 29, 1948, p. 10.

p. 181     ". . . for support rather than light." Henry A. Murray quoted in James H. Korn, *Illusions of Reality: A History of Deception in Social Psychology* (Albany, NY: SUNY Press, 1997), p. 61.

p. 181     ". . . and Hints by the "Prisoner, etc." MacKinnon, op. cit., p. 7.

p. 182     ". . . sometimes they physically attacked the stooges." Banks, pp. 66–67.

p. 183     ". . . by finding a computer program." John K. Singlaub, Major General, US Army, Ret., telephone interview, July 18, 2013.

p. 183    ". . . and to transform the individuals who comprised it." Nikolas Rose and Peter Miller, *Governing the Present* (Malden, MA: Polity Press, 2008), p. 152.

p. 184    ". . . who attended a weekly meeting of ward representatives." Brian Nicholl, "Bion and Foulkes at Northfield: The Early Development of Group Psychotherapy in Britain," Business Coach Institute, published online. www.businesscoachinstitute.com/library/bion_and_foulkes_at_northfield.shtml

p. 184    ". . . much of our time in various forms of exercise and activities." Quoted in S.H. Foulkes, *Introduction to Group-Analytic Psychotherapy* (London: Heinemann, 1948) p. 49.

p. 184    ". . . was dramatic enough for his taste." Malcolm Pines, "Foreword" in Martin Ringer, *Group Action* (London: Jessica Kingsley, 2002), p. 13.

p. 184    ". . . to make spontaneous readjustments to their environment." Tom Harrison, *Bion, Rickman, Foulkes and the Northfield Experiments* (London: Jessica Kingsley, 2000), p. 64.

p. 185    ". . . or asking him to help with a wounded comrade." Roy Grinker and John Spiegel, quoted in Ben Shepherd, *A War of Nerves* (Cambridge, MA: Harvard University Press, 2003), p. 214.

p. 186    ". . . do not necessarily provide insight." Ivan C. Berlien, *Psychiatry in the Army Correctional System*, Office of Medical History (US Army Medical Department, n.d.), p. 508.

p. 186    ". . . so that group pressure for social adjustment was effectively employed." Berlien, op. cit., p. 508.

p. 186    ". . . by individuals in front of the group, with good results." Norman Q. Brill, *Psychiatry in the Army Correctional System*, Office of Medical History (US Army Medical Department, n.d.), p. 289.

p. 186    ". . . by both medical and line personnel that it was beneficial." Berlien, op. cit., p. 511.

p. 187    ". . . and other questions of the same sort." MacKinnon, op. cit., p. 10.

p. 188    ". . . small groups of many kinds." Leslie D. Zeleny, "Selection of Compatible Flying Partners," *American Journal of Sociology*, 52(5):424–431, 1947.

p. 188    ". . . the lower his number of sociometric choices by others." French, R. L. "Sociometric Status and Individual Adjustment among Naval Recruits," *Journal of Abnormal Social Psychology*, 46:64–72, 1951.

p. 189    ". . . the higher their sociometric status." Personality correlates of sociometric status," Izard, Carroll E. *Journal of Applied Psychology*, 43(2):89–93,1959.

p. 189    ". . . as well as how many choose." Leo Katz, "A New Status Index Derived from Sociometric Analysis," *Psychometrika*, 18(1):39–43, 1953.

p. 189    "... success as a regular US Army officer." Bernard M. Bass, *Bass and Stogdill's Handbook of Leadership: Theory, Research, and Managerial Applications* (New York: Free Press, 1990), p. 179.

p. 189    "... at least in Naval Aviation." James Giordano, e-mail, November 27, 2013.

p. 190    "... for the conduct of T-groups." Scott Highhouse, "A History of the T-Group and Its Early Applications to Management Development," *Group Dynamics Theory Research and Practice* 6(4):278, 2002.

p. 191    "... in the early NTL workshops." Ibid, p. 279.

p. 192    "... he begins to understand himself." Alfred Jay Marrow, *Behind the Executive Mask: Greater Managerial Competence Through Deeper Self-Understanding* (New York: American Management Association, 1964), p. 53.

p. 192    "... and a more democratic leader." Nikolas Rose, *Inventing Our Selves: Psychology, Power, and Personhood* (Cambridge, England: Cambridge University Press, 1998), p. 141.

p. 193    "... appears to have resulted from T-groups." Highhouse, op. cit., p. 283.

p. 193    "... that they avoid the entire cult." George Odiorne, quoted in Highhouse, Ibid., p. 282.

p. 193    ... a more humane world? Jenna Feltey Alden pointed this out to me.

p. 193    "... would boost worker productivity." Todd Gitlin, "Grand Illusions," *Book Forum*, December/January 2013. http://bookforum.com/inprint/1904/10582.

p. 195    "... whom he credited with persuading him to complete his Ph.D." Thomas P. Hébert, Bonnie Cramond, Kristie L. Speirs Neumeister, Garnet Miller and Alice F. Silvian, *E. Paul Torrance: His Life, Accomplishments, and Legacy* (Charlottsville, VA: The National Research Center on the Gifted and Talented, University of Virginia, 2002), p. 6.

p. 195    "... and insure his own acceptance by his men." Mario Levi, E. Paul Torrance and Gilbert O. Pletts, "Sociometric Studies of Combat Air Crews in Survival Training," *Sociometry* (17), 1954.

CHAPTER EIGHT

p. 200    "Liston has the image of a man who will conquer." Murray Rose, "Psychiatrist Sees Liston KL winner," Associated Press, September 24, 1962.

p. 201    "... courting America's culture of celebrity." Graham Henry Lazar, "Psychodrama: The Word, The Practice, the Project," Honors Thesis, Department of the History of Science, Harvard University, Cambridge, MA, March 2012, p. 42.

p. 204    "... of Carl Rogers and Abraham Maslow." "The Group: Joy on Thursday," *Newsweek*, May 12, 1969, p. 104.

p. 205  "'Why can't it always be like this?' she asked." Jenna Feltey Alden, "Bottom-Up Management: Participative Philosophy and Humanistic Psychology in American Organizational Culture, 1930–1970," Doctoral Dissertation, Department of History, Columbia University, New York, NY, 2012, pp. 104.

p. 205  ". . . in social psychology now." Ibid., p. 106.

p. 205  . . . a new religious cult. Ibid, p. 104.

p. 206  ". . . and action methods from psychodrama." Jenna Feltey Alden, "Bottom-Up Management: Participative Philosophy and Humanistic Psychology in American Organizational Culture, 1930–1970," Doctoral Dissertation, Department of History, Columbia University, New York, NY, 2012, p. 446.

p. 208  ". . . empathetically into the private world of the client." Irvin Yalom, "Introduction," Carl R. Rogers, *A Way of Being* (New York: Houghton-Mifflin, 1995), pp. ix–x.

p. 211  ". . . and so on." Abraham H. Maslow, "A Theory of Human Motivation," *Psychological Review* 50(4):375, 1943.

p. 211  ". . . as an outpouring of their very personality. . . ." Edward Hoffman, *The Right to Be Human* (Los Angeles: Jeremy P. Tarcher, Inc., 1988), pp. 187–88.

p. 212  ". . . as legions of admirers promoted Maslow's approach." Hoffman, Ibid., p. 266.

p. 213  ". . . you have to sweat," he told Leary. Hoffman, Ibid, p. 266.

p. 213  ". . . the I-Ching and Jewish mysticism." Hoffman, Ibid., p. 330.

p. 213  ". . . as Herbert Marcuse, J.L. Moreno, Thomas Szasz, and Norman O. Brown." Anderson, op. cit., p. 184

p. 214  ". . . for admission to our various graduate schools." Henry Murray, quoted in Jessica Grogan, *Encountering America: Humanistic Psychology, Sixties Culture and the Shaping of the Modern Self* (New York: Harper Perennial, 2013), p. 131.

p. 214  "from the humanistic psychology movement." Robinson, op. cit., p. 354.

p. 215  ". . . his own dramatic form of group therapy." Walter Truett Anderson, op. cit., p. 96.

p. 215  ". . . narrative-of-who-I-am 'in here." Jeffrey J. Kripal, *Esalen and the Religion of No Religion* (Chicago: University of Chicago Press, 2007), p. 162.

p. 216  ". . . the more crying and volume, the better." Frederick S. Perls, *Gestalt Therapy Verbatim* (Gouldsboro, Maine: Gestalt Therapy Press, 1992), p. 163.

p. 216  ". . . to wipe their own ass." Walter Truett Anderson, op. cit., p. 97.

p. 217  "If not, it can't be helped." Anderson, op. cit., p. 90.

p. 217     "I'm Popeye the Sailor Man." Kripal, op. cit., p. 164.

p. 217     ". . . not only people." Frederick S. Perls, *Gestalt Therapy Verbatim* (Gouldsboro, ME: Gestalt Therapy Press, 1992), p. 143.

p. 218     "Great," John C. Lilly, *Center of the Cyclone* (Oakland, CA: Ronin, 1972), p. 97.

p. 218     ". . . will you just accept your greatness?" Anderson, op. cit., p. 97.

p. 219     ". . . with his rudeness than his skill." Quoted in Kripal, op. cit., p. 159.

p. 220     ". . . her long blond hair streaming." George Leonard, quoted in Kripal, p. 209.

p. 220     ". . . or concepts or thinking,' he adds." David Dempsey, "Love and Will and Rollo May," *New York Times*, March 28, 1971, SM29.

p. 221     ". . . but rather by laymen or 'hippiephrenic' individuals." J.L. Moreno, "The Viennese Origins of the Encounter Movement, Paving the Way for Existentialism, Group Psychotherapy, and Psychodrama," *Group Psychotherapy* 22(1–2):7, 1969.

p. 221     ". . . and stimulating them to violence," Ibid., p. 12.

p. 223     ". . . into present-day transactions." Thomas A. Harris, *I'm OK–You're OK* (New York: Harper Collins, 1972), p. 62.

p. 224     ". . . with an original idea in this regard." Eric Berne, "A Review of Gestalt Therapy Verbatim," *American Journal of Psychiatry* 126(10):164, 1970.

p. 225     ". . . in some cases forty years earlier . . ." Will Schutz, *Here Comes Everybody* (New York: Harper and Row, 1971), p. 201.

p. 225     ". . . derived from Moreno's work." Kurt W. Back, op. cit., p. 97.

p. 225     ". . . were originally invented by Dr. Jacob Moreno. . . ." Abraham Maslow, Letter to the Editor, *Life Magazine*, August 2, 1969, p. 15.

p. 225     "Convalescing nicely." J.L. Moreno to Abraham Maslow, August 9, 1968. J.L. Moreno papers, Countway Medical Library, Harvard University, Cambridge, MA.

p. 225     "one thousand self-actualizing people and their families." Abraham Maslow, "Eupsychia—The Good Society," *Journal of Humanistic Psychology* 1:5, 1961.

CHAPTER NINE

p. 229     ". . . experiencing 'great success with psychodrama.'" Quoted in Michael E. Staub, *Madness is Civilization: When the Diagnosis was Social, 1948–1980* (Chicago: University of Chicago Press, 2011), p. 85.

p. 229     ". . . from his experience at St. Elizabeths." Michael Pettit, "The Con Man as Model Organism: The Methodological Roots of Erving Goffman's Dramaturgical Self," *History of the Human Sciences* 24(2):138–154, 2011.

p. 231   "... environment that valued individual self-expression." Matthew Gambino, "Mental Health and and Ideals of Citizenship: Patient Care at St. Elizabeths Hospital in Washington, DC, 1903–1962," Doctoral Dissertation, University of Illinois at Urbana-Champagne, 2012, p. 292.

p. 232   "... angry people speaking their truth." Lewis Yablonsky, *The Therapeutic Community* (Lake Worth, FL: Gardner Press, 1994), p. 20.

p. 232   "... viciously raining down blows on the pillow. ..." Ibid, p. 108.

p. 233   "... you wouldn't be here." Lewis Yablonsky, personal interview, May 21, 2013.

p. 236   "... he should be buried. ..." Press Release, Eichmann Trial, June 5, 1961, Jacob L. Moreno Papers 1911–1977, 69:1155.

p. 237   "... into anything else." Gideon Hausner to J.L. Moreno, 18 June 1961, Jacob L. Moreno Papers, 1911–1977, 69:1155.

p. 237   "... to acquaint you with my point of view." J.L. Moreno to Gideon Hausner, June 24, 1961, Jacob L. Moreno Papers, 1911–1977, 69:1155.

p. 237   "... the main business of the A.P.A." "The Kennedy Round," *Time*, May 15, 1964.

p. 238   "... describing his work as 'psycho-theatre.'" David Feldhendler, "August Boal and Jacob L. Moreno," Mady Schutzman and Jan Cohen-Cruz, eds., *Playing Boal* (London: Routledge, 1994), p. 88–89.

p. 239   "... to deliver slowly a theatrical piece." J.L. Moreno, "Foreword," *The Theatre of Spontaneity* (Ambler, PA: Beacon House, 1983), p. d.

p. 239   "... for people in our present-day civilization." Jerzy Grotowski, quoted in Robert Landy, *The Couch and the Stage* (New York: Rowman and Littlefield, 2008), p. 166.

p. 240   "... you feel cool, warm, alone and loved." Ralph Novak, "Hangups Dissolve in Liquid Theatre," *Pittsburgh Press*, December 1, 1971.

p. 241   "... to also disrobe emotionally." "The Group: Joy on Thursday," *Newsweek*, May 12, 1969.

p. 241   "... and more innocent about their minds, as well." Abraham Maslow, quoted in Paul Bindrim, "A Report on a Nude Marathon," Robert W. Siroka, Ellen K. Siroka, and Gilbert A. Schloss, eds., op. cit., p. 151.

p. 242   "... gave it a full page." "Love Thy Analyst," *Time*, March 24, 1975, p. 76.

p. 242   "... a useful part of the psychotherapeutic process." Cited in Phyllis Chesler, "The Sensuous Psychiatrists," *New York Magazine*, June 19, 1972.

p. 242   "... had difficulty maintaining an erection." Ibid.

p. 243   "... into the orbit of the group therapy movement." Naomi Braun Rosenthal, "Consciousness Raising: From Revolution to Re-Evaluation," *Psychology of Women Quarterly* 8(4)309, 1984

p. 244   "... as long as a feminist practiced it." Ellen Herman, op. cit., p. 302.

p. 244   "... and denounced them as "little more than a 'T' group." Ibid., p. 316.

p. 244    "... including 'dramatic relief' through psychodrama and role playing." Cancer Prevention Research Center, "Transtheoretical Model." http://www.uri.edu/research/cprc/TTM/ProcessesOfChange.htm.

p. 244    "... and talk to each other from their new positions." Charlotte Ellen and Howard J. Clinebell, *"Counseling for Liberation," The Intimate Marriage*, (New York: Harper & Row, 1970). http://www.religion-online.org/showchapter.asp?title=1898&C=1703.

p. 249    "'... just keep battering at the limits' of the ideas." Werner Erhard, personal interview, New York City, July 10, 2013.

p. 252    "... promotes the vision of recovery, humanity, and hope." Joseph Patrick Powers, e-mail, February 21, 2014.

## Chapter Ten

p. 253    N.A. Christakis and J.H. Fowler, "The Spread of Obesity in a Large Social Network Over 32 Years," *New England Journal of Medicine* 35:370–379, 2007. http://christakis.med.harvard.edu/pages/research/r-images.html

p. 254    "... fewer than six degrees of separation between them." Jeffrey Travers and Stanley Milgram, "An Experimental Study of the Small World Problem," *Sociometry* 32(4):425–443, 1969.

p. 255    "... barely scratching the surface." Russell Brandom, "The Future of Facebook Was Born in 1932," Buzzfeed, May 21, 2012. http://www.buzzfeed.com/tommywilhelm/the-future-of-facebook-is-from-1932

p. 255    "... raised over $1.8 billion." "Twitter Raises $1.82 Billion In Biggest Tech IPO Since Facebook," *AdAge*, November 6, 2013. http://adage.com/article/digital/twitter-raises-1-82-b-biggest-tech-ipo-facebook/245154/.

p. 255    "... as many as 100,000 pieces of type." Will Durant, *The Reformation* (New York: Simon and Schuster, 1957), p. 259.

p. 255    "... no less an objective than the whole of mankind." J.L. Moreno, *Who Shall Survive?* (Beacon, NY: Beacon House, 1953), p. 1.

p. 256    "... what robots mean to us." J.L. Moreno, *Psychodrama Vol. 3* (Beacon, NY: Beacon House, 1975), p. 263.

p. 256    "... which are inherent within his organism." J.L. Moreno, *Who Shall Survive?* (Beacon, NY: Beacon House, 1953), p. 598.

p. 257    "... the scale and reach of the practice of psychodrama." Lazar, op. cit., p. 49.

p. 257    "... of the visual telephone by millions." J.L. Moreno, quoted in Lazar, op. cit., p. 49.

p. 257    "... a kind of televised psycho-drama." Alvin Toffler, *Future Shock* (New York: Random House, 1970), p. 231.

p. 257    "... a psychodrama, three news commentaries, a football game. ... "
Arthur C. Clarke, *2001: A Space Odyssey* (New York: New American
Library, 1968), p. 287.

p. 258    "... increase of machinery nor robot races of the future." J.L. Moreno,
*Who Shall Survive?* (Beacon, NY: Beacon House, 1953), p. 596.

p. 258    "... through submission, actual destruction, and social revolution."
Ibid., p. 595.

p. 258    "... fragmentariness and imbalances." J.L. Moreno, *Psychodrama Vol.1*
(Beacon, NY: Beacon House, 1959), p. 390.

p. 258    "... destructive to therapeutic filming." J.L. Moreno, *Psychodrama Vol. 1*
(Beacon, NY: Beacon House, 1959), p. 396.

p. 259    "You should call it, 'From Love to Facebook.'" Lewis Yablonsky,
personal interview, May 21, 2013.

p. 259    "... to back up that insight." Clay Shirky, e-mail, August 2, 2012.

p. 259    "... they do not substitute for conversation." Sherry Turkle, "The
Flight from Conversation," *New York Times*, April 21, 2012. http://www.
nytimes.com/2012/04/22/opinion/sunday/the-flight-from-conversation.
html?pagewanted=all.

p. 260    "...in tying it up with technological devices." J.L. Moreno, *Psychodrama
Vol. 1* (Beacon, NY: Beacon House, 1959), p. 403.

p. 260    "... people use them for different reasons." Cameron Marlow, telephone
interview, August 2, 2012.

p. 261    "... encounters enhance warmth, mutual understanding and health."
http://www.meetup.com/Humanistic-interpersonal-Meetup.

p. 261    "... in new and surprising ways that their designers did not intend."
Alan Rosenblatt, personal interview, October 31, 2013.

p. 261    "... who had no one to talk to about it before." Liba Wenig Rubenstein,
telephone interview, January 3, 2014.

p. 262    "... Psychodrama became a significant activity in the Free U. ... " John
Markoff, *What the Doormouse Said* (New York: Penguin Books, 2005),
p. 113.

p. 263    "... may now be turned to human ends." Charles A. Reich, "Reflections
on the Greening of America," *The New Yorker*, September 26, 1970.

p. 263    "... was not politics, but mind." Fred Turner, *From Counterculture to
Cyberculture* (Chicago: University of Chicago Press, 2006), p. 36.

p. 264    "... for its cyberspace initiative." Fred Turner, Ibid., p. 163.

p. 264    "... turn on, boot up, jack in." For a guide to Leary's later views on
networks see: Timothy Leary, Michael Horowitz, Vicky Marshall, *Chaos
and Cyber Culture* (Berkeley, CA: Ronin Publishing, 1994).

p. 265    "... in some cases forty years earlier. ..." Will Schutz, *Here Comes Everybody* (New York: Harper & Row, 1971), p. 108.

p. 265    "... in six 'flavors' no less." R. Nave. "Quarks," *HyperPhysics*. Georgia State University, Department of Physics and Astronomy, 2014, Atlanta GA. http://hyperphysics.phy-astr.gsu.edu/hbase/Particles/quark.html.

p. 265    "... but was not used much in their original design." Clay Shirky, e-mail, August 2, 2012.

p. 266    "... looking to create something of interest." Joseph A. Konstan, e-mail, June 10, 2013.

p. 266    "... often uses social network analysis in its efforts." Sergio Sismondo, presentation, Department of History and Sociology of Science, University of Pennsylvania, Philadelphia, PA, February 17, 2014.

p. 266    "... the deluge of data that they are producing?" Michael Kearns, personal interview, November 5, 2013.

p. 266    "... describing the data stream left by Internet communications." Tim O'Reilly, telephone interview, November 8, 2013.

p. 267    "... created the terrain for being able to use social network analysis." Nicholas Christakis, telephone interview, October 21, 2013.

p. 269    "... and we take the theory seriously." Barry Spodak, personal interview, November 1, 2013.

p. 270    "You have to experience it." David Swink, personal interview, November 23, 2013.

p. 271    "... grounded in empathy, not sympathy." "Psychodrama and the Training of Trial Lawyers: Finding the Story," 21 N. Ill. U. L. Rev. 1 (2001), p. 18. http://www.aals.org/profdev/newideas/cole.pdf.

p. 272    "... happens almost by accident." Alan Arkin, *An Improvised Life* (New York: Da Capo, 2011), pp. 184–185.

p. 272    "... that stands in for President Bush." Erin Overby, "The Tina Fey Years," *The New Yorker*, March 7, 2011. www.newyorker.com/online/blogs/backissues/2011/03/saturday-night-live.html.

p. 272    "... they love Chicago-style sketch comedy!" Tina Fey, *Bossypants*, (New York: Little, Brown, and Company, 2011), p. 90.

p. 272    "... since the mid-1970s." Joy Behar, e-mail, April 13, 2014.

p. 272    "... where you reverse roles with the other child." Justin McCarthy, NewsBusters, "Behar Denounces a Violent Game. . .Tag," April 16, 2008. http://newsbusters.org/blogs/justin-mccarthy/2008/04/16/behar-denounces-violent-game-tag#ixzz2kdDZ2rV.

p. 273    "... almost a psychodrama." Joy Behar, Joy Behar Show Transcripts, Interview With Jane Fonda, August 10, 2011. http://transcripts.cnn.com/TRANSCRIPTS/1108/10/joy.01.html.

p. 273    ". . . played out on the national stage." *Barack Obama, The Audacity of Hope* (New York: Random House, 2006), p. 56.

p. 273    "The Psychodrama of the Obama Presidency." Peter Wehner, *Commentary*, October 3, 2011 (www.commentarymagazine.com/2011/10/03/psychodrama-obama-presidency/).

# INDEX

9 781934 137840